The Red Fog

The Red Fog

✦

A Memoir of Life in the Soviet Union

By Lilija Zarina
Translated from Latvian
by Gunna Dickson

iUniverse, Inc.
New York Lincoln Shanghai

The Red Fog
A Memoir of Life in the Soviet Union

Copyright © 2006 by Gunna Dickson

iUniverse books may be ordered through booksellers or by contacting:

iUniverse
2021 Pine Lake Road, Suite 100
Lincoln, NE 68512
www.iuniverse.com
1-800-Authors (1-800-288-4677)

ISBN-13: 978-0-595-40257-1 (pbk)
ISBN-13: 978-0-595-84632-0 (ebk)
ISBN-10: 0-595-40257-7 (pbk)
ISBN-10: 0-595-84632-7 (ebk)

Printed in the United States of America

Contents

Foreword

I stood at the window of the florist's shop, mesmerized by the extravagant blaze of color. I had never seen such a profusion of beautiful, bright flowers all in one place. The richness of the sight was overwhelming.

Of course we had florists in Latvia, but their windows were mostly bare. Any hope of getting something there depended on whether you could offer the shopkeeper a half kilo of sugar, a bag of flour, or some kind of Western medicine. Even then, you couldn't choose the flowers you wanted—you had to take whatever they had. Here, you could actually buy what you saw in the window.

It was hard to believe, but I was really in the Free World.

Mostly it felt like a dream. How lucky I was to have attained the very thing that so many others—hundreds of thousands, perhaps even millions—wanted so badly.

I stared at my reflection. Yes, that really was me. And this was really the West. I was not as smartly dressed as the other people hurrying by—all of them with somewhere to go and something to do. I was not like them—not yet. But I was free.

I wanted to shout with joy that I had escaped the Communist prison that passed for life on the other side, but my heart was still heavy with pain for my homeland and the people I had left behind.

"Tell them how difficult our lives are!" a friend had urged me.

How many others would have begged me to do the same, had they only known I was about to escape. Over here, people's lives revolved around material things—homes and cars, refrigerators and clothes.

Yet, whenever I tried to tell them how disturbingly different things could be, they would just look at me with suspicion. How, I wondered, could these comfortable and contented Westerners seem so immune to the suffering of others?

Would their indifference melt away if I could make them see what life was like in that other, faraway world?

Come. I will show you. Allow me to take you to Russian-occupied Latvia. I will start by making one thing very clear: Life under Communism is more tragic and difficult than anything you might expect from the wildest, most dramatic tales of fiction.

As you read this memoir, try to imagine yourself in our shoes. Do not be too self-righteous or too quick to jump to conclusions. And do not judge anyone too harshly or say you would have behaved differently in similar circumstances.

The situation is complex. To protect the people who still live there, I have changed their names, as well as some of the settings.

But, regardless of how careful I may be about safe-guarding certain details, I will never bend the truth, so the world can see Communism in its true light—the way it is, the way it always was, and the way it will always be.

Whether the principal players are called Josif, Nikita, Mao, or by any other name, the ideology of Communism itself does not change. Whether they use their guile or military might to bury the Free World, the goal of Communism is—and will forever remain—to destroy freedom.

That is the message I want you to take from my story.

—LILIJA ZARINA

During World War II, the sovereign Baltic States found themselves caught between the armies of Hitler's Nazi Germany and Stalin's Communist USSR. By the summer of 1944, the Red Army had defeated the Germans at the Eastern Front, and that autumn the Soviets began the brutal occupation of the Baltics that lasted for nearly half a century.

1

We Stay Behind

The shrill ringing of the telephone jangled every nerve in my throbbing head.

"Hello—3289."

"Lita, is that you? Your voice is so faint, I can hardly hear you. Lita, I've seen the Russians! I don't know what to do. I'm alone, and I'm scared. We can't stay here. Please…say something!"

It was my schoolmate Karina.

"I'm ill, Kari," I said weakly. "I have an inner ear infection, and I'm burning up with a fever."

There were muffled sobs at the other end of the line. "But…but…I was counting on you," Karina stammered. "I don't know where my family is. Your father is so wise…I thought…all of us…together…"

I felt helpless. "Don't worry, Kari. Of course we'll go! If we stay, we'll be killed. My father isn't here right now. He's helping with bridge patrol. But we're definitely going to leave….Hello…Can you hear me?…Hello…"

A split second later, the world exploded. A powerful force propelled me out of bed, into the air, and back to the ground with a sickening thud. Then everything went black.

I'm not sure how long I was unconscious, but, when I opened my eyes, I was lying on the ground under some thick shrubbery. The giant oak tree near our house was in splinters, and the air smelled of dust and charred wood.

Beside me on the grass was my mother, wiping her eyes with a corner of her apron. "It was a bomb," she whispered, her voice hoarse. "You're alive. Thank God."

I wanted to lift my head, but it was too heavy. My brain felt thick and dull, like it was wrapped in layers of gauze. I tried to think back over the last weeks, when the red fog started to creep into our lives.

◆   ◆   ◆

July 1944, Jelgava, Latvia.

War was closing in. The Bolsheviks were coming from the East, and were advancing along the main road—the same road on which I used to ride my bicycle home from school. We listened to the daily reports in denial and disbelief.

My childhood along the banks of the Svete River had been golden, but now a feeling of dread, like a gathering storm, threatened to destroy everything that had once been good.

Armed raiding parties roamed the area, making life even more uncertain. One night tragedy struck close to home. We were awakened by terrified cries for help from our neighbors' housekeeper, but, by the time my father arrived, it was already too late. Our neighbor's wife, stabbed through both eyes, lay on the floor beside her husband, whose lungs had been slashed open. Their baby, his tiny arm broken in three places, was squirming in a pool of slippery blood.

After that night, I never saw my father smile again.

Then the air raids began. Bolshevik planes—huge, gleaming, metal birds—droned in and out of the clouds over Jelgava. Engines shrieking, they swooped downward. Seconds later, deafening explosions shattered the night, and flames lit the sky already thick with dust and smoke. I watched in sick fascination, frozen in terror that turned quickly to blind confusion.

People were streaming out of the city, carrying suitcases or just rucksacks. Their faces all wore the same expression of worry mixed with fear and uncertainty about what was yet to come.

Our farmhouse was filling up. Every new group of arrivals brought increasingly disturbing news. The bombs had destroyed the train station, the main street, the factory district. One night, our neighbors' grain silo vanished in a blinding flash, and another bomb landed in their herd of livestock. The dying screams of the mortally wounded animals shattered the darkness and sickened our hearts.

The next day, my father came home exhausted and covered with grime. "Start packing," he told us. "We have to be ready for anything. I've got to go out again, but, if things get worse, I'll be back. Then we'll hitch up the horses and leave."

He got on his bicycle and rode away.

That evening there was another air raid. The earth shook with each powerful blast as the explosions came one after the other. Jelgava was engulfed in a sea of flames. We were in a boiling cauldron in the middle of hell itself. People were shouting at each other, not making any sense. One woman was running in circles with a pillow over her head.

We sought cover, choking on acrid smoke and dust. Near the shelter in our yard, we saw Simon and Marija, who had spent the last year doing odd jobs on our property. They were standing with a small group of other Russians and a man who had recently called himself a refugee. Gesturing broadly, he was calling for power for the downtrodden. Revenge, he said, would be sweet.

◆   ◆   ◆

Soon fighting erupted in the streets of Jelgava. Our soldiers fought hard to defend every inch of ground, and had succeeded in destroying ten Russian tanks. But the onslaught was relentless, and the Red Army was advancing toward Riga, the capital, and the Baltic seashore.

Eventually, the air assaults subsided, but then came an alarming new sound—chains clanking on asphalt. There were Russian tanks on the main road. My father still had not returned.

Our house was packed with people when the door burst open with a splintering crash. "Hands up!" came the order in Russian.

We found ourselves face to face with soldiers, who were standing with guns drawn.

Suddenly, my mother went crazy. "Dysentery!" she shrieked, flailing her arms. "My daughter has dysentery!"

Cursing, the soldiers disappeared almost as quickly as they had arrived, tripping and shoving each other in their haste to push back through the doorway.

"We know what these soldiers were after," Mother said wearily. "But the next time it might not be so easy to scare them away. Being robbed wouldn't be the worst thing. I must go find Anton."

Anton, our wise old farmhand, didn't believe we had seen the last of the foot soldiers. His experiences from World War I had taught him what to expect, and he urged us to find a hiding place before more soldiers arrived.

Our house was near the road, with a garden on one side and an orchard on the other. To the right of the house was the silo and an open-air summer kitchen, to the left, a woodshed and storage space for farm machinery. Directly opposite was a long stable that housed our horses, cows, and pigs.

After dark, Mother and I climbed up near the feed chute in the stable hayloft, where we could see the road and carry on a hushed conversation.

"Remember that young man Strautnieks?" my mother whispered. "Yesterday, he was standing on top of the woodpile, a red kerchief in his pocket, shouting that 'the hour of liberation' had arrived. Everyone is afraid of him—except for Velta Sergeyeva, whose husband is a soldier in the Red Army. She insisted on staying in the house with her four-year-old daughter."

I settled into the straw, and must have dozed off. I was jolted awake by loud Russian voices and the barking of our dogs. The barks quickly turned to ferocious growls, followed by gunshots, high-pitched yelps of pain, and then silence. Trying to go back to sleep was futile. At dawn, I heard someone enter the barn. It must be Anton, I thought, with an explanation for the previous night's events.

Instead, Sergeyeva stood in the doorway, cradling a lumpy bundle in her arms. Stray locks of her wavy hair partly covered puffy eyes ringed with deep purple bruises. The young woman's dress was in tatters, and her stockings pulled down around her ankles revealed bare legs well above the knees. Moving as if in a trance, she sat down on the floor and slowly unfolded the stained blanket to reveal the nude, bloody, and lifeless form of her little girl. Sergeyeva's eyes were dry, but from deep within her chest came an anguished sound like the wail of a wild animal.

Later that day, my mother and Anton told me what happened.

A large group of soldiers had come to the house. Anton welcomed them as friends, explaining that he was only a simple laborer. He said he had not seen any Fascist troops or refugees.

When one soldier gave Anton a shove, the dogs sprang to his defense. But the shots that silenced the loyal animals also frightened Sergeyeva's daughter, who started to cry.

"Women!" the soldiers shouted and, ignoring Anton's protests, raced toward the sound.

They ripped the blanket off the terrified woman and tore at her clothing, oblivious to her cries that her husband was also a Red Army soldier. When the captain picked up the little girl, Anton lunged at him. But one blow from the officer's closed fist rendered the old man unconscious.

2

Life in a Strange Barn

Two Russian soldiers arrived on horseback one morning and told us we had two hours to get off our property.

When Mother and I went back inside the house, we got quite a shock: Our telephone and wall clock had been hacked to pieces, and the radio split in half. Books had been torn apart, pages scattered all over the floor, and on one open volume was a pile of human excrement. My beloved books! I was disgusted and confused. Robbery was one thing, but this was mindless. We tried to concentrate on what to take with us and what to leave behind.

Opening the wardrobe, Mother grabbed one of my father's shirts, a pair of his trousers, and an old raincoat. "Quick, put these on," she ordered. She picked up some scissors, and a moment later my blonde curls lay scattered on the floor. Mother walked to the stove, ran her hand along the top, and deftly smeared grime first on my face, and then on her own cheeks and forehead. She tossed me one of Grandfather's caps. I went to the wall mirror, and saw an unkempt boy looking back at me. Mother nodded her satisfaction.

We opened the barn and stable doors to free our remaining animals—first the pigs, then the cows, calves, sheep, chickens, and ducks.

The soldier brandishing a pistol told us to hurry up.

We were ordered to leave our own house. Mother didn't say a word, but the tears rolled steadily down her cheeks.

We left in two horsedrawn carts, with Anton in the lead and Mother and me following close behind. Her face grim, she suddenly looked like an old woman.

We searched in vain for Velta Sergeyeva, whose little girl had been buried in a corner of our garden. Much later we learned that Velta had killed herself.

People jammed the roads as we crossed Grivas Bridge. On Dobele's main thoroughfare, we were joined by another stream of refugees fleeing Jelgava. At the crossroads, the crush of people and carriages was so great we could hardly move.

Looking back, we saw that our heifer Zimala had broken from the herd and was trotting after our cart like a faithful dog, causing Mother's tears to flow anew.

We reached Kalnares, where every house was overflowing with people. But one farmer, a family friend, let us stay in his barn, where we made beds from dried bales of hay.

Anton took the runners from an old sled, and made a tripod on which to hang a soup kettle. Using meat we had brought with us and, with the farmer's permission, potatoes from his garden, we made soup. But it tasted burnt and, after a few spoonfuls, I pushed my bowl away, not knowing that in the weeks and months to come I would be thankful for food that tasted much worse.

My only joy in those days was petting Zimala and trying to find food for her.

I must admit I liked pretending to be a boy. I had always enjoyed whistling and climbing trees, though I had often been scolded for it. I could now indulge myself as much as I wanted. But I never strayed far from the barn, as I was too frightened of a chance encounter with soldiers.

The Russians were more active at night, stopping at farms to pick up sacks of flour, pigs for slaughter, or fresh horses to ride—and to help themselves to any woman foolish enough not to hide.

No one had any illusions about the Red Army anymore, and people were fighting back as best they could. Men, women, and children defended themselves with axes, canes, pitchforks—even boiling water. And if they had managed to hold on to some of their firearms, they used them as well.

Unnerved by the resistance, the intruders became more cautious, though they usually left several dead civilians behind.

The barn was well off the main road. If any Russians ventured near, Anton was ready with impressively stamped documents, which the Red Army—many of them illiterate—couldn't understand. He added that his babushka was ill, and a boy was helping to take care of her.

The story worked well for a while, and my mother, all bundled up, could indeed pass for sixty-eight-year-old Anton's babushka. Then one afternoon, a half dozen Russians arrived and, shoving Anton aside, headed straight for the barn.

"We are taking this land," they said. "But we'll leave you one of our horses, if, as you say, you really are 'one of us.'"

Anton's protests fell on deaf ears. They were preparing to take our brood mare, Flora, and three-year-old Kadra, my favorite. Hysterical, I clung to her mane and wouldn't let go, kicking and scratching like a cornered wildcat. I struck one of the soldiers in the face, and in return got a solid kick along with a string of curses before Anton could pull me away. I was inconsolable. The thought of losing my beloved horse, who turned her head and looked back at me as she was led away, was more than I could bear. I cried harder than I had ever cried before—and rarely since—in my entire life. It took all the strength Anton could muster to restrain me.

The horse the Russians left behind for us was small, and so run down it could barely stand. "He's more like a cat than a horse," I sniffed, and Cat became the pathetic animal's name for as long as it was able to pull our cart.

Besides Flora and Kadra, the Russians took many of our other things. Anton was convinced that someone in the main house had tipped them off. He later found out that the informer had been Marija, who had worked for us during the German occupation, then joined the Bolsheviks, and was now was a Red Army sympathizer.

"Marija recognized me, and guessed we must be together," Anton explained. "She told the soldiers where they could get better horses and more valuables. She said she is a member of the rifle brigade, but she's nothing more than a mattress for the Red Army soldiers."

But not all Russians were like her. There was Vasily, who had worked in our house for two years. Born in Ukraine, he had at first believed the tales of a Communist paradise—until he realized it was just a sham. By then he was an army officer stationed in the Baltics. During a battle in 1941, he had hidden in a forest from the retreating Red Army in order to avoid being sent back to Russia, where he knew there would only be poverty and oppression. I wondered what had happened to him.

Wherever there are a lot of people, there are as many opinions and, of course, no shortage of gossip. The descriptions of events Anton relayed to us grew more alarming by the day.

But the days stretched into weeks, and still nothing happened. Fall was in the air. In the damp, drafty barn, we burrowed deeper into the hay. On rainy days it was not possible to light a fire, so we had to do without soup. We had left our warm clothing back home. Home…would we ever be able to return there? Mother and I were sinking into a deepening depression. We still had no news of my father, although we asked about him at every opportunity.

I grew more and more homesick. I dreamed of sleeping in my soft, comfortable bed, bathing with floral-scented soap, and putting on a pretty party dress. I remembered my perfume bottles and cosmetics jars, and the hours I had spent in front of a mirror. I dwelt on the absence of once-ordinary things, like going to birthday parties or attending concerts.

I thought about how drastically my life had changed, and the things we had taken for granted. I felt sorry for myself. Worst of all, I couldn't see an end to my present misery.

Weeks passed. It was September and, as the din of war grew louder from the West and the Gulf of Riga, it seemed that help might actually be on the way. But once again our hopes were dashed.

The trees had changed color, their leaves turning red and gold before separating from the branches and drifting slowly down to carpet the barren ground. But we could not, like them, become dormant until the spring and then awaken to a new life. We had to go on.

We decided to go back home. Loading up the cart with what was left of our things, we hitched up Cat, who had made a fair recovery, and said our heartfelt thank-yous and farewells.

We had long dreamed of going home, yet there was no joy in anticipation. Our nerves were frayed, and our hearts were racing. What would we find when we got there?

As we rode past demolished homes, columns of Russian tanks were rolling in from Jelgava, and planes with blood-red wings and star insignia droned overhead.

While we thought the Bolsheviks would have been driven out by now, there were Red Army battalions just as certain that in a few months they would advance all the way to Berlin.

At Grivas Bridge we met one of our neighbors, Vigants.

"It's good to see you!" he exclaimed. "I'm going to get my wife to bring her home—or at least to what's left of it. The hayloft, woodshed, and sauna are still intact. I even caught a pig and put it in the sty. We'll stay in the sauna where it's warm—what else could my wife and I hope for? I'm eighty-three and still have my health, though it's hard to think about starting over." Vigants looked as though he had aged several years in only a few months.

"Your house is still standing but it's not in good shape. The Kontrazvietka, or NKVD secret police, or whatever they call themselves these days, have set up offices there. I haven't seen any of our other neighbors—maybe they were lucky enough to get to the other side. We seem to be the only ones left. I'll see you," Vigants said, tipping his hat.

We did not make the turn toward our house but went in the opposite direction, stopping at Zanders cemetery. It too had been vandalized, but at least our loved ones were at rest. We walked slowly through the gates and along the paths, reading familiar names on headstones in the tranquil setting, trying not to think about what lay ahead.

Eager to know anything that had transpired in our absence, we talked to everyone we met. I was happy that a woman everyone called "Grandma" was all right, although she was living in her own outhouse.

Then Anton came up with a plan. As we could not return to our house, he said Mother and I should go stay with my grandmother. "I don't have to worry," said Anton. "What can they do to me? As 'one of them' I might be able to get information that could prevent something bad from happening."

My mother agreed, but only with part of his plan. "You go." She gave me a stern look. "Nobody will harm a young boy. I will go with Anton. If your father returns, we can at least face the future together."

"Don't forget the security police are also there," Anton cautioned.

But Mother stood her ground, and Anton finally gave in. "All right then, let me make another suggestion. Please don't be offended, but let's go back to your house, both of us, as servants. The Communists won't be able to prove anything, as all the records in Jelgava have been lost or destroyed. Only Vigants would be the wiser, and he won't say anything." Anton smiled sadly and, drawing a long, slow breath, waited for a response.

Mother did not object, satisfied that at least she could go home.

As we rode together to the edge of the forest, I tried to pretend I wasn't nervous. I whistled a tune I had heard Latvian legionnaires sing.

"Careful. You might be taken for a Fascist boy," Anton chided. "Better to sing a Bolshevik song."

"No!" I scowled and stopped whistling altogether.

At the crossroads, I summoned a brave smile, kissed Mother, shook Anton's hand, petted Zimala, and hurried away, so no one would see the tears I could no longer hold back.

Later, having regained some composure, I began to reflect on the state of things. What had been the point of my education—all the emphasis on ethics, in particular? In class, Miss Dambergs told us to be honest, respectful, and kind because decency would always prevail. My classmates and I called her "Elizabeth, the Pure of Heart." I wondered what she would say now. These days, people had to lie to survive. Yet, when Miss Dambergs spoke of love, the girls in her class were enthralled. How grand and beautiful she painted the relationship between two people deeply in love!

I hurried along the forest path in the afternoon light, clambering over toppled trees and around the edges of deep bomb craters. There was the path leading to Diana's Hill—a tiny island deep in the forest. According to legend, a mighty castle had once stood there. Its stern ruler's only daughter, the beautiful Diana, had fallen in love with an ordinary boy, but was forbidden to marry him. Heartbroken, she leapt to her death from the castle window. The devil took her father away, and the castle sank out of sight, but a rooster could still be heard crowing every morning.

How exquisite it must be, I thought, to love someone so much you would die for him.

As I turned onto the main road, I saw a column of Russian soldiers coming toward me. Not daring to look at them, I thrust my hands deep into my pockets and kept walking. My ill-fitting shoes were rubbing my feet.

I thought back to a night when I had been getting ready for a party, but at the last minute had decided not to go because I couldn't find the right pair of shoes. Karina had begged me not to ruin my chances for a fun evening over something so trivial. She opened my storage chest. "Lita, you have thirteen pairs of shoes! There are blue, brown, green, and black ones. Surely one of them will do."

But, stubbornly, I had felt I just had to have new shoes, so I had stayed home.

Now, with painful blisters forming on my heels, I was just grateful I didn't have much farther to go.

As I turned into Lapskalna Street, the scene was all too familiar—burned-out and half-demolished homes, and, inevitably, among them some that had miraculously escaped damage.

I was relieved to see Gran's house intact. I opened the gate, and saw her cat on the path. Then Gran's gray head appeared in the kitchen window. She looked once, twice, then three times at the strange boy approaching. Suddenly she cried out, "My darling child!"

Moments later, safe in her arms, I sobbed as if my heart would break.

3

From the Ruins to Riga

The distant sounds of war kept rolling in from the flame-lit western skies. People spoke in hushed tones about battalions of American and Swedish soldiers arriving on Latvian shores.

Jelgava, my birthplace, was in ruins. Gaping dark windows lent a skeletal appearance to burnt-out buildings. The acrid smell mixed with the odor of rotting animal carcasses.

It took some skill to navigate what had once been the city center. People leapt from one pile of smoldering rubble to another and walked along ledges, past crushed and charred automobiles, scurrying about like ants trying to salvage the tiniest mementos. Some used shovels; others their bare hands, hoping to find their homes, or some part of their homes, intact. Occasionally a kitchen utensil—a knife, pot, or pan—took on renewed importance.

Some spent their days staring at the piles of scorched bricks, replaying in their mind's eye scenes of gaiety and laughter, climbing the steps to go home at the end of the day. It was hard for them to accept that a significant part of their lives was gone forever.

By some miracle, we had remained unharmed during those first months of the red fog. Gran maintained that it was the hand of God protecting us.

It was now mid-October, and Gran and I stored what little we had for the long winter ahead. I began to think about continuing my education. The war couldn't go on forever. If our country was to remain occupied, Gran said, a good education was necessary for a strong foundation.

The Red Army was gaining more of a foothold and already controlled Riga and Lithuania's major port of Klaipeda. We were still counting on the British, the Swedes, and the Americans to come to our aid. But what was taking them so long?

Still, our lives had to go on—even if it meant fighting the enemy all by ourselves.

One day, my father's friend Bruklis, who had been pressed into service driving a Red Army ambulance, confirmed that Riga had indeed fallen into the hands of the barbarians. Nevertheless, he managed to convince me that the best thing to do was to enroll in university there.

I did not know a soul in Riga, just the name of one family acquaintance. Perhaps it was foolish to take such a risk, but the thick crimson shroud made it difficult to see the future clearly.

The Red Cross vehicle picked up speed as we crossed the Driksnas Bridge. Sitting beside Bruklis, I nervously fingered the canvas rucksack that held all my possessions: the gold watch Gran had given me as a graduation present, a couple of gold coins wrapped in old newspaper, a loaf of bread, and a slab of smoked bacon. I slid my hand into a side compartment to make sure my school diploma was still there.

We passed the ruins of Jelgava's beautiful castle, designed by the Italian architect Rastrelli. I remembered once entering its swirling wrought iron gates and grand interior and being awestruck by the magnificent chandeliers, one of which now lay in shards at the roadside. There were broken tables and chairs and lots of torn books. A zinc coffin from a castle crypt had been pried open, revealing mummified remains hunched over the side as if in pain, or embarrassment.

The ambulance picked up speed. On the right were the chimneys of the former sugar factory and, just ahead, the first checkpoint, where four Russians in dirty green uniforms and armed with machine guns had encircled the car in front of us.

One barked orders at the driver while two others peered inside. It was forbidden to travel without official approval, so passengers had to show identification papers and explain where they were going and why. Sensing my apprehension, Bruklis reassured me that Red Cross vehicle checks were generally not as stringent.

The Russians finally came over and examined the driver's papers. When they turned to me, I handed them the only official paper I had—my diploma. The soldier angrily tossed it back at me and said something I didn't understand.

Bruklis translated, "He says, 'Why is your passport so big and written in German?' He also wants to know your destination and your permanent address."

"This is my school diploma. I am going to Riga to study to be a doctor," I answered in Latvian.

Fortunately, another car drove up, and he waved us through. I breathed a sigh of relief, but Bruklis just smiled. "That was only the first one…how many more before we get to Riga is anybody's guess. Thank God some of the guards are so ignorant that people have gotten through checkpoints using a cooking school certificate as a passport. Almost anything with an impressive seal seems to work. It also helps to curse in Russian and shake your fist." That sort of behavior went against the grain of everything I had ever been taught, but I was beginning to understand.

At the roadside, walking toward us was a woman in high boots, a purple hat, a red scarf, a black fur vest, and a long green jacket that clashed with her bright blue skirt. I recognized her—it was our history teacher, Akermane, whom the boys had nicknamed Aphrodite.

Akermane was a survivor. She was as white during the German occupation as she was red in the Bolshevik years. But even if she hadn't really been a Communist, her students didn't respect her. She was merely someone who, whether out of fear or self-preservation, had sacrificed her principles.

When two of our classmates were taken away to Siberia, she had said it was only right because "spineless people needed to be taught a lesson."

I wondered if she would now express the same contempt for anyone who had not joined Com-Youth since the first Bolshevik occupation in 1940.

We passed Akermane, and then we passed army trucks carrying Russian soldiers. There were more checkpoints, and I was grateful that Bruklis was there to interpret for me.

As we drove on, the devastated countryside took on a certain monotony—splintered trees, bullet-pocked stone walls, burned-out houses, and bomb craters filled with rainwater. Crumpled cars and pieces of furniture littered the landscape. In the broken branches of one tree hung a blue-gray soldier's coat, a Latvian flag emblem on its sleeve. A helmet with a bullet hole through it lay nearby on the frost-covered grass. I shuddered.

"That, my dear girl, is life," said Bruklis quietly. "Take it as it comes, and keep your eyes open." I swallowed hard. And, when at the next checkpoint I saw three young men being pulled out of their car, I did not say a word.

Finally, we arrived in Riga, a beautiful city with large, ornate buildings and broad streets. Bruklis let me off at the address on Barona Street. I thanked him, and we said good-bye.

I pressed the bell on the door, apprehensive about what or who was on the other side. What if the Baltins family didn't live there anymore? After what seemed like an interminable wait, the door opened, and I saw a familiar face. It was Olga. I was so happy I could hardly speak.

"What a nice surprise!" she cried, taking my hand. "Please, come in."

"I need a place to stay," I blurted out.

"We have lots of space. You can have the corner room," she answered calmly. "I'll be right back."

Left alone for a few minutes, I took in my surroundings. At the far wall opposite the window was a couch, with the remaining floor space in the midsize room taken up by two round tables, several unmatched club chairs, and a tall cabinet filled with sparkling crystal.

Olga returned with a tea tray. "You must be hungry," she said, setting it down.

4

A New Life

As I lay in bed the next morning, I reflected on recent events. I thought about my parents and what had happened to our home and to our lives.

I wished I could make the terrible events of the last several months disappear, to transform them into a book that I could put way up on the highest shelf, out of reach, never to be opened. But here I was in Riga, and everything was real—the ceiling, the walls, the windows. Above the traffic noise, I could hear the distant drone of aircraft.

Olga had asked me to go to the market for her, so I got dressed and went out into the streets of the city that would shape my future.

I paused at the intersection of Stabu Street and Freedom Boulevard, Riga's main thoroughfare, as wide and smooth as the motorway that led home to Jelgava. Here and there I could see some of the ravages of war, but things looked mostly intact.

Speeding along the boulevard were open trucks with Russian soldiers who held bayonets, their faces like masks. Some of them were quite young. Maybe they even wished they could be somewhere else, not in this strange city, uninvited and unwanted. Didn't they know their victory laurels were no more than crowns of rusted, blood-stained barbed wire? Perhaps that was why they took such delight in their battle benefits of rape and robbery.

Some were singing. The Bolshevik song—the one Anton had suggested I whistle to make it appear I was one of their own—grated on my ears.

Suddenly, the truck screeched to a halt in front of a shop, and the soldiers jumped off one after another. One had a half-empty bottle of vodka in his hand, and some, with faces flushed, were unsteady on their feet. They snapped the lock to the store, and minutes later came out with a large box, loaded it into the truck, and went back inside for more loot.

"Thieves!" a nearby voice hissed. "This is a bad corner. Look, here comes one of the Cheka. Let's get out of here."

I whirled round to see two women hurrying away and a man walking toward us, a malevolent smile on his face. *"Ek, krasavici."* (Hey, my beauties.)

I froze momentarily then, in a blind panic, started running as fast as I could. Shopping for food was the last thing on my mind. By the time I slowed down, I was short of breath and had completely lost my bearings. I saw a woman coming toward me and asked for directions to the market.

"It's right here, but what's the hurry?" Her sympathetic tone caused my throat to tighten. She had a nice face and looked to be about my mother's age. "You are so young. Let me give you some advice: Never give in to fear. Use guile as your weapon. I will give you an example. On the night Riga fell to the Russians, a band of them broke into my home. With no hope of escape, my only chance of survival was to 'fall in love' with one of our 'liberators'—the highest-ranking one. Of course there was a price to pay, but the final cost would have been far greater. My dear child, you must learn to deal with life as it comes."

Her voice was gentle, and her face had no hint of coarseness. I watched, bewildered, as she continued on her way. Then, seeing a much older woman, a basket hooked over one arm, reminded me of my original mission. I asked again for directions to the market. "Come along, dear," she said. "I'm going there myself."

On the other side of the market gates was a scene of destruction: The stalls had been vandalized—anything breakable had been smashed, metal twisted, and clothing shredded. A small group of people had gathered in the central area, some selling eggs, others selling smoked bacon. Still others arrived on bicycles with bags of potatoes and other farm vegetables.

I made my purchases and rejoined the old woman.

"I can tell you're a stranger here," she said. "I've lived a long time but have never seen anything like this. And it's only the beginning. May God help you young folks. Which way are you going, dear?"

Without hesitation, I told her my address.

"We'll walk part of the way together. I live at Barona and Aizsargu Streets. A man was shot dead in our building the other night, trying to protect his wife. The poor woman was raped and had a mental breakdown afterward." She continued talking as we walked along Matis Street to my corner. "Go straight ahead from here," she indicated, and we said good-bye.

As I turned, I was startled by a man leaping out of a broken display window with an armload of fur coats. I stifled a scream and, remembering the first woman's advice, curbed an impulse to run. The thief was so absorbed in his own crime that he didn't even see me.

Farther along, a large truck blocked a driveway as soldiers loaded it with carpets and furniture. Several of them were grunting and cursing under the weight of a grand piano. A thick volume of Beethoven sonatas fell at my feet, next to a score of Darzins's "Melancholy Waltz"—both quickly trampled by heavy boots.

I hurried past, eager to get back home and share my adventures with Olga.

She listened attentively, and then said softly, "Unfortunately, you will see a lot more of that. Learn to get used to it."

I felt safe with Olga; she was pretty and nice and easy to talk to. She was twenty-four years old but had already been married for eight of those years. Her oldest son was four, and her youngest had just turned two. Her husband, Andrejs, was a Latvian legionnaire, fighting to defend our country's freedom.

"When the enemy forces took Riga, Andrejs didn't want to send me and the boys to Germany. He and his friends put their faith in the British and the Americans, hoping they would arrive and eventually deal with Stalin as they had dealt with Hitler. But now they are all in hiding."

"But what will they do?" I asked.

"They're not sure," Olga said with a wry smile. "Surely there is someone somewhere in this world who won't allow this situation to continue forever. Andrejs says we cannot expect the British and Americans to fight Germany, Japan, and Russia all at once. He believes Roosevelt and Churchill have a plan. They have temporarily thrown in their lot with Stalin in order to defeat Hitler, but, when that is done, Stalin will have a surprise in store, maybe as early as the spring.

"I was ready to take our sons away to safety, but Andrejs was afraid we might never find each other again. There were lots of stories about refugee ships and hundreds of corpses floating up on the shores of the Baltic Sea. Our biggest worry now is how long Andrejs can stay in hiding."

"But what if the thieves I saw in the streets break into our house?" I asked fearfully. "There are so many nice things here. What will we do?"

"Whatever happens, we must learn to take things in stride," Olga replied, "if only to keep hope alive. My children depend on me, and, for now, we have no other choice but to accept things as they are." She drew in a deep breath and continued, "That furniture you say is so nice? I hate it. It's a reminder of everything that's bad right now."

I didn't know what she meant and didn't ask. I began to explore our living quarters. There were six rooms in all, three of them occupied by Andrejs's older brother, Roberts. I had seen him several times from a distance, but we had never spoken.

Roberts's rooms were full of beautiful furniture and other expensive objects. In the center of the largest room was a tall walnut shelf filled with books: Western classics, Latvian writers and poets—Blaumanis, Aspazija, Rainis, Virza, Dambergs, Eglitis, Lazda, Aigars—a literary feast.

"Your brother-in-law has many interests!" My gaze slid past the books to a German piano. "And he plays the piano!" I exclaimed, babbling excitedly about how happy I could be in these surroundings.

Olga, who had trailed behind me, finally broke her silence. "There is something you should know," she said. "You'll find out soon enough. I've never had much respect for Roberts and have even less now. He is just like the thieves you saw on the streets, only worse, because he is Latvian.

"During the first year of the Bolshevik occupation, when people were so terrified they didn't know where to hide, Roberts became drinking buddies with our oppressors. When fighting broke out, Andrejs and other Latvians fought against the Reds. But Roberts became active in the black market, and, when the Germans drove out the Russians, he changed his stripes to side with them. You want to know where this furniture came from? One night Roberts and some of his Russian friends got drunk and raided people's homes."

I felt like I'd been doused with a bucket of icy water. "And the library?"

"I doubt Roberts has ever read a book in his life! The books are stolen, as is everything else here. I have to accept that for now, but now you also understand why Roberts and I don't get along. Still, I have to believe that his brother's wife and sons will be his last resort as bargaining chips."

I felt terrible. That magnificent piano must have been at the center of many a happy occasion. I touched it gingerly then took my hand away. No, I thought. Mine was also a stranger's touch.

◆   ◆   ◆

One evening, I suppressed my moral outrage and went in search of a book to read. When a tipsy Roberts entered the room, I apologized for the intrusion.

"Go ahead, take one," he growled. "I can't hang on to that crap much longer anyway. The shelf might have some value, but those damned books could get me into trouble. I have no idea what they're about. Anything that doesn't support the Party has to go."

He took out one of the books and examined it. "Hmm, Edvards Virza—who the hell is he? Oh, wait, wasn't he somebody during the independence years?"

"Yes, Virza was one of the best-known Latvian poets of that time," I said.

"That's got to go," Roberts cried, tossing the book into the corner of the room. He took out more books and, cursing their authors, heaved them one after the other against the far wall, sending a large framed painting crashing to the floor.

"Purvitis? What kind of artist was he?" Robert muttered to himself. "Oh well, it's better to be safe," he said, splitting the canvas with his boot, leaving a dirty footprint on the delicate blue and white winter landscape.

He turned his attention back to the remaining titles. "*The Red Room*? Sounds like it could be pro-Party, but…August Strindberg? Berg? Sounds like a German Fascist! Burn it!"

The ruckus brought Olga into the room.

"Why don't you make yourselves useful," Roberts shouted. "These damned books are dangerous! Rip them up and burn them! Save any works by Stalin or Lenin."

Kicking more books onto the floor, he smirked at Olga.

"Do you really think if these books weren't here, they'd be sitting around waiting for their owners to claim them? Don't you know that Russians consider Latvian freedom fighters to be more dangerous than Hitler? They made Stalin crap in his pants. Me? I just want to live a comfortable life, so I do what I have to do. When I die, the worms will get me just like they'll get you. So, if I have to make a deal with the devil today, I'll do it. And, if St. Peter and a thousand angels led by Churchill arrive in Riga tomorrow, I'll find a way to do a deal with them too."

◆   ◆   ◆

In those days, the role of building superintendent was considered important. But ours—a short, nervous man with long arms and bug eyes—did not seem to care at all about our building.

One day, he announced a new rule. "You must register with the police in the next few days. And you'd better not be hiding anyone…or…" he made a threatening gesture with his fist.

We were apprehensive that night. Would I be sent back to Jelgava? Or maybe put in jail?

Olga had gone to see Andrejs to tell him about the development. The large cellar where he was hiding was full of able-bodied young men, who for one reason or another could not—or did not want to—escape to the West. It was time to make a decision, Olga told them, to take a risk and register, or to remain in hiding.

The young legionnaires discussed the possibilities of lending support to their units fighting in Kurzeme, or of joining the partisans still hiding in the forests. A number held on to the belief that help from the West was on its way. Some were just plain scared, and others, overcome by hopelessness, felt that whatever the consequence, coming out of hiding to register was the only thing left to do. Maybe if they told the truth, the authorities would go easy on them. There were also those who argued that hiding in the forest would mean certain death, and coming clean with the authorities would only buy them a one-way ticket to Siberia. All were in agreement, however, that the Reds were not to be trusted.

The answer seemed to be to get new identity papers and jobs that would not arouse suspicion—until the day they could again take up arms for their cause.

5

Registration

Our registration office was located right next to the market. People milled around outside and jammed the hallways as Olga and I tried to squeeze inside to observe the process.

In the first room, through a smoky haze, we saw three tables. At each table sat blue-clad police, two of whom had not bothered to take off their hats, while the third had placed his on the table alongside his gun.

In front of the tables were long lines of grim-faced people.

I got the feeling someone was watching me and looked up to meet the gaze of the genteel woman I had met in the street near the market. But today she looked shabby and wore a red scarf tied round her head. She nodded a greeting.

Olga and I stayed near the window, looking out every few minutes as if we were waiting for someone while straining our ears to hear what was going on behind us.

The nearest official, his hat pushed to the back of his head, had a wide, acne-scarred face. He was speaking to an old woman in heavily accented Latvian. A hand-rolled cigarette dangled from his lips as he punctuated his questions by slamming his fist on the table and spitting on the floor.

"All my documents were lost," the woman was saying in a tremulous voice.

"Was your son a legionnaire?"

"No, I do not have a son."

"How long had your husband served with the national guards?"

"He has never served, but…"

"You'd better tell us. We'll find out anyway."

"My husband is…"

"Your husband was in the guards!"

The woman finally managed to say her husband had been dead for twenty years.

"You'd better not be lying!" her interrogator shouted, giving her a date to return with witnesses who could vouch for her identity.

Next in line was the woman with the red scarf. She looked the official straight in the eye.

"What are you smiling at?" he demanded. "This is not a circus."

"Comrade, Soviet citizens are intelligent and educated people," the woman said evenly, "…and perform their duties courteously."

"Ah, so you've come here to teach me how to behave toward Fascists?"

The label "Fascist" was liberally applied to Latvian patriots or anyone who did not support the new regime or adhere to the Party line.

"These are not Fascists. They are workers," she continued. "Didn't you know that in the 1940 elections, 99.9 percent of them voted for the Party and Stalin? You should look for the real Fascists out where they are fighting the brave Red Army, not here among the common folk. Here are my papers. Please look them over and, if you have any questions, ask them politely."

He snatched up the papers with a snarl, but the longer he examined them, the less combative he became. Finally, he stood up and showed them to another officer, who appeared to be higher in rank as well as intelligence. Having examined the documents, he cleared his throat. "You see, comrade," he addressed the woman, "sometimes it's hard to tell who's who in wartime. I apologize for my colleague's brusqueness."

The woman took back her papers and, with a satisfied smile, left the filthy, airless room. The questioning continued, but fewer expletives were heard.

Men were grilled more intensely: Had they served in the Latvian legion or German police? If they had a home in the country, they were told to go back there.

Slowly, we moved forward. Olga asked the person in front of us to save a place in line, and we retreated to the hallway.

Putting her hands on my shoulders, Olga whispered, "Remember, you are an orphan. You have no relatives, and, until now, your only education was what your grandmother had taught you at home. The less you say the better. I'll come back here in a couple of days so I can make sure that whatever I say fits in with Andrejs's plans. Now, go!"

It was my turn to approach the table. Paralyzed with fear, I spoke in a mechanical, barely audible voice.

The man seemed satisfied. I didn't know if it was my embossed diploma, or whether he felt chastened by the red-scarfed woman's comments, but he even managed a little praise. "There's a smart girl! All Soviet citizens are intelligent."

Stepping outside, where Olga was waiting, I filled my lungs with the cool autumn air. "He didn't even ask if I had a husband!" I complained as we hurried to brief Andrejs.

"You, my dear, are such a fresh-faced country girl that it wouldn't even occur to them to ask if you were married to a legionnaire," said Olga, smiling her tranquil smile. "And they were never known for their brain power, and that works to our advantage."

"So what did you think of that woman?" I asked. "She was the one I met on the street, except she looked so different today. She recognized me too."

"Who knows what documents she showed them to bring about such a drastic change in attitude. These days, people do whatever they have to do to get by. Anyway, judging from what she told you, she's no Communist. And she knows how to handle herself."

We kept walking until we came to a gate. Olga looked around, as she had done several times in the last half hour, then, putting her finger to her lips for silence, she motioned me to follow her. We went down a flight of stairs and knocked on a door. It was opened by a gray-haired man.

"Good evening, Mr. Briedis," Olga greeted him.

"Good evening," I echoed as we stepped inside, and Olga reached around to close the door behind us.

A small candle flickered in the dark room, which also served as a kitchen. Next to the wall was a bed covered with an old striped blanket and above it a gold-framed picture of Lenin. In the corner was a stove, a wardrobe with some tattered clothes, and opposite the door a table and old-fashioned club chair. As my eyes adjusted to the dim light, I could see rickety shelves filled with books.

"It was good of you to come," Briedis said politely. "They are all waiting."

Sliding a ring of keys from a nail on the door, he led us into the courtyard and down more stairs. Homemade candles lit the way as we walked for what seemed like miles in the musty damp passage, past a large black furnace and an empty coal bin, climbing over stacks of firewood. Just when I felt we were hopelessly lost, we came to a stop.

"I'll come back for you in an hour," Briedis said. "It's better if I am back in my room in case anyone comes looking for 'Fascist' fugitives."

Among the many young legionnaires' faces, I recognized Andrejs, although he had changed somewhat. I was used to seeing him in uniform. Now he wore a sweater and jacket with blue-gray trousers and heavy combat boots.

The basement room was filled with canvas cots. Propped against the wall was a row of rifles, with revolvers on the floor next to them.

We sat down next to Andrejs, and the questions began to fly.

"Wait just a moment," Olga said. "First, let me tell you what happened today."

In a calm, clear voice, she related the events of the day, and, when she was done, the men sat in silence for a while.

Then a dark-haired, dark-eyed young man spoke up. "I'm not going to bow down to those fools!" he said defiantly. "There will be no compromise. We'll throw them out. They don't belong here."

"He's right!" cried a blond legionnaire. "He's talking like a man!"

"But how can we fight when we've lost everything?" a tremulous voice came from a dark corner. "What if the West never comes to help us?"

"History has plenty of examples where the little guy comes out on top," another hard-edged voice weighed in.

"This is a fight we can't win—one way or another, the Russians have got us. Maybe if we just give up, they'll go easier on us," said the timid voice, which belonged to a nervous young man named Peksis.

"Yeah, right, your mother can send you a nose-warmer in Siberia, because that's where you'll end up!" shouted Aivars.

"Boys, please don't argue," Olga interceded. "You can each make your own decision in the end. For now, let's just try to be realistic."

Sufficiently admonished, the men began a constructive discussion. By the time Briedis reappeared to lead us out, many had come to a decision.

◆   ◆   ◆

At breakfast several days later, Olga said, "Peksis is registering today. Let's go and see what happens."

She was concerned, as no one had been able to sway him away from the belief that, if he just told the truth, everything would turn out all right.

"Why were the other legionnaires so mean to him?" I asked.

"I guess they saw him as a weakling. Kindness wouldn't have worked either, believe me. I tried talking to him for several hours once," Olga replied. "I just hope he doesn't ruin it for the others. As a precaution, he'll be blindfolded while Mr. Briedis leads him out of the cellar."

"Tell me about Mr. Briedis," I said. "He seems nice, but also tough."

"You're right. He has a heart of gold but keeps it well concealed. He was once a schoolteacher and a good friend of Andrejs's father. The two fought with the revolutionaries and wound up in Russia in 1917. Andrejs's father quickly became disillusioned and returned to Latvia, which by 1918 was independent. Briedis ultimately came to the same conclusion about the false promises of Communism and was imprisoned when he dared to question it. When they let him out, he was old and in ill health and took any available odd jobs until it was possible for him to return to Latvia."

The story made me think again about how many ordinary people had been deceived, even kind old Anton.

"Let's go," said Olga. "We don't want to be late."

By the time we arrived at the registration office, Peksis had already taken his place in line. When his turn came at the interrogator's table, his round, apple-cheeked face looked more like a girl's. His hands shook so badly he had to lean on the table to steady himself.

"You are a Fascist!" the official with the pock-marked face shouted, taking advantage of the young man's fearfulness.

"B-b-but I had no choice...p-p-please...h-h-have...m-mercy."

"Shut up, you son of a bitch! Or I'll shut you up."

With lighting speed, Peksis was surrounded by police, one pointing a machine gun.

"Hands up!" they barked and led him away.

"Let's get out of here," said Olga, grabbing me by the hand.

6

The Streets of the City

I wandered the streets of Riga wearing my shabby coat and one of Olga's old scarves. I made sure to leave my watch at home, because I knew Russians had a weakness for them, mainly because they were so scarce. Occasionally you'd see one on an officer's wrist, though it was more the size of an alarm clock. Women's watches were not much smaller.

"Atdavai chasi!" (Give me your watch!) had become a familiar phrase. And if you happened to be alone, facing a group of Red Army soldiers with guns pointing at you, it was best to comply. Sometimes people who refused paid with their lives. The justification for shooting them was simple: "Fascist!" And that was the end of it.

These days, robbery and rape were a part of life and often took place in daylight. Russian soldiers would arrive with official-looking papers to check whether residents had registered or were harboring any Fascists. Two soldiers would ask questions to divert the residents' attention while the others went about scooping up valuables.

People were frightened to admit strangers, and no longer asked, "Who is it, please?"

Actually, words such as *please* and *thank you* labeled their users as having dangerous capitalist values. Instead people just shouted, "Who's there?" from behind a closed door.

A lock did not guarantee safety. Sometimes people were told they had a package or registered letter that required a signature. When they opened the door even a crack, it was kicked in. If only women were home, rape and robbery took place simultaneously.

Seeking to protect themselves, people asked *"Kto tam?"* (Who's there?) in Russian. That worked well if the voice was loud and masculine, as they had no wish to rob one of their own.

On the lighter side, a story was making the rounds among Latvians about a recording of a string of Russian expletives, followed by *"Kto tam?"* One variation: "Who's the son of a bitch on the other side of this door?" The recording was not cheap, but it was effective. If played loudly from behind a closed door, it conveyed to intruders that no Fascists were hiding within.

On one gloriously sunny day, I turned onto Freedom Boulevard and walked toward the Freedom Monument. Between Gertrude and Lacplesis Streets loomed the skeleton of a demolished building, though next door stood a brand-new shop that sold produce to people who were registered and had been issued food cards. This particular store was for ordinary folks. Political functionaries patronized their own special stores.

I arrived at the monument, a mother figure, calm and deliberate, rising silently above the chaos. In her hands, which were raised toward the sky, she held three golden stars whose brightness seemed to defy getting lost forever in the red fog. Standing at the feet of this great national symbol, I felt I had entered another world. I read the inscription—"For the Fatherland and Freedom"—half aloud to myself.

A loud Russian voice snapped me back to reality.

"I don't understand," I said. The man waved his machine gun at me and continued to shout. Just then an elderly pedestrian paused and translated for me in halting Latvian. "He says you must leave. It is forbidden to stand here."

I hurried away, careful not to show fear or any other emotion. To make sure I wasn't followed, I looked back over my shoulder, but no one was there.

A sign—Cafe Luna—caught my gaze, which quickly shifted across Kalku Street to a large pile of rubble and melted glass. This had once been the famous Opera Café, where Riga's social elite had come to bask in their reflections in the mirrored Grand Hall.

The Old Town section of Riga also had its share of devastation, but the worst was on the banks of the River Daugava. All the bridges and buildings along the embankment had been bombed, and no effort had been made to clear up the mess. People were saying—tongue in cheek—that the victors showed so little interest in rebuilding that they must know they wouldn't be staying long.

By now I had arrived at the President's Palace, which was still standing, though it showed signs of damage.

Passing the National Theater, I turned onto Kronvalda Boulevard, where the university chemistry building stood intact. Farther along, as I approached the anatomy building, my heart beat faster. Would I, one day, be walking through these doors as a student?

Cautiously I pressed down on the door handle. To my surprise, the door was open. An elderly woman sat at a table in the vestibule. "What is it, dear?" she asked gently. "Will you be coming to study here?"

"Yes, I would like to study medicine."

Upstairs, she indicated, was the main laboratory, and downstairs a morgue. On the wall above the staircase was a large painting of a doctor and his assistants grouped around a cadaver.

That was the second highlight of my day. Every medical student dreams of being able to dissect a human body—a prospect as frightening as it is exciting. My ambition was to stand in the lab in my white coat, a scalpel glinting in my hand, and methodically take apart a cadaver. Would I ever get to that point? And, if I did, would I feel sick?

I arrived home to find several parcels and a letter from Gran.

My darling girl,

Though you are far away, I worry about you all the time. Today was a good day. Mr. Bruklis stopped by to tell me you arrived safely. And he agreed to take you a little present. I've packed up some bacon, raspberry jam, and a loaf of freshly baked bread, also your winter boots and a scarf I knitted myself. I am making mittens for you now.

Anton and your mother are living in the kitchen of your summer house. The Cheka have occupied the main house, and, for that reason, it has escaped extensive damage. There are even some cows in the barn.

Your mother's nerves are badly frayed. She rarely sleeps and cries all the time. She is able to look out the window as people are brought to the main house for questioning, and one day thought she saw your father.

Please don't go out after dark, and remember to dress warmly. It's getting colder every day, and you might get sick. I send you kisses and pray every night for God to keep you safe.

Grandmother

◆   ◆   ◆

We kept up our visits to the boys in the cellar, where the conversation always returned to Peksis. It was a warning to anyone else who believed honesty might be the best policy. Andrejs continued to urge his friends to be patient until the time was right for action.

Olga came up with a plan: We needed to get Red Army uniforms for the boys, so that, even in broad daylight, they could move about undetected. The problem was finding enough of them. We had heard that, in the countryside, soldiers were going from house to house, ready to trade their uniforms for bottles of vodka. Some even took them to the central market.

"Leave everything to me," Olga said.

7

A Drunken Evening

"Girrrls? Laaadies!" Roberts shouted. "Don't even think about going out tonight. I need you to help me entertain my friends. There's some food in the kitchen. Now get in there and prepare it—I want everything to be perfect!"

"He's drunk again," Olga whispered.

"Hey! Are you two deaf?"

"We can hear you," Olga said calmly. "But we'd hear you just as well if you used a normal tone of voice. We'll set the table for you, but we can't entertain your guests. You'll have to do that yourself."

"What!" an enraged Roberts loomed in the doorway. "How dare you speak to me like that! Do I need to remind you who's been protecting you? Ingrate! Who the hell do you think you are?"

Olga's face turned serious. "I guess we'll have to put in a brief appearance," she said quietly.

As I helped prepare a platter of open-face sandwiches, my mind wandered back in time—home, Father, Mother, and me at dinnertime, in comfortable surroundings day after day, month after month, year after year. It never occurred to me that things would ever be any different.

My father was a generous, hospitable man who passed on to me his love of the land and respect for our flag and country. What would he say now if he knew I was preparing a meal for our oppressors? Tears stung my eyes, but I willed them back.

When Olga and I were done, the table looked beautiful.

"What the hell kind of tablecloth is that?" Roberts demanded. "I told you to use the red one! And the crystal dishes…the ones I just got from the shop window. I told you everything must be perfect!" Roberts slammed his fist on the piano and disappeared again, muttering in Russian.

"He's crazy," Olga whispered. "A red tablecloth and fruit plates instead of dinner plates, only because they're crystal."

"Look," I tugged at her apron, "a red flag with a hammer and sickle. And Russian books—Marx, Lenin, and Stalin—on the shelves."

Olga didn't reply as she went about changing the table setting.

Soon we heard Roberts greeting his guests.

I suddenly had the urge to hide, and I could see Olga felt the same, but it was too late.

Bowing obsequiously, Roberts entered the room, followed by four uniformed men. Two, with flashy epaulets, appeared to be officers. They were introduced as Mishka, Vasya, Kolya, and some other name I immediately forgot.

"Tovarich prokuror," Roberts addressed one of the men, who I thought must be the new boss he was trying to impress. As absurd as it seemed, Roberts, himself a thief, was now working for the crime unit to help catch thieves.

The guests threw their coats down in various parts of the room. Only the *prokuror* took off his hat and tie, placing them on the leaves of a potted plant. Fearing the delicate branches would snap, I took a step forward, but a sharp look from Olga stopped me in my tracks.

"Take these stupid little things away!" Roberts ordered, indicating the whiskey tumblers we had put on the table. "Bring the tea glasses."

Then the drinking began, with an entire glass downed for each toast. *"Za Stalinu!"* (To Stalin!) *"Za roginu!"* (To the homeland!) *"Za krasnuju armiju!"* (To the Red Army!)

I couldn't bring myself to take even a tiny sip. The only alcohol I had ever tasted was a small glass of my father's sweet homemade wine.

The Russians were getting annoyed. They seemed insulted that we didn't drink to Stalin.

Trying to distract them, Olga urged Roberts to sing for his guests, knowing he couldn't resist showing off what he believed to be a great baritone.

Standing next to the piano, he sang a song about Stalin.

The Russians were enthralled, but I didn't take my eyes off the floor. Whenever they spoke to me, I said firmly, "I don't understand," and Olga kept her answers to a curt yes or no.

Then there was another toast—to the beautiful song about Stalin. They jumped to their feet and, brimming tea glasses raised high, shouted in unison, *"Za Stalinu. Zapjom za Stalinu"* (To Stalin! Let's drink to Stalin!)

Holding his glass aloft, Roberts joined in.

"Za nashu daraguju Stalinu!" (To our dear friend Stalin!) "He gave us freedom, our dear teacher, father, and friend, beloved Josif Visarionovich! *Za Stalinu!"*

Moved by his own words, Roberts took out a large handkerchief, blew his nose, and dabbed at his eyes, sneaking a peek to see if he was making a favorable impression. His guests, unfortunately, were showing more interest in Olga and me.

"Za Stalinu!" said one, raising his glass and looking right at me, eyes narrowed.

"Drink up!" I heard Olga say as she picked up a glass.

I was stunned but, following her example, gulped it all down. To my total shock and immense relief, the glass contained water. While Roberts was singing, Olga had filled our glasses from the same container she used to water the plants.

We were safe, at least for the time being.

The guests' faces were becoming flushed with drink. One would not take his eyes off me and was calling me *golubchik*—his little dove.

I stood up, anxious to leave the room.

"You!" Roberts shouted. "Stay!"

I sat down, and he turned back to his guests, who, ignoring the cutlery on the table, were using their fingers to scoop food into their mouths. Soggy sandwiches were swimming in plates of spilled whiskey, and the men's hats lay on the floor amid scraps of food and shards of broken glass.

Roberts continued to entertain his guests. Picking up a top hat and cane, he did his imitation of a capitalist.

"Vot, nash chelovek!" (He's one of ours!) the Russians shouted gleefully.

Roberts left the room and came back, breathless and carrying a large suitcase.

"Guess what's inside!" he said excitedly, opening it with great pomp to reveal a smaller suitcase. "Guess again," Roberts urged, opening that case to reveal yet another even smaller one. The guessing began in earnest as he prepared to open the third case. In it was a blackened kettle, with hissing and scratching sounds coming from inside. That called for another toast.

Finally, Roberts, putting on a Red Army hat, lifted the lid. I couldn't believe my eyes. In the pot was the stray cat which prowled our neighborhood for scraps—barely clinging to life. Roberts grabbed it by the scruff and lifted it high in the air.

"Comrades, here is the Latvian president Karlis Ulmanis, to whom the victorious Red Army did...this!" he snarled, flinging the hapless animal through the open window.

"Urrah, urrah, urrah!" the guests brayed and drained another round of tea glasses filled with whiskey. By then Roberts was walking on the piano keys.

Olga grabbed my arm and led me out of the room.

"Thank God, we finally got away," I gasped, trembling so violently my teeth were chattering.

"Go to your room and lock the door," Olga ordered, disappearing into her own room.

I went to my room and put on my nightgown, but, when I turned to lock the door, the key, which had been there that morning, was gone. Too exhausted to start looking for it, I pushed a table, a club chair, then another table and chair up against the door until it held firm.

I closed my eyes, but I saw only the drunken faces of the Russians and Roberts teetering on the piano keys.

"*Golubchik, golubchik…Atkrivai, golubchik.*" (Open the door, little dove.)

Sleep. Don't think. Go to sleep.

"*Golubchik…golubchik…*" Someone was jiggling the door handle. Then came a hard shove and the familiar invective, "The devil take your mother!"

Suddenly wide awake, I stuffed a corner of the blanket in my mouth to stifle a scream. I watched as a large knife slipped under the door and was pulled upward. Just as the door lifted off its hinges, the blade snapped.

"*Vot.* The devil take your mother!" the Russian cursed again, as he shoved his way through my barricade of tables and chairs.

Blinded by fear, I followed my instincts. When he was halfway to the bed, I leapt up and crawled on the floor as fast as I could between the table legs until I was out in the hallway. I ran to the kitchen and slammed the door behind me. Again, no key.

Looking around in desperation, I saw the pantry, where Roberts had made several trips for replenishments. I leapt inside and locked the door. How lucky for me that Roberts kept his food and drink under lock and key.

In the cramped space, my head was butting against the smoked hams hanging from ceiling hooks. The shelves were filled with pots and jars…only the bottom one had nothing under it. I lay down on the floor and pushed myself against the wall, pulling one knee up to my chest.

I could hear the Russian snorting furiously as he tried to figure out where I had gone. Chilled and shaking uncontrollably, I knocked over a bottle, giving away my hiding place.

"Whore!" he pounded his fists against the pantry door and tried, without success, to lift it off its hinges. Roberts knew how to protect his liquor.

Then the Russian took a long bread knife from the table and jabbed it through the crack in the door toward a spot of white—my knee. I gasped with pain.

Encouraged, he thrust the knife in again and again. I couldn't pull back any farther, but somehow I managed to wedge a ham between myself and the door.

Go ahead and slice up Roberts's ham, I thought to myself.

My attacker soon caught on. Panting and cursing, he pressed his eye to the crack. The thin door was all that separated us.

Oh God, what if he breaks it down? If he did anything to me, I would kill myself, I thought.

"Slut. Whore. Bitch…" his words were getting slurred.

Then I heard the whack of the small kitchen axe near the lock. I was sure this would be the last hour of my life.

"Please, God, forgive me my sins," I prayed. There were times I didn't obey my parents and misbehaved in school…once I cheated in ethics class because I hadn't done my homework. There must have been other things, but I could not think of them as the axe fell methodically. "Our Father, who art in Heaven…deliver us from evil." I repeated the Lord's Prayer over and over again.

The whacks suddenly ceased.

"Vodka!"

My attacker had found an open bottle. I could hear gulps and gurgles, a deep, appreciative sigh, then the sound of shattering glass, a thud, and more breaking glass. I imagined he had finished the bottle and, too drunk to stand, passed out on the floor. I heard a snort and then heavy breathing punctuated by loud snoring.

"Thank you, God!"

◆   ◆   ◆

The next day, as we sat on the canvas cots in the legionnaires' cellar, Olga related our previous night's adventure.

"That does it. I am going to register in the next few days," Andrejs declared.

8

Three Legionnaires Start Over

University registration had begun. My application forms completed, I arrived at the admissions office, where Professor Stradins, head of the medical faculty, looked them over.

"Now, why do you want to study medicine? And please don't say it's because you want to heal people. It sounds so false coming from young folks who know very little about suffering."

I stared at him, not knowing what to say. Stradins's expression softened. "It's good that you want to attend university," he said, patting my arm. "Knowledge is the only thing no one can take away from you." Then his tone suddenly formal again, the gray-haired professor ended our conversation with a curt, "Good luck on your exams."

More than a thousand students, most of them women, had applied to the college of medicine. Only three hundred would be accepted. Except for those who came from Red Army ranks or recent arrivals from Russia who were deemed safe, candidates had to report for an interview.

The names of those who would go on to the next level would be posted on the university bulletin board, along with a specific date and interview time. Everyone else could abandon any hope of a higher education.

The first list of names held no surprises. A few days later, a second list was posted, and I was one of the lucky ones.

Olga again coached me on what to say. The tale we concocted was simple. I would talk about my grandmother, a retired schoolteacher who had raised me and educated me at home. It was important to make a good first impression.

"You must also quote the new constitution whenever possible. Do it at every opportunity, no matter how insignificant the reference," Olga said.

During the interview, a man in a Red Army uniform asked about my siblings, posing the questions in such a way that assumed I had brothers. But, since I did not, I didn't have to lie, and my answers sounded convincing. When he said he

35

knew a young man who looked like me and had the same surname, I just laughed.

Finally, he changed the subject: "So, why do you want to study?"

I was ready with my well-rehearsed reply. "The government guarantees an education for its youth and pensions for the elderly. The constitution says so."

For the first time, the officer smiled. The interview appeared to be over, and he had not even asked about my parents. He handed me a form with forty-eight questions and told me to answer all of them and to return the completed form in a few days.

The exam itself consisted of four parts: chemistry, physics, the constitution, and the Latvian language. I wasn't worried. I had been at the top of my class in physics, and my knowledge of chemistry was also good. I had already memorized the constitution and was supremely confident in my knowledge of Latvian.

All in all, I was optimistic.

◆   ◆   ◆

Olga and I tried to look inconspicuous as we made our fourth visit to the ante-room of the registration office. The day before, Olga had come to register but without her documents. She explained that her husband would bring them the following day, after submitting a request for a change of surname.

Now Andrejs had taken his place in line with Martins and Leksis close behind. The three friends had planned everything down to the last detail.

Fortunately, many records had been destroyed in the bombing raids and fires, saving a significant number of people from certain deportation to Siberia.

Andrejs approached the table and calmly untied a bundle of papers. He had recently grown a small mustache and we had to admit that in his raggedy sweater and patched trousers, with a cap pulled down over one eye, he looked quite the proletariat.

"Comrade, here are my papers," Andrejs said, tossing them down on the table. He immediately launched into a rambling explanation of how he came to be in Riga and of his work in law enforcement, helping to fight the Fascists.

"It's all here in black and white," he said. "As a matter of fact, my half-brother is working for Vasiliev as an interrogator. You can call him."

"That won't be necessary, comrade!" the official replied. "I can see it's all there in your papers. Smoke?"

"Of course!" said Andrejs, accepting a cigarette of pungent Russian tobacco rolled in soiled paper. "This, by the way, is my wife," he motioned toward Olga.

"Looks like you got yourself a pretty one," said the guard. "Our people are smart...not like the bourgeoisie. Say, how would you like to work for us? We can use more help to hunt down the Fascists."

Andrejs thanked him and said that, while he'd certainly enjoy the work, he had just promised his services to the VEF factory director. "You know how important it is to set up the technology that will help us defeat the Fascists and capitalists. And I did promise the director personally."

"I understand," the official said. "Come back tomorrow. Your papers will be ready." He winked at Olga and pinched her on the hip as she turned to walk away.

"Pig," she hissed from a safe distance.

Andrejs's friends also passed through registration without problems.

But the men faced one more hurdle...Red Army service. Those born between 1922 and 1928 were drafted immediately for five years, while the younger and older ones were signed on as reserves or given military-related desk jobs.

Neither Andrejs nor his friends were of immediately draftable age. Their papers attested to that, as did their promise of jobs at the VEF factory.

Olga and I had done some research and found that certain jobs came with special privileges. The so-called armored jobs—electricians, factory and railroad workers, and so on—were much sought after by men who wanted to avoid the military. For a Latvian man to serve in the Red Army was considered not only demeaning but absolutely unacceptable.

And so, Andrejs, Martins, and Leksis, the beneficiaries of our research, began their new lives as civilian factory workers, safe for the moment, but still apprehensive about the future.

9

Madame General

The atmosphere in Roberts's house grew even more tense after Andrejs moved in. The brothers, whose views were so different that even normal conversation seemed futile, avoided each other. The easygoing Andrejs was used to speaking his mind, though now he didn't dare, but at least he was living with his wife and sons again.

Roberts could no longer boss Olga around, so, when something had to be done, he turned to me. But he was never satisfied and always criticized my efforts. His demands increased just as my exams were about to start. At first he only wanted me to water the plants and clean the rooms, but then he started bringing home stacks of papers for me to copy.

The Latvian part was relatively easy, but there were also papers in Russian. Since we didn't have a typewriter, I had to write everything by hand, and I dutifully traced the Cyrillic script, not knowing what it said. Roberts often complained that I wasn't working fast enough.

One day, using a dictionary, Olga translated some of the papers. They were mostly lists of residents in occupied areas, farm workers, or so-called "troublemakers," whose names would be passed along to the Riga courts, effectively sealing their fate.

One day, in a fit of disgust and frustration, I tore up the lists, ripping them furiously as if the paper itself was somehow to blame. Lucky for me, Roberts was not due home that night, or I might have told him what I really thought of him for taking advantage of the fact I didn't understand the language and using me to pass along lies involving innocent people. I might have thrown the scraps right into his face.

When Andrejs came home from work, he was taken aback.

"Who would have thought you had it in you, kid? Of course I would have done the same. But have you given any thought to the possible consequences?"

"I don't care," I said. "Let them send me away. I'll be with my father."

I didn't dare think that he might have been shot in a prison, or even ended his own life in some filthy basement. I started to cry.

"So, what are we going to do with you?" Andrejs asked, putting his hands on my shoulders.

Then, from the next room, the boys' gleeful laughter grew so loud and excited that Andrejs went to see what was going on. Standing in the doorway, he started to laugh, a curious laugh. I went to see for myself.

"We're playing Christmas," little Andrejs shouted. "Look! It's snowing!"

"Snow…snow…" his younger brother echoed.

The boys had ripped the paper scraps into even tinier pieces and were tossing them up into the air, squealing with delight as they floated down, covering the table, chairs, and finally the floor.

Olga joined us at the door. As Andrejs started to explain, he realized that his wife didn't seem at all surprised.

"Did you tell them it was all right to play in here?" he whispered.

She just smiled.

After that, I knew I had to find somewhere else to live.

Olga and I went to see Mr. Briedis, who gave us several addresses. He put special emphasis on one—boarding with a general's wife—and urged me to go at once and tell her he had sent me.

"I refuse to live with any Russian general's wife!" I protested.

Briedis looked bemused. "So you've been living in a Latvian apartment, and look what has happened to you. Soon there won't be any apartments without Russians. Then where will you go? Please trust me, and do as I say."

Downcast and apprehensive, I went to the house. My heart raced as I rang the bell, bracing myself for the sight of an armed, uniformed general like the ones Roberts invited to his drunken parties. His wife would be like the other Russian women, who, within days of coming to Latvia, were seen all around town wearing stolen fur coats.

The more spacious apartments were turned over to political functionaries and Party members, who were arriving in growing numbers. Red Army officers were allowed to bring their families. Maybe this general's wife, like the other newly arrived Russian women, also washed her vegetables in the toilet, wore white ankle socks with high-heeled shoes, and a nightgown as formal wear.

"Who's there?" came a voice from inside the door.

I took a few steps backward, ready to bolt.

An elegantly dressed woman appeared. Much to my relief, it was the same woman who had spoken to me in the street, the one wearing the red scarf in the registration office. Tonight there were traces of tears on her cheek.

"It's good to see you, my young friend. I was just thinking how nice it would be to have some company. Even strong people have moments of weakness."

"Don't cry." I took her hand awkwardly. "Life is hard for everyone now."

"You're very wise for someone your age," she said as she smiled. "Please, come in."

We sat for several hours drinking coffee and talking like we had known each other for years. I told her everything…my hopes, fears, and plans for the future. She also told me about her life.

Her name was Aldona Vinerts, and she had traveled all over Europe with her husband, a prominent Riga attorney. They had a grown son, who only six months ago had fled to Switzerland with his father. She was going to join them, but, when her own father died suddenly and her mother suffered a heart attack, Aldona decided to postpone her journey. Then the Russians arrived, and it was too late.

When the first group of soldiers broke into her home, Aldona chose, in her own words, the lesser of two evils: She offered herself to one of the officers, who called themselves Latvia's liberators. Her mother died the same night.

"But somehow life had to go on," she continued. "When, several days later, more soldiers burst in, I again 'fell in love' with the highest-ranking one—a general. A short time after that, he said he wanted to marry me, and I agreed. It only took a day to arrange the papers for my divorce, and the general and I were registered as man and wife. After a week, he received orders to go and conquer Berlin."

"Today I learned that he was killed in action somewhere in Germany. It has been a long time since I've cried tears of joy," she said.

I listened attentively to this woman, who seemed so intelligent, spiritual, proud, and strong. I finally asked if it would be all right for me to stay with her, and she was delighted.

It would be safe enough, she said, as the sign out front proclaimed that the residence was occupied by General Smirnov's family, so no one dared to break in. As a general's widow, she retained certain privileges, and, though she could not be certain the apartment would never be further subdivided, it wouldn't hurt if she already had a boarder.

"And, since you are so young, I hope I will somehow be able to save you unnecessary heartache," she said softly. I had found a new home.

For hours, I lay in the darkness, my eyes open. There was a lot to think about. I was not the only one with problems. Even so, I had been lucky to find my way out of some difficult situations. Gran must have been praying for me.

◆   ◆   ◆

It was the first day of exams at university. We sat in the large auditorium, waiting for the Latvian language test to begin. Professor Stradins came in, followed by Professor Balodis, a tall man with snow-white hair. Behind them were five men speaking Russian.

For the exam, we had a choice of three topics. First: why we wanted to be doctors; second: the poetry of Rainis; or third: job guarantees offered by the new government.

Recalling my first conversation with the professor, I decided against the first topic, which I was sure would also be the most popular. The second would be easy; I was familiar with Rainis's verses and literature in general. If I chose number three, would I talk about the past or the so-called ideals of the future? Perhaps analyze the constitution?

I decided on number two, and, when I was finished, I was satisfied that I had done well.

When the results were posted, most of the grades were marked "Unsatisfactory" or merely "Satisfactory." My efforts were rated "Good" with "no grammatical errors." My treatment of the topic had been "broad and knowledgeable enough, but lacking in social relevance."

Over the next few days, we had verbal exams in chemistry, physics, and the constitution, all of which I passed with ease. To be accepted into medical school, Latvian students had to earn nineteen points out of a total of twenty. The Communist youth were exempt from the rule. I scored nineteen points. Out of more than two hundred and fifty students, only several dozen were accepted for further study.

At the welcoming ceremony, the speaker was Russian. I didn't understand what he was saying, and my mind wandered until he finished his speech with a loud, "Urrah for Stalin!" Next, a man speaking in broken Latvian praised the new government for allowing us the opportunity to study and grow strong as Soviet citizens so we could use our power to destroy the Fascists and the bourgeoisie.

Then Professor Stradins stepped to the podium. He wished us success in our studies and later in the battle against death and disease. He talked about the evolution of medicine. We could never be good doctors, he said, unless we put the needs of our patients first. "The important thing is the quality, not the length, of life. *"Non quam diu, sed quam bene vixeris refert,"* said Stradins, a brilliant orator who would also be conducting lectures on surgery and the history of medicine. Finally, the ceremonies were over, and we had to rise for the playing of the "Internationale."

I walked home along Rainis Boulevard toward Valdemara Street. Snowflakes floated down, and I reached out my hand to catch them. They were so clean and perfect. What a pity, I thought, that the snow could not transform all the ugly things in our lives simply by covering them with a pristine blanket of white. But today had been special: It had been the first snowfall, and my first day as a university student!

◆   ◆   ◆

In happier times, the Opera Café had been a popular meeting place for Latvian society. Now they gathered in the central market. It was the only way they could get money to buy food.

On most Sundays, women perched on stools, their belongings spread out before them on a blanket. They displayed ornate Chinese vases next to patched-up trousers and balanced delicate Rosenthal porcelain atop pairs of worn-out boots. There were wooden clogs, feather boas, Brussels lace, a hobby horse with a broken leg, a sewing machine, carnival beads, a fan from the Napoleonic era, and an oil painting. Items of great value were mixed in with rubbish—all of it for sale. The vendors were once socially prominent Latvian women; the buyers, Russian women.

10

Classes Resume

The academic year always began on September 1, and the first semester ended January 7, signaling the start of exams, which continued until February 7. Then there was a week's break before the start of the second semester, which lasted until the beginning of June, when we again had exams until mid-July. Summer vacation was six weeks—half of July and all of August.

Exams for each subject were taken at specified dates and times. Scholarship grants, two hundred and fifty rubles a month, were given to students who got grades of "Excellent" or "Good."

Registration was once a year—in August. Those were the rules.

Medical students, whose course of study was six years, were eager for the time they would be able to carve up cadavers, assist at surgeries, and examine patients with a shiny stethoscope. But all that was still far away. Anatomy lab was not until the second year, and we had to wait until the third year to intern at a clinic. Only the final year involved actual practice, when students, or subordinates, as they were then called, were permitted to work almost independently. First we had to master the basics: chemistry, physics, anatomy, Latin, Russian, Marxism-Leninism, zoology, physical education, and military training.

It was time for my first lecture. Pausing in the vestibule, I checked to make sure the seams of my stockings were straight. Then, as I spun around, I bumped up against a barrel-chested, middle-aged man. "Now, now, child! Whether we run or walk, we all wind up in the same place eventually...so, please, slow down just a little," he chided.

Child! My pride was wounded.

"Do you know who that was?" asked a woman I had met earlier at registration. "The students call him Cadaver Martins. He's in charge of the refrigerated vaults, where the bodies are kept." Duly impressed, I went on to my first class: anatomy.

The huge lecture hall was like a theater with a gently sloping floor. Most of the seats in the back were already taken, so I sat down in the front row and took out my notebook. The students were all talking at once, creating quite a din. Suddenly there was dead silence, and a moment later the customary shuffling of feet that signaled the arrival of faculty—in this case a chunky man in a white lab coat. He was accompanied by four similarly attired fourth-year students, who placed books and papers on the lectern and set up a skeleton on a stand.

The lecturer, Dr. Tavars, was a gynecologist and acting director of the anatomy division. Reading from a prepared text, he began with an overview: First, we would study bones, then muscles, nerves, the brain, and finally internal organs.

There were no textbooks, so for the next two hours we took notes at a furious pace. Then the lesson was over, and, to more shuffling of student feet, Tavars left the auditorium. My fingers were cramped from clutching my pencil as well as from the chill in the unheated building, where we sat shifting uncomfortably in our bulky winter coats.

"Some lecture," said a male voice behind me. It belonged to a tall, slender boy named Laimonis. "I heard the same stuff from Professor Primanis, except he made it a lot more interesting." But Primanis was no longer in Riga. I heard he had gone to the West, which was probably why it was forbidden to mention his name.

"Tomorrow I'm going to wear some old gloves with the fingers cut off. It'll be easier to take notes," said another classmate, Vaira, a vivacious girl with sparkling brown eyes and dark, naturally wavy hair that stopped just above the shoulders. Born and raised in Riga, Vaira, both physically and in her demeanor, was the opposite of me.

The auditorium had grown silent again. Then more shuffling of feet greeted the new lecturer. A bony man in a threadbare gray suit entered the room. A Russian soldier's cape hung over his shoulders, and a bright red tie created a stark contrast to his dingy shirt.

"That's Dimanis," Vaira whispered. "He lectures on Marxism and Leninism."

"*Vot tak,*" Dimanis began, leaning his full weight on the lectern, which responded with a sharp crack. "I will teach you—dammit to hell—the basics as they were laid down by Marx and Engels and carried out by Lenin and that great leader and teacher Josif Visarionovich Stalin! *Vot tak.* These are things you have to know—dammit—especially now—dammit—when the snake of Fascism is not yet dead—dammit to hell—and in parts of Kurzeme, they are still fighting against our brave Red Army. They dare, those Fascist dogs—dammit—to raise their weapons against us. But we'll show them! We'll show them! *Vot tak.*" As he spoke, he threw the cape at the lectern with such fury that one would think it was the enemy himself. There was suppressed laughter in various parts of the large room. No one was taking notes.

Dimanis continue to rant. I began keeping track of the number of times he said *vot tak* and *dammit*. He was grimacing, breathing heavily, and punctuating his words with elaborate gestures. After awhile, his jacket hung from the lectern and the soldier's cape had slipped to the floor. He tugged at his tie. Was he planning to shed that too? And what would be next?

"*Vot tak.* If you are not with us," he raised his voice, "you are against us! We will take you like brides on your wedding night! *Vot tak.* Every Fascist and counterrevolutionary." He demonstrated by looping his tie around his hand and raising it above his head like a noose. "*Vot tak.* And if you don't believe me—dammit—if you don't believe the power we can give you, well…just look at me!" He pounded his chest, causing his shirt, which was already missing a few buttons, to open even wider, revealing pale skin and tufts of thick black body hair.

"Dammit, look at me! In Ulmanis's time, I was a bottle washer. But now…now I am a professor. *Vot tak!*" Pulling himself up to full stature, Dimanis smirked as he strode to the blackboard, one hand in his trouser pocket, the other tugging on his dark chest hairs.

"Once a blowhard, always a blowhard," a lone voice cut through the muffled giggles.

Dimanis's face went crimson, and the veins bulged out on his forehead. "Bastard! Fascist! The devil take your mother!" he spluttered with rage, his fists clenched and his mouth gulping for air like a guppy.

We were aghast. We had come for a lecture, but instead we got a barrage of expletives.

Dimanis spat out more threats and profanities against Fascists and other "bourgeois elements" and ended the class by striding off and slamming the door behind him.

I looked at my notebook: I had tallied seventy-four *dammits* and ninety-two *vot taks* in just one lesson.

◆   ◆   ◆

Lectures and homework were taking up my daytime hours. Getting together with Olga was difficult, as evenings were her busiest time, when her husband came home and the boys had to be put to bed. Visiting them also meant possibly running into Roberts, which was something I was determined to avoid.

Roberts had been like a maniac for several days after finding the torn papers. Perhaps he hadn't believed the story that it was the boys who shredded them after all. He calmed down only when Olga told him I was not coming back, and that I moved in with General Smirnov's family.

A faithful Party lackey, Roberts could be crude and aggressive or smooth and persuasive as circumstances warranted. Above all, he was a survivor. So, when he heard the general's name, his demeanor changed. For all he knew, such a connection could prove to be useful.

Life went on. We were issued food coupons. Shops received produce once a week, but nobody knew exactly when it would arrive. So, when it did, anyone who happened to be in the vicinity quickly got in line and bought whatever they could. If you happened to be at work, you were out of luck.

There were, of course, "helpful" people who offered to buy produce with your coupons, on the proviso they would get half of everything. Working folks had no choice but to accept those terms. Of all the coupons we had, the least in demand were the ones for butter and meat because all you could get for them was rancid fish oil.

It was much better if you knew people who lived in the country and grew their own produce, though getting there was not easy. Train travel required written permission. In the absence of that, there were Russian delivery vehicles, whose drivers demanded one ruble per kilometer from each passenger. And that wasn't the worst of it. Travelers also had to contend with "auto inspectors," who expected payment in return for declaring a vehicle roadworthy and allowing it to pass. To cover their fees, the drivers collected an additional charge from passengers, whose expenses continued to mount. Anyone who set out upon such a journey was taking a gamble.

Traveling at night was even more risky, as cars were often stopped and passengers robbed at gunpoint. It was obvious the bandits were our "friends from the brother republics," but, even so, official reports always erroneously stated that the criminals were Latvian partisans.

I was pleased and relieved when Olga returned safely from a trip to Jelgava. "How are things over there?" I wanted to know.

"Not much has changed. Local women who were unable to prove they had a job were given picks and shovels and told to clear the streets of debris left from the bombs. At night they were put up in an empty inn near the Red Army post, so the soldiers didn't have to go far for their "comforts.""

"Oh my God," I exclaimed, remembering my narrow escape at Roberts's party.

Olga quickly changed the subject. "Remember the sugar factory that was once a Russian prison camp? It's filled with Latvians now. I was watching some prisoners being herded towards the camp when a woman slipped one of them a piece of bread. A Russian guard saw her and kicked the prisoner, who fell down but would not let go of the bread. I could see blood coming from his mouth."

"How dreadful!" I exclaimed. "And they call themselves liberators."

"There was another group with trousers rolled up, on their knees in a ditch full of snow. Guards struck them on the back with sticks if they moved even a muscle. I stopped, but one of the Russians thrust a gun in my face and told me to keep moving. I recognized Pauls Bunge from the neighboring parish. And beside Pauls was…well, I'm not really sure…"

I stared wide-eyed at Olga.

"Lita, I'm really not absolutely certain, but…" she took my hand, "I thought I saw your father."

"Father!" I thought my head would explode. My big, tall, strong father was being forced to kneel in front of his "liberators?"

Olga picked up on my disbelief.

"I'm actually only certain about Pauls," she said and changed the subject again. "Your grandmother sends her love and a little package—mittens, a sweater, and some food."

How wonderful it was to know that someone loved you. There was a time we all took it for granted, like breakfast every morning. But now, each little thing meant a lot. Dear, kind Gran, I thought. When I become a doctor, I will take very good care of you. I promise.

11

Ill-Gotten Bones

There was fallout from the disturbance during Dimanis's lecture. The hunt was on for Fascists—anyone with antigovernment sentiment—and students were told to report to the university's central division.

Intense interrogations were conducted, but no culprit was found. Then, as a warning to the rest of us, ten students were arrested, allegedly for having some kind of connection, however remote, to capitalists, legionnaires, or other anti-Bolshevik elements.

Laimonis was looking pale and jittery, which to me proved that he was the one they were really looking for. So I wasn't surprised when I was walking home with Vaira and Lija and Vaira brought up the subject of the arrests, saying the guilty one had to be Laimonis.

"What makes you so sure?" I asked.

"He told me so," Vaira answered calmly.

"But why are you telling me?"

Vaira smiled. "My brother and Laimonis were classmates at the French Lycee during the German years. Laimonis was sorry he lost control during the lecture and was ready to turn himself in, but my father talked him out of it. Even if he confessed, he said, the other students would not be let go. He advised Laimonis to learn from the experience and keep his mouth shut in the future."

"But, for God's sake, why are you telling me this?" I repeated.

"Well, maybe we know you better than you know us," Vaira said. "Our friend Dace lives in your building. You may have seen her in Zoology class, sitting next to Lija—the slender brown-haired girl with the nice legs. Her mother and Mrs. Vinerts are friends."

♦   ♦   ♦

Inorganic chemistry was taught by Professor Stals, but a variety of assistants, including the chemist Silins, helped supervise laboratory work. Today's exam required us to correctly identify the separate elements in each of fifteen solutions or repeat the course.

Experiments were especially difficult in the dead of winter. There was no heat and often no water. When the pipes froze and burst, we had to carry buckets of water up the stairs.

The university lab was so cold that any spillage would freeze on the floor. We wore winter coats and gloves with the fingers cut off and we crowded around the gas burner, whose light, at least symbolically, provided some warmth.

One of our classmates was named Alma. Now, I'm not a very tall person, but Alma only came up to my neck, and her thick rubber apron dragged on the floor. She was always asking for help, and at first we obliged. But we soon realized it simply was not worth the time and effort, as she didn't seem to retain any information.

Today she was barefoot and approached my lab partner, Dace.

"I can help you now, but what will you do during oral exams?"

"Maybe some other kind person will help me," Alma replied.

"Why aren't you wearing shoes?" Dace wanted to know. "It's very cold."

"The dean is coming today," Alma explained. "Maybe he can get my tuition lowered, or recommend me for a scholarship. I want to show him how frugal I am. We workers can't afford to be like the bourgeois."

Just then the door opened, and in came Silins with Professor Stradins, head of the medical faculty. Dace pressed the test tube back into Alma's hand.

The professor came straight to our table.

"My burner isn't working. That's why I'm here with my colleagues," Alma lied, taking a small leap sideways into a puddle on the cement floor, splashing water onto the professor's trousers.

He saw her bare feet, which were even filthier than the floor. Alma had accomplished her goal. "It's so hard to get by," she said, looking up at him. "I have to save wear and tear on my shoes and stockings."

Aghast, Stradins looked ready to take off his own shoes and give them to her on the spot. "Don't worry. Things will be better soon. I'll see to it," the professor said and left quickly, without checking anyone's results. It seemed Alma had touched his kind heart.

◆   ◆   ◆

Anatomy class presented the biggest challenge. We learned that every human being has more than two hundred bones of different shapes, lengths, and sizes, each with any number of bumps, grooves, and other indentations—and each with its own Latin designation.

But because the university had not escaped the Red Army onslaught, only one complete skeleton remained, and we saw it only during lectures. The course was also exceedingly difficult, and many students—even the ones from the Party ranks—were dropping out. It seemed they were unable or unwilling to learn the complex material. No self-respecting "worker" should have to work that hard! It was almost as if they expected to get a degree just for turning up.

One day, Lija confided that she knew where we could get a skeleton, if we weren't too scared. If it meant going to a cemetery at night, of course I would be scared, but I could handle that. It was still nothing compared to my fear of the Russians.

"So, you want to do it?" Lija asked teasingly.

"Sure. Why not?" I replied convincingly, if not truthfully.

It was obvious that Lija and another student, Agnis, were co-conspirators looking for someone to help them execute their plan. But I had to agree that studying a skeleton up close would help immensely in my studies.

"All right, then, let's meet at dusk tomorrow—St. Peter's Church. Don't forget to bring some sacks and a pair of sharp scissors. A candle might be useful, too."

It was all so mysterious. Nevertheless, the next night I made my way to the churchyard. Not wanting to be the first to arrive, I stepped back into the shadows and waited.

A young woman approached and sought cover in another alcove, which, as it turned out, was already occupied. There were more footsteps and muffled giggles. So we were all there after all, none of us wanting to be seen as the first.

"Shh!" Lija ordered, her eyes wide, her finger to her lips. "Follow me."

She led us into the church and down into the cellar, which held the ancient burial vaults. The air smelled of dust and rot. Flickering candlelight revealed pried-open coffins and decayed remains, skulls and bones scattered about. Our shadows danced grotesquely on the walls and across the floor. A rat scurried behind some debris.

"There's no shortage of bones here. They're everywhere, like candy! Just help yourselves," said Agnis, trying to lighten the mood.

As he continued to crack jokes, our thirst for knowledge won out, and we started gathering up skulls, tibias, and fibulas. We even bagged an entire corpse, cut up into parts. As we stepped outside with our sacks full of bones, we found ourselves surrounded by police.

"Ah, you are students. And you have been robbing the vaults at St. Peter's? Well done!" They took our names and sent us on our way.

After a moment, Laimonis asked Agnis: "Don't you think that, by desecrating those graves, we were serving the interests of our oppressors? Perhaps we're no better than they are."

Agnis, though shaken, tried to justify our actions. "I didn't mean any harm. I saw in the *Red Corner* newspaper that students were encouraged to find their own educational aids and that there were bones in the church vault."

"I believe you," Laimonis said sadly, "but we've also given the Russians a trump card they can use against Latvian students. We should be more cautious when it comes to anything posted in the *Red Corner*."

"What's done is done," Vaira said. "We committed a sin, but we did it for a worthwhile cause. We can use the knowledge we gained to save our patients' lives."

I felt no sense of satisfaction as we said good night and went our separate ways.

◆   ◆   ◆

The remains had to be cleaned, and Agnis sought advice from Cadaver Martins, who suggested adding chemicals to boiling water to break up the leathery skin and dried tissue.

I volunteered our kitchen, as Mrs. Vinerts was away, visiting friends.

The laundry kettle was on the stove, bubbling away with the witches' brew, filling the candle-lit room with vapors so thick we could hardly see each other's faces. As Agnis, Laimonis, and Lija emptied one of the sacks, Vaira and Dace slipped the body parts, one by one, into the steaming pot. The way we had come by the bones still bothered me. But Vaira and Dace, happy at the prospect of doing well on exams, had no regrets, so I kept my guilt and my opinions to myself.

Time passed quickly, with Dace chattering away, telling Red Army jokes. But the wooden kitchen chairs grew uncomfortable, so around midnight we brought in some of the soft padded chairs from the living room.

The next thing I knew, daylight was seeping through the curtains. The flame under the kettle had gone out, and the water was cold. Vaira and Dace were sound asleep in their chairs. Sleepy-eyed and sheepish, we arrived at university in time for the second lecture.

The next night, we managed to stay awake. We found some amazing books about medicine, including an anatomy handbook, all of which must have been key to Mr. Vinerts's legal practice. We pored over the illustrations—the elbow joint, the shoulder socket, the skull. Things were starting to make sense, and suddenly the Latin terms were easier to remember.

We fished an arm out of the water and pulled away the tissue until we could compare the illustrations with the smooth, clean bones. By daybreak, we not only had a complete skeleton, but heads full of invaluable information. We were well pleased with ourselves.

12

Poor Eugenie

Eugenie was a very pretty girl with black hair, a Greek nose, and great figure. While the rest of us were busy taking notes, Eugenie would simply file her nails as she sat and listened. She frequently cut class, but when she was there she always made it a point to speak to me.

After the lecture, she took my arm. "Do you mind if I walk with you? The professors all tell me what a good student you are."

I was surprised, and flattered.

"Oh, don't look so shocked," Eugenie smiled sweetly. "I work in a place where I have access to all kinds of information. I like you, though. Would you come and visit me sometime?"

I couldn't think of any reason to say no.

"I've got a two-room apartment on Freedom Street. Won't you stop by Sunday afternoon for coffee and a liqueur?"

I wanted to say I didn't drink, but it didn't seem appropriate, so I just accepted her invitation.

◆　　　◆　　　◆

As I prepared to visit Eugenie, I was feeling quite the society dame. Mrs. Vinerts had told me all about Sunday afternoon coffees, where the proper guest was expected to bring flowers for the hostess. But where would I get flowers? I had nothing to give to the shopkeeper. And Eugenie was so nice. I wanted to bring her something special. I opened my dresser drawer and took out a silver five-lat piece that had been made into a brooch. I loved wearing it but could also imagine how good it would look on Eugenie. I wrapped it in a piece of colored paper and put it in my pocket.

An hour later, I was sitting on the couch next to my hostess. On a low table in front of us were two cups of aromatic fresh-brewed coffee and an assortment of delicious cookies. There were also carnations in a crystal vase. Had she gone to all this trouble just for me?

Eugenie's nails were lacquered a bright red, to match her lips, and black mascara made her long eyelashes even longer and thicker. She wore a violet hostess gown that was slit up the side, and there was a dark seam up the back of each of her stockings—altogether very fashionable. As I stared at her pretty, made-up face, I was reminded of a doll my father had once brought me from Riga. Her eyes would open and close, and she had long, thick, dark lashes.

Eugenie was delicate, not like the rest of us more athletically built girls, whom the boys treated more like their sisters. Whenever Eugenie appeared, they just stared as she walked past. She always looked straight ahead, though she was well aware of the effect she had on them.

Eugenie thanked me for the brooch, choosing her words carefully. It was hard to tell whether she liked it or not because her facial expression never changed; it remained like a lovely mask, suitable for all occasions.

"Have some of this, dear," she said, offering me a piece of cake with whipped cream. She used the term *dear* liberally, and somehow managed to sound sincere every time. "And then you can try a bit of the liqueur." Eugenie kept her voice low and cheerful.

The cake tasted divine; it had been a long time since I'd had anything like it. I didn't want to admit I had never tasted alcohol, so I put the small glass to my lips and took a sip. I coughed involuntarily as it burned my throat going down, but it also left a pleasant chocolaty aftertaste.

"Don't worry," Eugenie soothed. "It takes a while to get used to it. Then we come to realize how it can make our lives seem more pleasant."

Bravely, I finished the first glass, and then another. A wave of warmth flooded my body, and I felt so light-headed I just wanted to laugh and laugh.

Then Eugenie told me a sad story.

There was a man in her life, she said. They loved each other very much, but in order for them to be together, she had to take a job as his secretary. Because she was working, she could not attend all her lectures and therefore had no notes and had not completed any lab experiments. She felt so helpless, at her wits' end, she said, leaning closer. And that terrible Silins was expecting her to report to chemistry lab tomorrow morning. What was she going to do?

I tried to calm her by telling her a story from my own experience, to show that the professor was really a nice person. "He handed me a test tube and asked me to analyze its contents. I immediately ran the tests for cobalt, bismuth, silver, barium, but came up with nothing. Finally, I told him the tube could only contain

H_2O, because I couldn't find anything else. 'You're absolutely right,' he said, slapping me on the back. 'And you're also the first to come up with the correct answer!'"

"But, what is it…this H_2O?" asked Eugenie.

"You don't know?" I stammered. "It's…it's…water!"

Eugenie sighed. "…and, just imagine, tomorrow I have to face that terrible man."

I felt truly sorry for her then. It must have been difficult to hold down a job and keep up with your studies all at the same time. "I'd like to help you," I said hesitantly. "Maybe I can just show you how it's done, but Silins will certainly chase me away."

Eugenie seemed to perk up, the polite smile returning to her face. "You are so sweet. Would you really do that for me, dear? I would be ever so grateful. You could do my experiment while I stand next to you. And don't worry about Silins. He won't chase you away. The professors know they have to treat me differently."

Again, I couldn't see any reason to refuse. Eugenie was nothing like Alma. She was so nice. And I had noticed that people really did treat her differently.

"Thank you so much, dear," she cried. "I didn't think you would refuse. You're such a kind-hearted girl. I also know how highly the professors regard you. It would've been pointless to ask somebody stupid."

Then, quite abruptly, she changed the subject. "Have you ever been in love?"

I tried to think of an answer that wouldn't make me look naïve or foolish. "Well, yes, once…kind of," I said in a half-whisper, looking at the floor.

"There's a big difference between true, lasting love and infatuation," Eugenie said with great conviction. Lowering her voice, she motioned me to come closer. "Now, I will tell you a very big secret. My lover is Health Minister Grigorash. He comes to see me every Saturday, stays all night, and leaves at noon on Sunday."

I was stunned. Still, it did not diminish her in my view, quite the opposite. I now thought of Eugenie as a woman of the world. I felt honored, even after she let on that the faculty members were also in on her secret.

"The teachers all know I am with Grigorash. So you see I am not really worried about exams. None of them will dare to fail me," she explained. Her tone had hardened, but her smile was still dazzling.

As we said good night, I was convinced that Eugenie's personal fate as well as her future at the university was in my hands. I assured her that not only would I do her chemistry and physics experiments, but I would help her prepare for all the other exams. I also promised not to tell anyone about our agreement.

13

Pain and Hopelessness

I was miserable. I wished I were dead and laid out in a coffin. Maybe then some-one would take pity on me.

It was the first time I had ever failed an exam.

In preparing, I had been so sure I had known every single detail of the skeletal system. I couldn't tell you the number of times I examined each of the bones in the box in the corner of my room. One by one, I went over them with Vaira and Dace, then Lija. I even spent a couple of days with Eugenie just to make sure she was at least familiar with the basics.

She was not a particularly attentive student, but she had been right about one thing. The chemistry lab assistant really didn't seem to notice, or care, that I was the one who did the experiments while Eugenie stood and watched.

So when it was time for exams, I was a bit nervous for her.

But she surprised all of us by emerging just a few minutes later with a big smile and a mark of Excellent.

What also came as a surprise to us was that Dace got only a Good.

At last it was my turn. I strode in, supremely confident. Professor Erdmanis was seated on a wooden chair, a box of bones in front of him. He selected one, handed it to me, and asked me to describe its function.

Insignificant in appearance, the bone could only be a metacarpal or metatarsal. First, I had to say if it was from the hand or foot and then whether it was from the right one or the left one. But it was such an odd little bone, I just couldn't be sure. I was mortified. I honestly did not know. There was only one thing to do.

I told Erdmanis that I didn't feel adequately prepared and, before he had a chance to say anything, I left the room.

As I was telling my tragic tale, Irma, the chemistry professor's daughter, started laughing.

"It wasn't a bone, silly! It was a smooth stone deliberately put into the same box with the bones. Teachers have been pulling that trick for years!"

I was stunned. First resentment, then anger welled up inside me, and finally grim determination. I vowed I would never again be too complacent or overly confident. And never, ever again would I allow myself to be tricked.

◆   ◆   ◆

There is a saying that bad things happen in threes.

Mrs. Vinerts returned from Jelgava with fresh produce. She had also visited my grandmother.

"In the last few weeks, there were many arrests and deportations," she said. "The Cheka arrested Krastins in a case of mistaken identity. They were looking for someone named Krumins, couldn't find him, but still had to make their quota."

"But, I asked you to tell Gran what Olga said about the man at the sugar factory," I interrupted her.

"Yes, Lita, the man Olga saw really was your father. Your grandmother gave him some food while the Russian guard wasn't looking. But on January 25, he was taken away, God only knows where."

As a chill traveled down my spine, I suddenly felt frightened, and very helpless.

◆   ◆   ◆

Still, life had to go on, along with the fear and uncertainty that had become the norm.

It was beginning to dawn on us that the long-awaited Allies may not, in fact, be coming to our rescue. There was no Swedish coastal blockade, no Americans.

It was May 8, 1945.

On every street corner, loudspeakers blared forth praise for the "victorious" Red Army. Latvians, who had hoped for an eleventh-hour miracle, could only listen and shake their heads in disbelief. Was this our new reality, or a cruel test of nerves?

That afternoon there was a parade. American-made cars formed an agonizingly long procession, followed by cannons and tanks with open hatches and sullen Russian faces. People had been hastily recruited to line the streets and cheer the "invincible army," which had won "against impossible odds."

Rounding up willing participants was not easy. A bottle of vodka was offered to anyone willing to smile, applaud, and throw paper flowers, which were provided by the parade's organizers. Most of the takers were youths or former convicts. Even so, the crowds of "happy and grateful Latvians" were sparse and, to help photographers document the event, the same groups of people went from one corner to another, shouting encouragement to each arriving regiment of Red Army "liberators." Also in the crowd were many Russian women who had only recently arrived in Riga and were now joyfully pelting the soldiers with flowers. Newspapers would later describe the women as Latvian.

The truth was that most Latvians did everything within their power to avoid the tragic spectacle. We had been told—ordered, really—to show smiling faces on this "joyful" day, but I was finding it impossible to swallow the lump in my throat. I saw Dace, whose face mirrored my own despair. We put our arms around each other and wept for the misfortune that had befallen us and our homeland.

Photographers recorded many similar sad tableaux, and the next day, the Communist papers would describe them as scenes of "overwhelming relief" and "tears of gratitude."

◆   ◆   ◆

At university, at least we could immerse ourselves in our studies. It was time for another exam, and Dr. Tavars had placed himself next to a cadaver.

"Meyer...the rotator cuff."

My classmate described the shoulder muscles, detailing how, together with the connective tissue, they allowed the arms to move.

"Facial expression muscles," the doctor said.

Meyer winced only slightly as she indicated points on the cadaver's face.

"Thank you. Your grade is Good. Next!"

The pathetic, barefooted Alma stepped forward.

"Peterson, *musculus gluteus maximus.*"

"That would be here," Alma said, indicating her upper arm.

"Come, show me on the cadaver."

Alma approached and pointed.

"That is the bicep," Tavars frowned. "Show me the *gluteus maximus.*"

"Oh, yes, of course, here...on the stomach."

Her response drew muffled giggles.

"Peterson, you are obviously not prepared," said Tavars testily. "You will have to repeat the exam."

"No! I can't!" Alma squealed angrily. "I am a member of the working class and cannot, like the bourgeois, come back any time at all."

Startled by her outburst, Tavars paused, then reaching for her notebook, said quietly, "Very well, I will let you have a mark of Satisfactory then."

"I won't accept Satisfactory; I need Excellent," she shouted, refusing to relinquish her notebook. "I am a worker. I must have a scholarship."

"But that would not be fair to your classmates. You can't even identify one of the largest, most obvious muscles."

"Oh, now I know! It's here!" Alma exclaimed, slapping herself on the bottom.

"Well, on the third try, you've come close, but it doesn't show any knowledge on your part."

"I don't care! I said I don't have time to come back. Here!" Alma thrust her notebook at him. "I am a member of the Communist Youth!"

Tavars took the notebook and wrote in it. Judging from Alma's reaction, she was satisfied.

We later learned that teachers had been told that all Communist Youth were "polite, honest, intelligent, and diligent" and to be sure those commendable traits were reflected in their grades.

In the coming months and years, this rule would come into play over and over again. The Com-Youth students got the best grades because, naturally, they were "the smartest." Com-Youth and Party members always got priority for jobs because they were "the hardest workers." Even court rulings favored Party members, because they "never lied." Non-Party members could not, except in the rarest of cases, even consider lodging a complaint.

◆   ◆   ◆

Censorship was most blatant when it came to the postal service. Much of the mail was simply not delivered. The letters that did arrive took weeks and had obviously been opened and sloppily resealed. We had to be careful what we wrote.

One day, a letter arrived from Gran saying she wanted to see me. I had not been back to Jelgava since I began university—going back wasn't wise. But this was too important. After nearly a half hour's wait at the roadside, I managed to get a ride.

Back in familiar surroundings, curled up on the sofa with Prince the cat on my lap, I felt safe at last. I told Gran about the scruffy glassblower Dimanis, who was now a smartly dressed gent blowing off his mouth about the joys of Communism and the zoology lecturer Traubergs, who loved the color yellow and showed nothing but disdain for the girls. Boys who wanted to get a good grade from him would wear a yellow shirt during exams. What Traubergs didn't know was that it was the same yellow shirt being passed around. I told her about Roberts, his drinking orgies, and the horrible night I had had to lock myself in the pantry.

I also talked about my friends—Dace, Agnis, the fashionable Lija, Eugenie, and my zoology lab partner, Peteris. Gran seemed to like all of them, all except for Eugenie. She couldn't understand why I would do her homework and lab experiments.

"But you've always said that helping people is the Christian thing to do," I tried to justify my actions.

"Yes, child, but only for those who are truly in need," Gran said emphatically. "You said Eugenie has an apartment with expensive furniture and a closet full of gowns and furs that are too big for her. Maybe she and Roberts have more in common than you think."

"No, she's not like that," I insisted.

"There are many different kinds of people in this world," Gran said, fixing her clear blue eyes on mine. "You mustn't be so trusting, especially now. I don't know how many years I have left."

"Oh, Gran, don't even think about dying!"

"The time will come for all of us. I'm not afraid. I'm only worried about you. I pray every night that God will help you."

Gran had been raised in the country, where people loved nature and were deeply devout. She maintained a serene dignity, even in the most stressful times.

"Now, my girl, don't you even want to know why I asked you to come?"

"Yes, of course!"

"Well, there are some people here who are truly in need of help."

"Here?" I looked around. "Where?"

"In the bunker, near the barn."

"But who? How did they get there?"

Gran explained. "One night I heard a tap on my window. It was Sergeant Emils, and he had six legionnaires with him."

"You mean the same Emils who came to visit us with his brother?"

Gran nodded and proceeded to relate their stories of the last grim days of the war. The Latvian legionnaires had not been fighting to help Hitler or further his plans for a national-socialist Germany. Their homeland was in danger of being crushed again by the Russians. Until the final day, the BBC radio reports had remained encouraging. While giving few details, they had made it clear enough that British warships would arrive and order would be restored. But, in the end, those reports had turned out to be tragically wrong.

The war was over. Germany had capitulated on its Eastern Front, and the fate of the Baltics was sealed—the Russians had won. Confusion turned to chaos. The overwhelming instinct for most people was to get away as fast and as far as possible—to board trains and ships that would take them to a safe place and a new start. Our soldiers, whose courageous struggle had come to naught, faced deportation. Many legionnaires were arrested and sent to places such as industrial Tula near Moscow, the Arctic coal mining town of Vorkuta or Omsk and Tomsk in Siberia. Others, hiding in the forests, were tracked down by dogs and sentenced to hard labor in other parts of Russia.

Riveted by the stories, I stroked Gran's cat, which was now purring and sound asleep.

"The Russians found Emils's detail in hiding, and a battle ensued. Seven men managed to escape and found their way to Jelgava, where two of them used to live. And that is how they got to my house," Gran told me.

"For now, they are safe in the bunker under the haystack. One entrance is behind the goat pen; the other is under a pile of mulch by the lilacs near the neighbors' property. When Russians came looking for Fascists, they thrust long knives into the hay but found nothing."

I was suddenly very worried about Gran. Her house, set back from the main road, was accessible by a narrow, badly lit path. Was the presence of the legionnaires putting her in danger? Yet there was no doubt they needed assistance. And, as Gran couldn't hide them forever, I knew that their fate rested in my hands.

14

Changes

Until the fall semester, lectures at Latvia University had been read in Latvian, but, more and more, Russian instructors were starting to take over. It was clear that the "heroes of the liberation effort" were getting preferential treatment. Among their many perks were fully equipped apartments ready for immediate occupation—"in perfect living condition." They had, of course, belonged to Latvians who either had fled to the West or been loaded into cattle cars and deported to Siberia.

Riga had become a magnet for educators from Moscow and Leningrad. They arrived "by special invitation" and were entitled to bring friends or relatives, generally fifteen to twenty per "invitee."

There were other changes as well. A public address system was installed in apartments, broadcasting just one Riga station. It was illegal for ordinary citizens to own a radio or a typewriter. The few typewriters that remained had to be registered, along with typeface samples, twice a year—in May and October. That was to make it easier to track down anyone who might try to use them to spread anti-Communist sentiment.

The head of histology, Augureikins, gave our first lecture in Russian. We could not follow along, as our knowledge of the language was scant or, for many of us, nonexistent. So some students took advantage of the situation to make money. They translated the lectures, writing them by hand and also using carbon paper, so they could sell more copies.

Since we couldn't understand the lecture, we often passed notes to each other. Soon the instructor became paranoid that the "bourgeois nationalists" were trying to sabotage him, and students would periodically be called in for interrogation about their "secret organization."

Augureikins zeroed in on one particular Latvian student named Skaidrite. He spoke to her in Russian, but she just smiled and answered in Latvian. He had no clue what she said and took it as a sign of disrespect, not only to him but to all "brother Russians."

So Skaidrite was summoned to his office time and time again until her nerves were shattered. One day, in the middle of a lecture, he moved slowly toward her and, when he was a few feet away, started to sing at the top of his lungs. She let out a scream and, trembling violently, collapsed on the floor. She had finally broken under the strain. And, although her physical health improved with time, Skaidrite couldn't keep up with the lectures and had to drop out, her dream of a higher education forever lost.

In anatomy class, Dr. Tavars was replaced by a Russian-Estonian named Kalbergs. He was learning to speak Latvian, and within several months was conducting classes in two languages. He lectured in Russian for the Russian students and a mixture of Latvian and Latin for us. He was also paid two salaries for his efforts. Kalbergs was known for extending special kindnesses to his female students. The downside of that was that they were expected to reciprocate, and he never forgot a rebuff.

◆   ◆   ◆

One Sunday afternoon I went to visit Olga. I wanted to ask her and Andrejs's advice about the legionnaires hiding on Gran's property.

Andrejs opened the door.

"Hello! Is Olga home?"

"Yes…in the kitchen."

After a brief warm handshake, Andrejs and I walked down the hallway. Feeling right at home, I missed his silent signal to go into the living room and headed straight for the kitchen.

Roberts was sitting at the kitchen table, a bottle of whisky in front of him.

"Well, if it isn't our illustrious student!" he exclaimed. "You know, of course, it's only the dummies who go to school. The smart ones find out all they need to know just by living. *Prozit!*" (Cheers!)

"And where do you think all your smarts will get you?" Olga challenged him. "You don't have one shred of decency. Even your boss could see that. That's why he got rid of you."

"Got rid of *me*?" Roberts pounded a fist into his chest. "That's nonsense! He just wanted to take the credit for my work." Refilling his glass, Roberts raised it toward Andrejs. "Prozit, old man! Now I have a job where the bosses aren't too clever. Everything I can get my hands on goes into my own pockets. Those Russians are so dumb! Their brains are in their pants."

We left him alone with his bottle.

"So, what is his new job?" I whispered.

Olga explained: "Out in the country, they are dividing up land, giving each ten-hectare section to the new landlords, who take over the farm, along with the livestock. Previous owners were given responsibility for overseeing an area of up to thirty hectares. They were also given the derogatory name of 'kulaks.'

"The new landlords were not required to pay any duties or taxes in the first year. Later, they were to be assessed a reasonable fee. There was a different set of rules for the kulaks. Aside from the high duties they had to pay on milk, butter, grain, potatoes, and other produce, they were required to pay fifteen to twenty thousand rubles in cash, sometimes as much as fifty thousand a year. Yet their barns were empty, their farm animals taken away, the fields torn up, and their homes subdivided. Where were they to get the money to pay the state? Whatever belongings they had managed to hold on to were impossible to sell. The markets were strictly controlled with permits issued only to those who had paid all their dues to the government. Their backs were against the wall.

"So they found that, by using the black market, they could sell grain, smoked ham, sausages, clothing, housewares, and whatever else they had. But, with no direct access to black marketeers, they needed an intermediary. And that is where Roberts comes in."

No surprise there. We changed the topic.

"Whatever happened to legionnaire Martins?" I asked.

Andrejs told me his story. "He was given urgent orders to deliver to the front. He arrived at the designated place and time, but then came the capitulation and much confusion. In regrouping, the partisans—or Greens, as they called themselves—had been joined by other soldiers as well as civilians.

"When it came Karlis's turn to go for provisions, he borrowed Martins's coat. Upon his return, they were to meet up with another group of Greens in the forest. But, as it turned out, the leader of the new group, so full of energy and good ideas, had betrayed them. As soon as they had all come together, the military KGB (Cheka) surrounded them and started shooting. Of course, the men, Martins included, fought back but were overpowered. That was the Russians' latest ploy, to send one of their own to gain the others' trust, and ultimately to betray them."

Andrejs drew a deep breath and went on: "On his way back, Karlis wasn't far from the arranged meeting place when the bloodbath began. He ran until he came to a stream, jumped in to avoid Cheka tracker dogs, and stayed there for several hours, submerged up to his neck among the reeds. He heard the Russians say they had captured some partisans, though a few were badly wounded. Having been in the water for such a long time, Karlis became ill but was nursed back to health by a kind farmer's wife, who gave him one of her son's suits. Using Martins's papers, which had been in the coat, he managed to get through various checkpoints."

Andrejs was deeply concerned. Not only did he feel sad for his friends, he was worried that some of the military documents that had been in the possession of the dead or wounded Latvian soldiers might have fallen into the wrong hands.

Only time would tell, but if the Russians got a hold of the papers, the identities of Andrejs, Leksis, and many of the others' could be revealed, placing them in jeopardy. At that point, I thought it best not to add to their worries by mentioning the legionnaires hiding at Gran's house.

◆   ◆   ◆

In Riga there were coupons for everything—butter, meat, and milk, but, because demand always exceeded supply, those items were available for only an hour or two after delivery to the stores. The idea of the coupons, it seemed, was as unrealistic as the promised "happy land" of Communism. The only food that was readily available was bread—it was dark and dense and tasted of sawdust. We were entitled to a half loaf and one slice every two days, and we had to stand in line for an hour to get it.

It was tempting for students to try to sell their bread. One loaf in the black market cost seventy rubles—a considerable sum, as our monthly stipend was two hundred and fifty rubles.

The problem was that nobody wanted to buy half a loaf. So Lija and I devised a plan. She would buy a two-day ration—one loaf and two slices. Two days later, I would do the same. We took turns selling the whole loaf at market, keeping the two slices for ourselves to eat.

Our main diet consisted of potatoes—boiled or fried in fish oil. All of Riga reeked of fish oil, its foul smell permeating everything from the apartment walls to our clothing.

Students who did well in political courses were rewarded with what was called the "first warm coupon," redeemable for a bowl of soup and potatoes with gravy. Those who earned good grades in general got the "second warm coupon," good for a bowl of porridge, and, if we were really lucky, a glass of imitation fruit drink.

We'd dream about the first meal we would buy with our doctor's salary. It would be a large pork steak, with lovely golden brown potatoes that had been roasted in pig's fat. And for dessert we would have real fruit compote, sweetened with sugar, not saccharine.

◆   ◆   ◆

Because of frequent document checks, we always had to carry our temporary IDs, which had taken the place of our passports. There were many stories of ID papers being stolen and the subsequent great difficulties in replacing them.

The streetcars we used as public transportation were always overcrowded, especially in late afternoon, and sometimes I had to stand on the outside platform. One particular day, people seemed more ill-tempered than usual, pushing, shoving, and swearing at each other.

It was not until I had gotten off at my stop that I realized my book bag had been slit crosswise with a razor, precisely at the spot where an inside pocket held my money and ID. The contents, of course, were missing. Distraught, I went to report the theft to the police. I explained how it had happened, but the officer refused to take down my complaint.

"Comrade, there are no thieves here," he stated emphatically. "You lost your things because of your own carelessness."

"I didn't lose them. They were stolen."

"You lost them!" the officer raised his voice.

"No! I…"

"Nonsense! Maybe you sold them to some Fascists. That's what usually happens, and then people come and try to tell us they were stolen."

"I'm telling you the truth. I…"

"And for the last time, I'm telling you that there are no thieves here. I'll say in the complaint that you lost your things. For that you have to pay a fine of one hundred rubles and wait six months for a replacement ID."

"One hundred rubles!" I gasped. "Six months! What if I need to show my ID?"

"If that happens, allow yourself to be brought back to the police station, and we'll sort it out."

"But why so long? Why six months?" I asked, thinking of the trips I needed to take to Jelgava to help the legionnaires.

"It can't be done any faster. Besides, the only way you'll get the papers in six months is if you admit that you lost them. If you keep saying they were stolen, it could take much longer. Go home, comrade, think it over, and come back tomorrow when you've decided."

Early the next morning, I was awakened by the doorbell. "Who is it?" I asked.

"Your papers," came the reply in accented Latvian.

I cracked the door and saw a young man, who repeated the words with a heavy Russian accent: "Your papers. I found them. If you give me one hundred rubles, you can have them back."

"Where did you find them?" I asked, pronouncing the words slowly and distinctly.

"Your papers. I found them. If you give me one hundred rubles, you can have them back," the Russian repeated, word for word. It seems that was all he had learned. It also meant he had not understood my question.

"Nehokike, nenada?" (You don't want them?) He switched back to his native tongue and prepared to leave.

"Wait, I want them!" I called after him and ran inside to borrow the money from Mrs. Vinerts. I had not yet received my monthly stipend. In spite of the unpleasantness, I was glad to be able to buy back my papers, if only to avoid going back to the police station.

"Finding lost papers" was a popular way to make money in Riga and was often used by former soldiers working in teams. They would pick a target, create a disturbance, and, in the melee, one would slit the victim's bag or coat pocket with a razor blade and take its contents. If any victims protested too strongly, the razor would be held to their faces, accompanied by a threat, which more often than not was carried out. The thieves would never be apprehended because, according to the police, there were no thieves here. Robbery victims were later given the chance to buy back their own possessions.

◆　　◆　　◆

Our study requirements during the first two years included physical education and marksmanship. Those who excelled in sports had a promising future and were granted special privileges, which included the right to shop in stores that stocked real butter.

And if they were preparing to go to the sports festival in Moscow, they were given a suit of clothes, shoes, and sports gear. Athletic benefits were also extended to those in the workforce, who were allowed to spend all their working hours in training.

The thinking behind it was that "Communist countries must be the best in the world at everything, so they could defeat the capitalists, who in time would be drawn into the Communist fold."

Military training was the most difficult. The boys caught on quickly, but for the girls it was dry and dull. For four hours each week, we had to study army regulations and military strategy and learn the individual parts and assembly of a variety of weapons.

The classroom contained a large sandbox, where the instructor—a Russian officer—built hills and valleys and placed houses, bridges, trees, and a Fascist or capitalist enemy, a black block with a stiletto blade attached. Then he called on a student to plan and execute the attack, using red blocks representing the Red Army. This was considered one of our most important classes.

Four more hours a week were spent learning to march. On our way to the practice field, we must have looked quite comical: Girls, sometimes wearing high-heeled shoes, marched in formation along the cobbled street, rifles or automatic weapons on their narrow shoulders. Then the drills began, with commands shouted in Russian: Get up! Drop down! Right face! Left! Present arms! Missing a military lecture was tantamount to a political transgression, with harsh consequences.

I was standing next to Dace, who had been sick and did not know the drill had been rescheduled. It happened to be her birthday, and she was wearing a light blue suit her mother had re-made to fit her, along with a hat with a veil—also a present from her mother.

"Right! Left! Run! Drop down!"

Not wanting to soil her new clothes, Dace remained standing at attention. The drill instructor cursed at her and ordered her to step forward. "Right face! Present arms!" he barked.

Confused and nervous, Dace caught the tip of her rifle barrel in the netting of her hat, sweeping it into a large puddle left by the previous night's downpour. The Russian students burst into laughter as the instructor brought his boot down to crush the delicate hat, simultaneously splashing muddy water all over the front of Dace's new suit. Fighting tears, Dace no longer resisted and followed all the ensuing commands—including the one to drop down.

15

The Illegal Masquerade Party

It was almost Martins' Eve—Halloween—and we all agreed that it should be observed in true Latvian fashion.

Vaira's older sister used her sorority connections to find a medium-size room on Valnu Street, across from the former army store. From our class, which had grown to three hundred and fifty including the late-arrival Russian students, we would invite only fifty. And, because there were relatively few Latvian boys, we chose fifty more from the engineering and agriculture colleges, both schools known to be non-Communist.

We didn't have much choice when it came to the food—it would have to be whatever was available, or whatever we could trade in for a couple of days' worth of rations. No matter. We were poor and our future was far from certain, but party fever swept over us. Our biggest dilemma was what costumes to wear. Dace dug into her grandmother's storage chest and came up with some lace blouses, a fan, a long black slip, and crumpled paper roses. It was a good start.

Finally, the day arrived. The room was festively decorated, and the students' costumes were testimony to what could be done with a bit of imagination. And, with all the sacrifices that had to be made for days or even weeks in advance, the same could be said about the party food.

We pulled out all the stops that night. We had boiled peas, traditional goose—and, best of all, Lija's home-brewed beer. We sang Latvian songs—the "language of dogs," the Russians called it. Even the professors, in a light-hearted mood, climbed up on chairs for some of the more rousing choruses.

I felt glamorous and invincible dressed as Madame Pompadour. Dace was a cowgirl, with a human tibia stuck in her leather belt. We were very popular with two boys in particular vying for us as dance partners. If they couldn't get a dance with us, they seemed to prefer standing on the sidelines. Both wore plain dark suits and no masks.

Hiding behind my mask, I lost my country girl shyness and had no trouble keeping up with my witty dance partner, whose name was Hugo. When the musicians took a break, Hugo and his friend, Noldis, sang and played the guitar and accordion. They were a big hit with the girls, who crowded around, smiling and applauding. But, when it was time to dance again, the boys asked only Dace and me. We were in seventh heaven.

Midnight arrived much too soon, and it was time to take off our masks. Suddenly shy, Dace and I headed for the cloakroom, but our young admirers followed us, begging us to spend the remainder of the evening with them. Dace finally gave in, but all my inhibitions had returned, presenting a challenge for Hugo, who was used to girls falling all over him.

"May I see you home?" he asked.

"No."

"Why not?"

Silence.

"May I see you again?"

"No."

"Why?"

"I'm busy."

"But, maybe...sometime?"

More silence.

Finally, I persuaded Dace to leave. Noldis came along, with Hugo trailing behind. He caught up with me at the stoop, but I ran inside and quickly closed the door.

The next day at university, Lija and Vaira were called in and asked to explain why they had taken part in "illegal" activities. It was forbidden, they were told, to meet in groups of more than a certain number without a permit. Any large gathering had to be registered with the police and fire departments. And, although the evening had gone without a hitch, it became clear afterward that, had we sought permission in advance, it would have been denied. Stories in the student newspapers condemned the "bourgeois spirit" of the medical school, citing our gathering as a classic example of what not to do.

As the evening's organizers, Vaira and Lija had to publicly apologize to the higher faculty, who in turn apologized to their superiors for allowing such a terrible thing to happen. The two girls lost scholastic aid for two semesters, and all student guests had written warnings put into their records. But, even so, nothing could diminish our memories of a joyful night.

♦   ♦   ♦

Hugo was turning up more frequently with stories that everyone found amusing. I was the only one who didn't laugh. To be honest, I wasn't sure why I was being so standoffish.

Hugo was studying veterinary medicine, so his lectures were near the medical school, making it easy for him to hang around and wait for me. It also made it easier for me to see him coming and try to avoid him.

Noldis was having more success with Dace. They had gone to the movies together, and, although Dace didn't say much, I knew she liked him. Through her, I learned more about Hugo. He was a former legionnaire, who by some lucky break was able to cover up that "blemish" on his background and allowed to register for classes. Noldis, a fellow legionnaire, described his friend as a brave but foolhardy soldier who had won several medals. Spoiled, vain, and charming, he invariably found himself surrounded by women.

Dace also told me about Hugo's sad childhood. His father was German, his mother Latvian. His parents split up, causing him emotional conflict that was made worse when his mother remarried. Hugo had told Noldis he had never met such a stuck-up girl as me, and that he just didn't understand me.

"And he won't, either," I said stubbornly. "I don't like him or his silly jokes. I doubt he's even capable of a serious conversation."

"But so many girls are absolutely in love with him," Dace persisted. "If one of them managed to snag him, wouldn't you care?"

"Not a bit! I'm just not interested," I told her.

♦   ♦   ♦

As the eighteenth of November—Latvia's Independence Day—approached, word spread that there would be a gathering at the Cemetery of Brothers to honor our war heroes. Dace and I made plans to attend.

But, as I was getting ready, Eugenie arrived unexpectedly. Noting my confusion, she came in nevertheless, tossing her fur coat onto the nearest chair. Draping one leg casually over the arm of a club chair, she started talking about her favorite subject—her lover, the health minister.

"You can't imagine how much he adores me! But he has so many other obligations," she said, taking out a small silver cigarette case. "Do you mind if I smoke?"

I felt awkward listening to her. The things she told me were too private, and in the cold light of day took on a certain banality.

The doorbell sounded again.

Ignoring it, Eugenie said, "I thought you might help me prepare for my physiology exams, dear. You know I'd be lost without you. My fate is completely in your hands. Won't you please help me?"

"Of course," I answered mechanically and hurried to open the door.

It was Dace. She was surprised to see Eugenie but quickly composed herself and took off her coat, as if she had been planning to stay a while.

"Am I interrupting something?" asked Eugenie, lighting another cigarette. "Perhaps you had other plans?"

"Oh, no!" replied Dace. "We were just going to study."

"Oh, homework. Actually, just before you arrived, Dace, we were talking about something much more interesting—my love life."

"Ah, yes, I've heard all about that," Dace said casually, "but, if you're so much in love, why don't you get married?"

"Married?" Eugenie sniffed. "How common. My lover says he will never turn me into his servant. That's what any wife is to her husband, just an unpaid maid."

"But if you love someone, every chore is a pleasure," Dace persisted.

"Washing socks? Ironing shirts?" Eugenie wrinkled her nose. "It's the death of romance. We'll never get married, so we won't lose the magic of our love."

By the time Eugenie left, it was too late to go to the cemetery.

"I don't trust her," said Dace.

"Oh, it's just your imagination," I said, but I had to admit I was starting to question my own loyalty to Eugenie. "She's completely under Grigorash's spell. I've read it's like that when you're really in love."

"Maybe," Dace said hesitantly, "but she talks about her affair to anyone who'll listen. It's almost like she's bragging."

All of a sudden I felt foolish. I thought Eugenie was confiding in me because I was the only one she could trust with her "secret," but it did indeed seem to be common knowledge. I realized she had just been taking advantage of my generous nature.

I walked to the bookshelf and, reaching behind some books, took out a small Latvian flag. "This should be on display today," I said, placing it beside a homemade candle. Dace opened a book, *Touched by Fate* by Aleksanders Caks, and started to read out loud.

On that poignant Independence Day, it was important for us to show that we loved our country and honored the memory of its fallen heroes.

◆   ◆   ◆

The next day, there were a lot of empty chairs in our class. We learned that everyone who had attended last night's gathering at the cemetery had been arrested.

Laimonis, Lija, and some other students had been delayed by a streetcar accident. Later, as they neared the gates, they had seen figures hiding in the bushes. It was clear that the area was crawling with secret police, so they left.

Dace and I realized how close we had come to being arrested.

I asked Lija how she had learned about the gathering.

"Vlasova told me. She is a Russian-Latvian who recently joined our class and is always complaining about the 'damned Communists.' I don't know why I believed her."

16

Betrayed by Sweden

I was so proud of myself. I had been able to help the legionnaires hiding on Gran's property.

I had found a woman in the passport division who was willing to prepare travel documents for a fee, though only two of the young men's families could come up with the required five thousand rubles after selling whatever valuables they had left.

There had been a three-day wait for the finished documents. With great trepidation, I had set off with the money, hoping I was not walking into a trap.

But everything had gone smoothly, and in the end I was as happy for Emils and Guntis as if they had been my own brothers.

Now, many years later, I know they both fared well.

◆　　　◆　　　◆

Then I got more good news. Our neighbor, Vigants, told Gran the NKVD had moved on, and I could go back to my father's house.

In the meantime filtration camps had been set up all over the country to identify and detain "troublemakers." Some people were held for a day, others for weeks or even months. The drill was always the same: The ones who were able to spout Communist propaganda sailed right through, while others were arrested and deported for no apparent reason. The weak or frightened ones—who under interrogation usually admitted to things they had never even done—were pronounced guilty and sent to Siberia.

The most severe grilling was reserved for those who had fled to the West and returned home, mistakenly believing the threat was over. They were perceived as the most dangerous, because they were able to draw comparisons with a life other than Communism. Free thinking was not permitted; the Communist leaders would be the ones to tell people what they were supposed to think. Bilingual or multilingual people were also feared because they could read books or papers that might give them "dangerous" ideas.

Speaking Russian, however, was encouraged. We were told it was the most beautiful language in the world and the richest in expression. It was the only language that could show people the true path to Communism and the future. That kind of verbal and mental slop was fed to the barbarians in the troughs of Stalin's pigpens. And now that they had invaded our land, they wanted to force-feed it to us.

Lost in thought, I walked along the edge of the forest. I saw familiar houses with strangers' faces at the windows. In the best of circumstances, the former homeowner's family was allowed to stay in one room. More often, they were told that the sauna or barn were more suitable for "their kind."

From Diana's Hill, I could see my father's house in the distance. There was a gray-haired woman in the yard. My God! It was Mother. She had aged so much that for a moment I didn't recognize her. Tearfully, we fell into each other's arms.

Thanks to dear Anton, she had escaped physical harm, but her nerves were frayed and every few moments she looked out the window. Was she afraid more soldiers would arrive? Or was she hoping to see Father coming down the path.

Anton's health was not good, but still he resisted going to the hospital.

"I will get better, if it is God's will," the old man said philosophically. "I am more worried about how you will get along without me. But it is all in His hands."

The conditions in the hospitals were not good. They were inadequately staffed and overcrowded.

"There is a great shortage of doctors," our friend Dr. Veide said. "We have only one surgeon and one infectious diseases specialist. I am an internist, but I don't know how much longer I can remain effective in my job. The women's ward is full of teenagers and children who have been raped, beaten, stabbed, or shot. Today, a six-year-old rape victim died of her injuries."

The tragic story reminded me of Velta Sergeyeva and her little girl. I squeezed my glass so hard it cracked, cutting my hand.

Mother then told another story, about Latvian soldiers who were turned back by Sweden and kept penned up in barbed-wire enclosures. She had managed to talk to them and give them food after bribing their Russian guards with cigarettes. The soldiers' trust had been betrayed—more proof the Allies had forgotten about us. It was something I didn't want, or dare, to believe. There had to be some kind of misunderstanding.

Back at school, the list of things that were forbidden grew longer than the list of things that were allowed. Books not written in Russian were bad. To be really "good" students, we were urged to "see things in the proper light" and get high marks in the main courses—Marxism-Leninism, military studies, and the Russian language—the very subjects we found the least palatable.

Every one of our absences had to be explained by a doctor's note, or we risked losing scholastic aid. Although the student monitors were from our own ranks, there was another group watching them. And, if they failed to report an absence, they would get a black mark for disrespect toward a government institution.

Some of the older students complained that Latvia University used to encourage academic freedom, character development, and independent thinking. In Communist universities, taking any sort of initiative was frowned upon.

Laimonis had begun his studies during the German occupation, so the Communists made him start over. He found Professor Kalbergs's anatomy lectures especially useful, but his interests extended to veterinary medicine, and he took it upon himself to attend those lectures as well. When he was asked to explain why he had missed some classes, he made no effort to hide that he had taken on an extra course load. But his actions were labeled inexcusable, and he had to give up his scholarship. Even excellent marks in Marxism-Leninism and Russian could not save him.

"I won't allow the *comrades* who dream up the rules to tell me what to do," a frustrated Laimonis said as he walked with Dace and me. "I'll get a job."

"I hope you can find one," Dace said. "But what if they keep harassing you?"

Our conversation was interrupted as Eugenie caught up with us.

"She must want something again," Dace said under her breath.

She was right. Eugenie wanted me to be her partner for anatomy exams. She showed me two Russian medical books she said she had just purchased.

"If I didn't have the right books, none of my friends would believe I was studying medicine," she explained.

"But where did you get them? How much did they cost?" I asked.

"I have connections. I work for the ministry, remember?" she said smugly.

◆   ◆   ◆

Exam time was approaching, and Cadaver Martins had asked some students to help bring cadavers up from the basement and place them on lab tables. As he and Laimonis brought in the first stretcher, I stared, horrified at the formaldehyde-soaked body of a man, his head bashed in on one side.

When Laimonis headed back downstairs, I followed him. The stench took my breath away and stung my eyes. Along each wall of the large cement room, I saw a row of tubs filled with formaldehyde, each holding a cadaver with a numbered metal tag in its ear.

"That's how we know when each of them died," Laimonis explained, leaning on a long hooked pole used to fish the cadavers out of their preservative baths. My stomach was churning. I felt sick. It struck me then that only a naive young medical student would consider carving up one of these bodies as a great accomplishment.

"They look pretty fresh to me—only maimed," I said, wanting to break the ghastly silence in the chilly room.

"Most of them are from KGB interrogation headquarters on Stabu Street. They've been beaten, shot, or otherwise killed, but we mustn't talk about that. Martins has been threatened with deportation if that information leaks out," he whispered. As we stood looking at those poor victims, I touched Laimonis's hand and said a silent prayer. Maybe he was doing the same.

◆　　　◆　　　◆

That evening, Dace arrived in an agitated state. "You've got to help us."

"What is it? What's wrong?"

"Not here. You have to come to my place. My mother and I need to know what to do."

"But how would I know what to do if your mother is at a loss?"

"We must put our heads together," Dace said impatiently. "Come on."

As we entered her house, a young man stood up to greet us. He was quite a sight, with trousers barely to midcalf and a jacket too tight to button. Either he had long ago outgrown his clothes or had borrowed someone else's.

"This is my cousin," Dace said. "Now, Jaksis, start from the beginning."

"Well," he said. "I joined the legionnaires like all my friends and left my sweetheart back home in Daugavpils. When our forces in Kurzeme were defeated, I hid and tried to think of some way to get back to her. I traveled a few miles every night, and after a while I reached Daugavpils, which by then was in ruins and filled with strangers. It was not wise to ask too many questions. Then, quite by accident, I met two fellows like myself, and we came up with the idea to escape to the West via Poland. I won't go into the details, but one of them was shot dead and I was wounded and captured. While in prison, I recovered, and the unrelenting interrogations began. I finally admitted to every possible crime, even ones I knew nothing about. It was common knowledge that the Cheka would go easier on you if just answered yes to all their questions.

"They offered me freedom, on the condition I become an informer, something my conscience would not allow. Nevertheless, I signed a paper and was given my first assignment—to learn the whereabouts of a certain dentist's husband. To make it easier, they set me up in an apartment next door to hers. Since I knew the family, I advised the dentist to tell everyone her husband was killed in the war, though in reality I had heard he was in Germany. When I reported back to the Cheka, I related the story I had concocted.

"For my next assignment, they took me to Riga to find out one professor's views on the present state of affairs. I met with him on a variety of pretexts, but after a while it seemed he was asking me even more questions than I was asking him. This time I told my contact the professor appeared to have Communist leanings. What else could I have said if I didn't want to bring him any harm? But the Chekist was not satisfied and said I would be punished for failing to cooperate. Only later did I realize the professor probably had a similar assignment, and he might have given the Cheka a less benign report on me."

Jaksis looked at me wearily. "Dace should not have brought you here," he said, rising. "I'd better go."

"No!" Dace cried. "They'll send you to Siberia! They'll torture you."

I remembered the anatomy lab, and it occurred to me that Jaksis might wind up like the cadavers there. I wanted to weep along with Dace for what had happened to our country. I was angry with the Americans, who supposedly cherished freedom and yet had abandoned the Baltics and half of Europe to the Communists. It was clear we had to find a way to help ourselves.

Suddenly an idea struck me. "I know! Jaksis can stay with my grandmother in Jelgava. It will give us all more time to think."

"But he'll be stopped at the first checkpoint."

"We will come up with a plan," I said with all the resolve I could muster.

◆   ◆   ◆

At university, the big day had arrived. Wearing white lab coats and rubber gloves and brandishing scalpels, we gathered outside a locked classroom door. Soon we would be like the doctor whose portrait dominated the large entry hall. We took ourselves very seriously indeed.

Professor Kalbergs arrived, and we entered the lab. Before this moment, all our knowledge had come from boxes of bones, jars of organs, and previously dissected cadavers. Now the time had come to show that we ourselves knew how to locate, isolate, and identify the network of veins and arteries, muscles and nerves that made up the human body.

"The body is not symmetric like a chess table," Kalbergs was saying. "Only in theory are all people formed from the same bones, muscles, nerves, and organs. In practice, there are many irregularities, which is why you will dissect the hands of one cadaver, the feet of another, the stomach cavity of still another, and the head of yet one more. Be sure to watch your classmates as well."

I was paired with Dace, and our first assignment was to work on the hands—one each. At the feet of the same cadaver was Eugenie, paired with Sergei.

Having cut through the skin of one foot, Eugenie was looking for help. "Sweetie, won't you tell me what we're meant to be looking for?" she asked, looking at me.

"*Musculus rectus femoris* is at the top," Sergei replied.

"Sweetie, won't you help me?" Eugenie directed her question at me.

Leaving the cadaver's hand, I went to her aid.

"And what is this big nerve here?" Eugenie asked.

"That is the *vena saphaena magna*," Sergei again responded.

"Yes, but this one, is this the big nerve—ischias?" Eugenie persisted.

"Ischias?" Sergei looked surprised. "You seem to be under the impression the *nervus ischiadicus* is found at the back of the foot. This is an artery."

"You're not being a very good lab partner," Eugenie complained, acting the wounded damsel. She quickly turned back to me. "I have so little time…Sweetie, I need to be somewhere very soon. Won't you help me?"

I did what she asked.

Eugenie's eyes kept darting toward the door. "Why is he late?"

I wanted to ask who "he" was, when the lab door—with the sign "Unauthorized Entry Forbidden" in Latvian as well as Russian—swung open. A man in a Red Army uniform stood holding an enormous old camera. He looked around, saw Eugenie, and, with all eyes on him, strode toward her.

A solemn-faced Kalbergs held up his hand, as if telling the visitor to stop.

"Hallo!" the uniformed Russian shouted at Eugenie.

Taking a few steps forward, she waved her scalpel coquettishly and stepped between the two men. The three were now the center of attention.

Eugenie smiled sweetly at Kalbergs. "You know, Professor, Serjosha—I mean, Health Minister Grigorash—would like a photograph of me in the anatomy lab. He didn't have time to come and see for himself. You could join me so it would look as if we were sharing our views on a matter of great medical importance. Ser-josha would be so happy."

Kalbergs looked uncomfortable.

"Very well…But why not a photograph of me with the whole group of lovely ladies," he said, motioning for the other students to join him.

As the photographer was setting up a tripod to mount his cumbersome cam-era, Eugenie said sharply, "All right then, go ahead and take one photo of the group, but then take several of me by myself and also with Professor Kalbergs."

17

The General's Wife and Kirchenstein

The food markets in Riga were drying up. Making things more difficult was the fact that farmers were not allowed to sell produce unless they complied with government regulations. The government's seal of approval could be bought with the right connections, but the demands were impossibly high—as an "incentive" for farmers to join a cooperative "of their own free will."

For country folk, necessities such as shoes, soap, nails, or sugar were in short supply. An exchange of goods was an obvious solution for both sides. But that was considered a provocation—a crime against the government, because it "hindered economic development."

Economic development? It didn't take a genius to see that chaos ruled, and the right hand had no idea what the left hand was doing.

The loudspeakers were a daily reminder for us of the "right path" to take. "Only the disillusioned would consider engaging in such criminal behavior as barter, because the truly honest people are the workers who contribute to the grand scheme of socialism," they blared in their unrelenting attempts to "educate" us—the "backward" people.

For the most part, people remained apathetic. Among friends, they made the occasional critical remark, "They're lying to our faces, and saying black is white. The real criminals are running the country."

Jobs were assigned at random, with no consideration for aptitude, interest, or established skills. Residents in the countryside were not permitted to leave, except to go to school, so some parents pushed their children to study. They also knew there would be no work on their farms, as the autumn would not bring the usual bountiful harvest. That much was clear, to both generations. City dwellers had their own problems. Factories, offices, and other workplaces were all run by Russians, so other Russians and Russian speakers got preferential treatment. In short, the only people who could get ahead in Latvia were those who knew Russian or were willing to learn it.

A similar situation existed in the schools, where Latvian and Russian students were segregated. Bilingual instructors read each lesson twice. But the Russian teachers spoke only in Russian, and students had to sit through their lectures whether they understood them or not.

We hated the things the regime forced upon us, but if we wanted to graduate and find work in our profession, we had no choice but to comply. And while loudspeakers boasted about "unprecedented" economic progress, in reality we had never been more destitute.

Still, we thought, maybe someday, somehow, things would change.

◆   ◆   ◆

Mrs. Vinerts had privileged status. No one could order her to work or threaten her if she refused. But she was also one of the "criminals" who went to the countryside for food, because all the rubles she got as the widow of a general could not buy the food that did not exist in Riga.

She had a lot of free time and her own Russian chauffeur on call. Even when he had other driving assignments, he would take her along, particularly if the destination was near a market. Through an elaborate system of bribes, he and the other chauffeurs would drive their ladies where they wished to go, sometimes picking up other passengers and even sharing the spoils at the end of the outing. This time, Mrs. Vinerts had a double reason for going shopping. Besides bringing back food, she would help Jaksis escape.

There were chairs, tables, and shelves set up in the hallway to be taken to Jelgava. It was obvious Mrs. Vinerts could not manage by herself.

"Come on, let's go," the chauffeur shouted to Andrejs and Mr. Briedis, who were struggling to load a large kitchen cabinet into the car.

"Have a good trip!" I waved as the car sped away. "Good luck!"

◆   ◆   ◆

I had a genuine feeling of satisfaction that evening as I sat in the large club chair drinking coffee. Very few people could afford real coffee in those days, and the rich aroma was making me swoon. It seemed to me that here, in Mrs. Vinerts's rooms, the West began. My impressions of it were formed by her stories and all the beautiful things from faraway places.

"To celebrate our recent good fortune, let's use my Rosenthal china," she said, arranging apple strudel, miniature pastries, and sandwiches on a platter. "My husband and I bought it. Who knows how long before we'll have to trade it in. We must enjoy things while we have them. Too many people are leaving everything in God's hands, when they should be trying to help themselves. I really admire Martin Luther, who said that first you must do everything in your own power. When you have done all that you can, leave the rest to the Lord and pray that things will come out all right. What if we hadn't helped Jaksis?"

Taking a sip of coffee from the delicate white cup, she related the events of the day.

"We had no problems getting to Jelgava. My chauffeur even helped Andrejs carry the heavy cabinet into your grandmother's garden shed. I gave him an extra large tip for his efforts. It was only later that a pale and shaken Jaksis was able to crawl out of the cabinet to stretch his cramped limbs. Then we drove to an excellent Lithuanian market in Janiski.

"What about the border crossing?" I asked.

"Border? What border? Don't you know we are all one brotherhood?" she said dryly.

Even though I caught the irony in her voice, her comment made me angry. "Latvia is a free country, and it will always be. I refuse to believe that, in the eyes of the world, we are part of the Communist republics."

"If only we hadn't been sold out. Did you see the newspaper photos of Churchill, Roosevelt, and Stalin at Yalta, smoking their long Russian pipes and mapping out the future of the world? Sly old Stalin probably blew smoke in that naive American's eyes to keep him from seeing the truth."

I didn't say anything, but I too had seen the smiling trio, with a photo caption describing the cordial atmosphere of the talks.

"On the way back, we stopped in Jelgava again," Mrs. Vinerts went on. "That was when I learned Anton had died. Who knows how your mother will get along without him. She might be better off giving up the house."

"My mother will never do that! She has to wait for my father," I said.

Mrs. Vinerts changed the subject. "Now I have something funny to tell you. As of yesterday, I am no longer the general's widow." She started to laugh, as if enjoying a really hilarious joke.

"It's right here in black and white—a letter in Russian: It seems that General Smirnov was already married. His wife and children have requested his pension, which will now be taken away from me.

"But, that means you'll lose your income and status..."

I failed to see any humor in her situation, but Mrs. Vinerts just kept laughing. "I have no intention of giving up any privileges. I told Kirchenstein I did not know the general already had a wife when I married him. Not that I could ever understand why I got his pension in the first place. It's a perfect example of how disorganized the regime is. The pension came directly from Moscow, and if I didn't make a huge fuss over losing it, the high-placed fools in Riga would never be the wiser."

I didn't know whether to believe her. I was sure she would be all right, but at the same time I worried that if the payments stopped, the landlord would notice. I voiced my concern.

"If that happens, you must remember that victory belongs to the one who attacks first," the newly deposed widow said calmly. "I will attack the Russian general's honor, expressing my shock and outrage that a man of his stature would stoop so low. I'll shout until they beg me to be quiet. I will tell them that, in my mind, I am still married. As far as the pension, whether or not I keep getting it doesn't matter—the main thing right now is our safety.

"Anyway, I've taken care of the landlord. I am now his supervisor."

"What? How?"

Mrs. Vinerts was full of surprises. "It was simple. There is no paper or document that can't be bought these days. It's only a question of the price. Our Russian housing director has always paid me compliments, so I invited him over to drink vodka. I even stuffed three bottles into his canvas carry bag. Then I told him I needed a document stating that I am employed by the housing authority as his assistant. He was honored to do a favor for a general's widow and just a few hours ago, I waved the official paper in our landlord's face."

"A while back, you mentioned talking to Kirchenstein," I said, unable to contain my curiosity any longer.

"Oh, yes, I digressed. It has been such a strange day. This morning a Russian in a lieutenant's uniform stuck his boot in the doorway and said he was sent by the housing authority to reclaim two rooms. I knew if I let him put his bags in the hallway, I would lose the right to turn him away. In the eyes of the housing authority, "inviting" a visitor in was a friendly and binding agreement that he was welcome to stay. It was getting more common, with the number of Russian immigrants increasing, encouraged by the regime to promote "the brotherhood" and "preserve" our culture.

Since no one would willingly allow Russians to move in, the housing authority came up with a directive: A Russian was given papers that entitled him to one or more rooms in the larger apartments, with the understanding he would be in charge from that point on. The Russians would not take no for an answer, some gaining access with threats or brute force and others with overblown promises to pay three hundred to five hundred rubles a month rent, which they conveniently forgot after moving in. All of these methods were unofficially sanctioned. So instead of talking, I acted."

Mrs. Vinerts savored the look of disbelief on my face. "The Russian was trying to push his way in, so I grabbed an umbrella and drove the point as hard as I could through the top part of his boot, near the laces. He shouted and swore but didn't budge. Then I slapped him across his insolent face. While he was still in shock, I grabbed the large floor vase my husband had brought back from Greece and, with the water still in it, cracked it over his head, screaming all the while that he was getting what he deserved for disturbing our peaceful household. 'Don't forget, you stupid little lieutenant, that I am a general's wife!' I carried on like that for quite a while until he finally gave up and left."

I laughed out loud. The lieutenant would not forget that encounter and no doubt made his retreat thoroughly convinced that she was one of their own. "But I still don't understand where Kirchenstein comes in."

"Well, immediately afterward, I got dressed and went to the Agricultural Academy. I said I was a general's widow and had urgent business with Professor Kirchenstein. I threw my papers down in front of his secretary and said it was a matter of great importance, that my heroic husband had not given his life in vain defending Communism alongside Comrade Kirchenstein in the ranks of the Red Army.

"The secretary phoned the professor at home and sure enough, the old guy arrived ten minutes later, huffing and puffing. I started right in on him. 'Comrade, thanks to you and other clear-minded people, we Latvians have been allowed to join the mighty Russia to form a brotherhood and together take Communism to the rest of the world. Only when capitalism is vanquished and all the people of the world live happily in a Red paradise will we reap the fruits of our labors. Fight! Fight until the final victory—that is our duty.

"My husband, General Smirnov, gave his life fighting the Fascists in Berlin. Yet I, the general's wife, have been insulted and abused. A stranger tried to force his way in, like I was some kind of Fascist. And worse, he showed me papers that had been prepared by the housing authority without my knowledge. Comrade, he overstepped all the boundaries.

"To my own ears, my outburst sounded almost comical, but after a brief pause the old man bellowed at his secretary, 'Maria Janovna, get me the phone number of the housing authority!' Before I left, I had a paper stating that my apartment was off limits, in honor of a fallen hero," she finished with a flourish.

In bed that night, I had trouble falling asleep. Maybe it was the caffeine or just an overly active mind. It was odd, I thought, that Mrs. Vinerts and Roberts, while vastly different people, had some things in common. They both maintained that only the strong survive, and both were capable of coping in any situation. Except that Roberts would bow and scrape to anyone of higher rank, yet happily trample lesser beings, even his own family, if it meant material gain for himself.

Mrs. Vinerts had no interest in material things, except to hold on at least to some of what she had. And so, in fighting the occupiers, she occasionally borrowed some of their own methods.

While I had no desire to be like her, I admired her deeply.

18

Sometimes It Doesn't Pay to Be Nice

Andrejs and Olga had a third son, Juris. When I arrived at the christening ceremony, Roberts was circulating among the small number of guests.

"What is he doing here?" I asked.

"He simply announced he was coming and bringing his new girlfriend," Olga shrugged. "I asked why he wanted to attend a Latvian christening, and he replied, albeit with false humility, that he too was Latvian."

"Since when has he had any national pride?"

"Maybe since he lost his job again."

We were in the kitchen, preparing food for the party.

"As you know," Olga continued, "Roberts was making quite a lot of money, and even more on the side by putting the squeeze on landlords who owed payments to the government. He'd wait until their backs were against the wall and then push even harder until they paid him just so he wouldn't report them. But one day Roberts picked on someone with friends in high places, and his little game was exposed."

"They didn't lock him up?"

"Obviously not. But he had to grease so many palms to get out of his predicament that he lost all his ill-gotten gains."

"He's broke?"

"Not exactly. He still has money, at least for now," Olga went on. "No doubt you've heard about the latest housing changes. Everyone is being urged to give up a room to a new arrival from our 'brother republics.' So Roberts sold one of his three rooms for thirty thousand rubles. The buyer assured him he was single, but, when he moved in, he brought along a wife, two kids, and a mother-in-law."

"So why the humble act?"

"I think I know," Olga said, but didn't finish. The guests had started to arrive. I sat next to the minister, Lija's father, listening intently as he told stories about student life during the independence years.

Across the table, Roberts muttered about the "lousy idiots who had come to rob our country." He also cursed the British, Americans, and Swedes for doing nothing to help us.

I couldn't believe my ears.

Soon, he felt the urge to perform and sang one opera aria after another. Roberts was in his glory as some guests complimented him, and his girlfriend, Ance, gazed at him adoringly. But I was still trying to figure out why he wanted to be there.

I was helping Olga bring more food from the kitchen, when, as if reading my mind, she said, "Ance's mother is on her deathbed. Her father, a Latvian army officer, was killed in 1940, and she hates anything to do with Communism. But apparently there is some kind of inheritance, so it is important for Roberts to convince her of his feelings for her and for Latvia."

"Ah, so he wants to impress her with his nationalistic relatives. Poor Ance. Shouldn't somebody warn her?"

"I don't see how. Roberts doesn't leave her alone for a moment. Besides, she's young and obviously smitten. She might even misinterpret our intentions and tell him."

I knew Olga was right.

After a while, Roberts's behavior became so repugnant to me that I decided to say good night. Reverend Peteris was also leaving, and we walked in the twilight, talking about my studies, our country's problems, and the teachings of Christ.

I was so wrapped up in our conversation I didn't realize we had walked right past my house. "I was enjoying our conversation so much I lost track of where we were."

The minister paused for a moment, and then said, "I'd like to get together, maybe once a week, with young folks who are also interested in hearing how things used to be. We'd be taking a risk, but what wonderful gatherings they would be!"

"That would be fantastic!" I agreed. "Let's form a club. We'll invite people we know and meet once a week, each time in a different place. We could say it was a name day or birthday party."

A plan was beginning to take shape.

◆   ◆   ◆

I went back to Jelgava again to see Gran and, on the way, met a woman who was working as a seamstress. We started to chat, and I told her about my studies.

"That's nice. Everybody works so hard here. On the other side, Latvians are just plain lazy, sitting around making silly plans, while the Brits and Americans feed them. I couldn't take it. So when that nice repatriation officer told us how wonderful things were back here, I came home."

"But where have you been?" I asked.

"I went to Germany and lived in a number of refugee camps, the last one near Hamburg. When I came back to Jelgava, I made no effort to hide the fact that Latvians were living a slothful existence abroad. The comrades here were so happy with my powers of observation they offered me one hundred rubles to sign a letter to send to other refugees. Wasn't that fantastic?" she said excitedly, watching me, as if expecting praise.

"Did they give you a room? A job?"

"Not yet," she replied. "But those gentlemen, comrades, said I should move in with some friends, and they would find me a job."

"It's true there are no Brits or Americans throwing parcels of food and clothing at us, but there are people here as well who do absolutely nothing," I said emphatically.

"But that's not possible," the seamstress said.

"I have to go. Good luck finding a room and a job!"

I walked away quickly, leaving behind a very confused woman.

I was happy again just being with Gran, where I always felt safe and loved. We exchanged stories and laughed and cried together. Then, quite unexpectedly, she asked, "Who is Hugo? You never mentioned you had such a good friend," she sounded a bit hurt.

"Hugo? Hugo who?" I was taken aback.

"The slender lad," Gran explained. "He came to see your mother and offered to help. He said he had heard from a friend of his, Noldis, that she was having a difficult time."

Noldis? So that was it. His relationship with Dace was getting serious, so she must have told him I was worried about my mother after Anton's death. And Noldis must have told Hugo.

"Hugo must like you very much," Gran said thoughtfully.

"But I never asked him to help!" I protested. "I don't like him, and I don't like what he's doing! I don't care if other girls are jealous of me, Gran. The person I choose to share my life with will be tall and smart and spiritually strong, someone who makes me feel safe."

"Of course, dear, a lot of intelligent and attractive women feel that way, and they end up alone. Sometimes we need to be more flexible."

"I know that. But I will never marry Hugo."

"I'm not saying you should marry him; I don't even know him. But life is easier if you have someone to share your burdens with. I just worry that you might be too idealistic."

"Maybe so, Gran, but it's still nice to dream."

"There is plenty of time for dreams. You must be tired. Come on, I'll tuck you in." She stroked my hair. "I worry about you all the time."

I hugged Gran and kissed her wrinkled cheek.

Before falling asleep, I thought about Hugo. Not about marrying him…I would never do that. Why was he going to such lengths to please me? I wondered if I should behave differently toward him now.

It was Sunday. I was sitting in Gran's garden bunker with six miserable young men who had been hiding there since the capitulation. Emils and Guntis, with their newly acquired passports, had been working in Riga for six months already.

The radio was on night and day. The soldiers dreamed of taking up arms with the Allies and driving out the enemy. The three most powerful men in the world were talking about peace and understanding, yet America was looking the other way while Russia annexed one country after another. Not only Roosevelt, but now Truman as well. All those speeches about freedom were starting to sound like hollow rhetoric.

Our local news consisted of unremitting boasts about progress that didn't exist and threats against anyone who had still not registered with the government. Nobody believed the assurances that no harm would come to "illegals," if they would only come forward. There were too many examples of innocent people who had complied and been deported.

Typewriters and radios were still forbidden, but the boys had managed to get their hands on both. They had repaired a damaged typewriter they found in a bombed-out house and were using it to write resistance materials. To distribute them, they took turns dressing up as an old man or woman out for a late-night walk.

"Our mission was to reassure our countrymen and anger the occupiers, and we have succeeded," Jaksis explained. "But our efforts have also resulted in the arrest of innocent people, and we are starting to question whether we are doing the right thing."

"We want to…but," Uldis began.

"I agree," Jaksis continued. "All of us—and hundreds of thousands of others—want to believe we can take back our country. But when? And, if we ourselves are starting to have doubts, what hope have we got of convincing anyone else?"

"And we don't want to bring harm to our two benefactors," Uldis added.

I was touched by their concern but modestly denied having made much of a contribution. I brought them up to date on the filtration camps and compulsory registration.

My plan was patterned on the one used by Andrejs—to go register, armed with false documents and a made-up story. Jaksis said he was willing to take the risk and, as I had hoped, his enthusiasm was contagious.

It would be more difficult to explain the time lapse as more months had gone by since the Communists took over. But still, it was not impossible.

I told the story of a young man who came back, after several failed attempts to get to the West. He arrived at a filtration camp with a plan: to say he had been captured by the Fascists and put in prison for refusing to join their army. Later, when he learned the heroic Red Army had liberated Latvia, he had managed to escape.

"What a good idea!" Jaksis cried. "We can all pick up some pointers from his story. What do you think, boys? It's worth a try."

"Yes, everything is risky these days," Uldis said thoughtfully. "I wish my brother was here."

"Where is he? You said he was a minister."

"He was," said Uldis, "and he wouldn't approve of this, because he always believed in telling the truth. He even thought that keeping silent could be the same as telling a lie. So when the Russian soldiers broke into his house, he identified himself as a minister, and his wife didn't hide. They dragged her into the bedroom, and, when my brother tried to come to her aid, they shot him. When they were finished with his wife they shot her as well. Their adopted son—a curly-haired blond twelve-year-old my brother took in after his parents were killed—began crying hysterically. At first the Russians joked about their good fortune—that they had found a house with not only a woman but a girl as well. They were temporarily taken aback, but then took turns sodomizing the boy until he lay half-dead on the floor. His old nanny, hiding under the bed with a scarf stuffed in her mouth to keep from screaming, witnessed the horror."

We sat in silence, sickened and feeling helpless. These stories were becoming commonplace. We wanted to know what happened to the boy.

"The nanny nursed him back to health. But his personality changed completely. He took pleasure in torturing animals—pulling wings off butterflies and putting out frogs' eyes. Once, left alone for awhile, he drowned the family dog in the well. One day the nanny noticed he was spending a lot of time at the nearby creek. She went to look and saw he had thrown a cat into the water and, whenever the exhausted animal got near shore, he shoved it farther back in the water.

"He'll be dead soon," the boy said gleefully. When the nanny struck him, he glared at her and shouted, "When I grow up, I'm going to kill you!"

"How horrible," I said, unable to hold back tears of anger.

"'Love your enemies,' my brother used to say, but I despise them," Uldis said bitterly. "Maybe the Almighty will forgive me, when the time comes."

"I think it's time to make a decision," I said.

"The more I think about your plan, the more I think it will work," said Uldis.

"It might be our only chance," Jaksis agreed. "What do you think, boys? Maybe in a few months we'll meet up again as students. For now our hopes rest with one special person. Our hearts ache every time she leaves."

I was blushing crimson from the praise, but I was also very glad to hear it.

"All right, you can stop joking now. Let's get down to business."

"Let's do that," said Jaksis, taking my hand. "But at some time in the future, you can expect a visit from six lovesick young men bringing six bouquets of flowers and six proposals of marriage."

"Oh, do be serious," I said, gently freeing my hand. I tried to compare Jaksis and Hugo. If Hugo were anything like that, I could definitely see losing my heart to him.

Serious again, Jaksis said, "What happened to Uldis's brother is another lesson that decency will get you nowhere with the Communists. So lying to them may not be the worst thing."

"Sadly, we are all forced to become liars these days," Uldis interjected. "If my brother had not been so honest, he might still be alive. In these times when people worship Stalin, Christians must bow only to Christ, not the antichrist that is put before them every day."

I remained silent. I had nothing that profound to contribute.

That night, Gran, who knew almost every word of the New Testament by heart, comforted me. "Each of us has an inner voice. Uldis's brother died true to his beliefs. But, if our entire nation followed his example, we'd be sacrificing ourselves to the Communists. I am breaking the law by hiding legionnaires, but if I didn't I would be condemning six young lives to Siberia or death. So I obeyed my inner voice. You must learn to listen to your own inner voice, my child. Then you will be able to live with yourself and in God's grace."

The next day, as I said good-bye to Gran and the boys, I had a clearer idea about the definition of absolute decency. Life was a compromise; we just had to be careful not to go too far.

Who could tell how we would judge ourselves in the future? Who could tell what our relatives, friends, and acquaintances would think of us? Would we all be godless Communists in the eyes of Westerners? Perhaps to them, the only true Latvians would be those who were deported to Siberia, and the rest of us would remain forever tainted and therefore dirty, dangerous, and deserving to be shunned.

19

Our Neighbors from Georgia

The loudspeakers in our hallways continued to broadcast Communist propaganda "for all to enjoy." Anyone who dared to complain risked being called an insect and too backward to appreciate the "breath of fresh air" that had been allowed into our lives.

To add insult to injury, we received a bill—149 rubles—for installation costs.

Those deafening monstrosities were not only impossible to shut off; they amplified every other noise in the building. It was enough to give you a migraine.

I had gone to visit Olga. She and Andrejs had been my best source of advice regarding the soldiers hiding at Gran's.

"The most important thing is to get the right papers," I was saying. "But we have to be careful because the Communists have put informers in our midst." Suddenly, the door opened and an unkempt woman burst in. She had dark hair and a thick body with short arms and legs. She paused for a moment, then sat down and began asking questions. I understood enough Russian by then and was able to reply using simple words.

Olga introduced her new neighbor, Zoya, who lived in the room Roberts had sold to her shoemaker husband for thirty thousand rubles. They had a fifteen-year-old son and two small daughters. "My husband, Joske, and I are Georgian," Zoya said. "As you know, there are only rich people in Georgia—no peasants and no Party members. We are neither Jewish, which many take us for, nor Russian, which some think we are. In reality, you know, we are of Latvian descent. I know how to speak a lot of Latvian: *hello, how much does it cost,* and many other words." Then, as abruptly as she had arrived, Zoya left, waving her hands in the air.

"She's all right," Olga said, "just messy and nosy. Her husband makes shoes from inexpensive Georgian leather and sells them at a big profit. He has five workers in the basement.

"So how many of them are there in one room?" I asked.

"Well, Joske arrived alone, followed by Zoya and two of their children. Then a grandmother brought the remaining child. Last week, another grandmother appeared. It's hard to keep track."

"Seven in one room!" I exclaimed.

Olga nodded, but, before she could say anything, Zoya burst through the door again, this time pushing a baby carriage. "So you are a student. Maybe you can use some of these beautiful things. Look."

She spoke in a loud voice, punctuating her speech with theatrical gestures as she emptied the contents of the carriage on the table. There were high boots, ankle boots, slippers, and other leather goods. "These would be perfect!" Zoya showed me a pair of high army-style boots.

I had seen them around Riga as well as at university, but I didn't like them. I shook my head no.

"What?" Zoya was taken aback. "You can have them—cheap."

Simply curious, I asked, "How much?"

"Only 2,000 rubles, but I can let you have them for 1,900," she said. "Or I can make an exception and say 1,875 rubles…no, 1,850!"

I finally said that I didn't like them and wouldn't take them, even if they were a gift.

"But of course, you are right. These modern shoes with the tire-tread soles are more for someone like yourself. You won't believe me, but the rubber was taken from Stalin's old car. You know, Stalin is also Georgian. What a history these shoes have! We also have some with rubber soles from Churchill's car. You know he was at Yalta! These historic shoes are remarkably cheap—only 1,500 rubles—but I can give you a special price."

Zoya bargained with herself until I could hardly contain my amusement, but that didn't seem to bother her. She did the same with each pair of shoes. When she ran out of shoes, she pulled out handbags and a Georgian lambskin hat—quoting the "ridiculously low price of 5,000 rubles."

I soon grew weary, but her sales pitch was unrelenting.

Then Olga said what turned out to be the magic words: "Your son is calling."

Zoya packed up her wares, and was gone in a flash.

One of Olga's own sons was crying, and she went to comfort him. When she came back, she told me, "It goes on like that all day—sometimes ten times a day. Zoya watches to see if anyone comes over and barges right in to gauge the visitor's customer potential. It doesn't stop at night. When Andrejs comes home, she wants to know if any of his coworkers need shoes or leather goods.

"It looks a lot dirtier here lately," I said. The once gleaming parquet hallway was marred by black, red, and white chalk marks and bits of paper.

"Zoya's children did that," Olga said in response to my critical gaze. "She either doesn't see it or doesn't want to. At first, I would clean it up but not anymore, because it's all messed up again an hour later. Neither Roberts nor Zoya seem to care, so it's pointless trying to clean up after them!"

I noted that Olga herself was uncharacteristically on edge.

"Well, every morning at six we're awakened by that horrid squawk box playing the so-called Soviet-Latvian anthem. Then comes the exercise program in Russian. And so it goes until midnight, when they play the anthem again. Knowing how much I hate the Russian language, Roberts turns it up full blast. And he hasn't had to look for work, because he still has the thirty thousand rubles Joske paid him." Olga's eyes filled with tears. I felt sorry for her, but didn't know what to say to make her feel better.

"Maybe they will leave soon," I tried. "Maybe all the occupiers will leave. And then we can have our own lives back, like before."

"Yes...like before..." Olga echoed, deep in thought. But her words sounded so hopeless.

◆   ◆   ◆

It was my fourth semester studying medicine and my fourth set of exams. The physics exam didn't worry me; it was Marxism that gave me problems, with its empty phrases that I had to force myself to remember. I had read the lesson over and over again, but my brain refused to absorb the information.

I reminded myself how lucky I was to be staying with a woman as worldly as Mrs. Vinerts. Our central heating didn't work, but we had several small space heaters that kept our rooms warm and cozy. Mrs. Vinerts had kept her radio, while claiming, of course, that she had never had one. So when the loudspeaker arrived, she explained to the installer that, since she had never even owned a radio, she could not possibly take advantage of the new leaders' generosity by accepting such a gift. Before he could say a word, she slammed the door in his face.

So we sat every night, the radio turned down low, listening to the news from abroad. Occasionally we'd hear something that gave us hope, but mostly the Free World broadcasters spoke in an unconcerned monotone.

One night when I knocked on Mrs. Vinerts's door before the evening news, she was listening to music. I was eager to tell her about my visit with Olga.

"So it looks like Roberts has found the ideal tenants," she said a bit sarcastically. "But you can't keep two cats in the same bag for very long. Sooner or later they will fight, and one will win. I feel sorry for Olga, though. This apartment sharing has gotten to be a real problem. At first it was 'by invitation,' but now it has become the law."

"Really? But how do you know?"

"Of course it's not published anywhere. It gives them an advantage if anyone protests. One of my husband's friends, a lawyer, explained it to me."

"What did he say?"

"Basically, that everyone is allowed nine square meters of space; seven in the center of town. The housing committee targets chiefly older women whose children either escaped to the West or were deported to Siberia. They start by intimidating them, reading their names over the loudspeakers and calling them criminals for not sharing their homes. When the woman is reduced to a nervous state, she is brought in before the committee members, who also zero in on the personal lives of her relatives, who are denounced as Fascists. When the victims are totally confused, they are shown the new nine-meter law and asked to sign a paper, whereby they accept only five or six square meters for themselves, while allowing the remaining space to be divided up by their 'liberators,' who, of course, have the necessary documents that override any previously existing property claim."

"What if the 'guilty' woman refuses to be squeezed into a five-meter maid's closet?" I persisted.

"Of course, people don't have to do everything they're told, but they do have to know how far they can push the limits before they risk being locked up. So we need to be familiar with the laws, as well as all the right Communist phrases."

"But why not just go to a lawyer?"

"Ah, but why make it simple when you can make it complicated?" Mrs. Vinerts mused. "The more confusion and lack of information there is, the more it works to the regime's advantage. Lawyers must be careful because they, like doctors, are paid a monthly salary by the regime. Riga has been divided into sections—Kirov, Stalin, Lenin, Molotov, and others. Each has its own consultants seated together in one room. Clients wait outside until they are called and must use whoever is free. Discussions are not private, and payments are made to a cashier."

"So there is no client privilege."

"Exactly. Lawyers overhear each other's conversations and mistrust each other and even their clients. In political matters, an attorney must refer the client to

one of the supervisors, each of whom has his own office. But any appeal is generally futile."

"How foolproof!"

"Like so many things these days. That's why I went to the attorney's house.
He had been to the West and so was labeled a criminal. When he returned he
found his house filled with Russians. He now lives in one room."

"He came back?" I was incredulous. "They allowed him back in his house?"

"Allowed…yes, allowed…but for a fee," she replied, her voice dripping sar-
casm. "When he made it through the filtration camp, mandatory for anyone
repatriated from the West, he had no job, no food, no house, and no relatives. He
was a stranger in his own city. He came to our house but fled when he saw General Smirnov's name on the door. He spent several nights on a bench in the railway station, but the repatriation committee officers kept after him until he agreed
to sign a paper that he was happy to return to his liberated homeland. They even
persuaded him to write a letter to a relative in Sweden, inviting him to come back
because life was wonderful. Starving, and at the end of his tether, he did as he was
told and bought a room in his own house. The more you learn about Communism, the more you know that deceit always plays a key role. My lawyer friend
had heard, in a radio broadcast to Latvians in exile, that his wife and children
wanted to be reunited with him. What he did not know is that they were actually
in Britain."

I wondered how that could happen, but I kept quiet.

"I see you still don't understand," Mrs. Vinerts said as she smiled. "The
woman's plea was broadcast a number of times, begging her husband to return to
her and their children. His wife's voice sounded a bit odd, but he knew that air-
waves often caused distortion, so he applied for repatriation. The lawyer and I
met by accident in Meza Parks, when I was visiting mutual friends who had
received a letter from his wife saying she and the children had managed to get to
England from Germany, but that she still did not know the whereabouts of her
husband."

I studied Mrs. Vinerts's strong profile, admiring her determination and perse-
verance. I did not doubt for an instant that anyone could ever make her do anything against her will. I reminded her that we had gotten off the topic of the nine-
meter law.

"Yes, it's very important to know your rights, such as they are. So be sure to
tell Olga and your other friends. Officially you are allowed nine square meters per
person, with four more square meters per family."

"Three times nine equals twenty-seven; plus four comes to thirty-one," I calculated. "Olga's three small rooms come to thirty square meters in all, so she will be able to keep them. But, still, they could try to take some of them away, as each has access to the hallway. I will warn her."

"Also, single people cannot be made to share a room with another person, even if that room measures twenty or thirty square meters. The same applies to connecting rooms. You see, I can access my bedroom only through the living room, but not from the hallway. Both rooms together are fifty square meters, but, according to the law, no one can share that space, except with my consent. I intend to keep these two rooms for myself and have a document to that effect. I have signed up a woman and her young son for my husband's two rooms, and I'll find another Latvian tenant for my son's room. And then there's you. So we are now full up."

I could only look at her in awe.

"There's one more thing you should know. If some of the larger apartments have to be given up to the new order, the old inhabitants have the right to keep the room or rooms of their choice. And they have three months to choose their next-door neighbors. That is what the law allows. But be wary of anyone offering to pay an inordinately high rent. Naive folks are more likely to be taken in by this, but more often than not the prospective tenant already has the necessary document in his pocket and once allowed to move in cannot be evicted. And, of course, the promised high rent is never paid."

"So people are deliberately deceived?"

"Yes. That's why I want to make sure you understand the rules, so you cannot be tricked into agreeing to something you don't want. But, I repeat, you must also know your limitations before trying to push any matter too far.

◆   ◆   ◆

Dace, sounding very mysterious, had invited me to come over.

"Are we going to study Marxism?" I asked.

"No. It's kind of a surprise. Wear your blue dress. It's very flattering."

"All right. I won't ask any more questions, but why the blue dress? It's not your birthday or your name day...Oh, never mind, I'll see you later."

"Until tonight then," Dace said, a smile in her voice.

When I knocked on Dace's door, Noldis opened it. "It's only a small gathering, Miss Lita," he greeted me, as I looked past him and saw Hugo sitting on the couch inside. "Don't worry, we won't bite."

"Speak for yourself," Hugo said, looking straight into my eyes.

How vulgar. I shuddered. I was angry with Dace for putting me in this position, but it would have been rude to turn around and leave. They were Latvian boys, after all. Anyway, Dace and Noldis might even get married, so I guessed I'd better get used to Hugo's being around.

A large bottle of home-brewed wine was on the table.

"Our family vintage," said Noldis as he filled our glasses. "We have to drink it before someone else does. Now let's toast to our very good health!"

The wine was delicious; it tasted a lot like the kind my father used to make.

"Why don't you say something, Miss Lita?" Noldis asked. "You could at least say thank-you. Hugo has earned it. He and his friends have been to your mother's house twice already."

"Yes, that was nice. But I never asked him to do it," I said curtly.

"Ah, so you acknowledge only the deeds that are done because you ask? You really should think of your poor mother all on her own. The fields and the garden won't wait."

I knew Noldis was at least partly right, though I didn't like the way he was letting me know. I forced a smile and turned to Hugo. "Please consider this my official thank-you."

"Such formality! I think I'd prefer your unofficial thank-you instead," Hugo said with a suggestive smirk. "But we can discuss that later."

Dace came in with a plate of sandwiches.

"Miss Lita," Noldis continued in his mock formal tone. "See this ham? It came from your house. Your mother gave it to Hugo, and he was kind enough to bring it to our little celebration. Tomorrow, he may have to go hungry. And look at this freshly baked bread!"

I touched my lips to the rim of my glass so I wouldn't have to reply.

"*Prozit!*" Hugo said, downing his wine in one long gulp. He sat down at the piano and, joined by Noldis, sang some old drinking songs, then moved on to more risqué, double-entendre ones.

Oh, well, boys will be boys. I chided myself for being so standoffish. And though I still didn't like Hugo, I made an effort to be more polite.

Dace couldn't take her eyes off Noldis. In truth, both boys were good looking, interesting, and resourceful. I really wasn't sure why I didn't like either one of them.

Hugo said he had brought me a package from my mother and that he had lots to tell me. I finally relented and said it was all right for him to come and visit me.

20

A Deportee Returns

The doorbell rang just as Mrs. Vinerts and I were sitting down to dinner. She went to the door and, leaving the security chain in place, repeated the now familiar ritual of "Who's there?" and "What do you want?"

We had to be cautious, as robbers had lately been using a decoy—a neighbor, usually a woman—to make sure the door would be opened at least enough for them to push in. Some gangs were made up of women, who had learned polite phrases in Latvian to facilitate access.

A moment later, Mrs. Vinerts returned, frowning. "There's an odd-looking man wearing a fufaika and burlap pants at the door, asking for you in broken Russian. I told him to wait outside."

Alarmed, I hurried to the door.

"Are you still there?" demanded Mrs. Vinerts, who was right on my heels.

"Da, da…yes," came the heavily accented reply as Mrs. Vinerts opened the door a crack.

On the stoop stood a raggedy man, his feet tied onto slabs of tire rubber. On his head was a filthy Russian soldier's cap. He looked like one of the droves of the destitute flooding in from "prosperous" Russia. Word of mouth had reached locals there that the Baltics were like a wonderland. I felt sorry for this vagrant because, even though our present life was far from the promised "paradise," it was obviously better than any life he had ever known.

I was thinking of what I could give him, when I heard a familiar voice. "Lita! Hello! Thank God, I've finally found someone I know."

"Excuse me, but I don't know you," I said backing away.

"My name is Arvids Krastins."

"Arvids? My God, is it really you?" I cried and, missing the warning look from Mrs. Vinerts, flung open the door. "I heard you were deported. Come in. Put down your satchel and take off your coat."

"I can't do that," he replied awkwardly. "I'm not wearing a shirt."

Mrs. Vinerts quickly grasped the situation. "You've come from Russia, haven't you? You're one of the deportees."

"That's right."

"Run a warm bath," she ordered me, then left and soon came back with clean towels, one of her husband's shirts, a suit, and shoes. "You're much too thin for these clothes, but it could be worse," she said, handing the items to Arvids. "At least you'll look and feel much better. Throw those Russian rags into the fire. I'll reheat our dinner; there should be enough for all of us."

The young man's eyes brightened at the mention of dinner, and the word "food" escaped his lips in a moan.

Mrs. Vinerts brought in a plate with bread and a slice of smoked pork. "I'll leave this here on the bench by the bath, so you can have a nibble while you're soaking."

Arvids followed her into the bathroom, where the first thing he did was to take a mouthful of bread. Only then did he close the door behind him.

When he emerged, dressed in clean clothes and rid of several months' worth of beard, he was a totally different person.

"Ah, now I recognize you!" I said.

"They always shaved our heads; the last time was a couple of months ago," he said, running his hand sheepishly over the still-damp stubble.

"So, you've been traveling for two months?"

"At least. Maybe even longer."

"Let's eat," Mrs. Vinerts interrupted. "We can talk later."

"There's certainly a lot to talk about," said Arvids, helping himself. "But first, Lita, I must tell you, your father sends his greetings."

"My father?" I cried. "He's alive!"

"Yes. We spent the last two years together," Arvids said, keeping a tight grip on the edge of his plate, as if he were afraid someone might take it away. With his other hand, he shoveled in mouthful after mouthful of food.

I peppered him with questions. There was so much I wanted to know.

"Let the poor man eat first," Mrs. Vinerts scolded gently.

After a while, she issued another command, this time to Arvids. "Stop. That's enough food for now or you'll get sick. You can have more in a couple of hours."

The three of us settled into the comfortable club chairs.

"I can't believe I'm back in Latvia, that I've gotten rid of my rags, and that I've actually had a real meal," Arvids began.

"So tell us. How did you find us?" Mrs. Vinerts asked pointedly.

"The last leg of my journey back to Riga was on a freight train," Arvids began. "When it stopped at night to unload, I jumped off.

"First I went to my relatives' house in Marija Street, but they weren't there. Maybe they are in the West; maybe, like myself, they were sent to Siberia. Then I thought of the Baltins. There the door was opened, just as cautiously as here, but by a small boy. I asked him if his name was Andrejs, and he answered yes. Heartened, I asked if his mother was home. He shook his head no and said he was not allowed to open the door to strangers. Did he know where his mother was? 'Shopping, or maybe she's with my godmother, Lita,' he told me. I immediately thought you might be the same Lita for whom I had the message. To my surprise, the boy told me your address."

I urged him to back up and start from the very beginning.

Arvids resumed his story: "After graduation from technical school, I worked as a security guard in the rail yards. I did this for the first year of the Communist occupation and continued during the German occupation. I was soon labeled irreplaceable, which meant I could not be drafted into the army. I was happy, because it meant I could further my studies at the Agricultural Academy. When there were reports of fighting around Jelgava, some of my colleagues fled, but I kept working. I had no interest in politics and had never joined any organizations or been in the military. I had no land or possessions to speak of and it didn't make sense to run away, so I continued to work even after central Jelgava was demolished. I was criticized for lacking idealism and national pride, but I had never harmed anyone and my entire world consisted of my work and studies. For better or worse, that was how I was. I now know that scope was too narrow.

"When the Jelgava railroad station caught fire, I wouldn't leave my post: I felt I had to stay by the phone to make sure the switch was thrown at the right time to avoid a collision of arriving and departing trains. But the smoke got too thick, and I finally staggered out—just as the waiting room ceiling caved in. I had been living at the station since our apartment house was leveled, so with nowhere else to go, I set off along the main road. It was dark and cold and only then did I realize I was in shirtsleeves. Because of the heat from the fire, I had removed my jacket and left it at my work station.

"Suddenly I was surrounded by armed Russians. I tried to say who I was, but they told me to be quiet and locked me in a basement with many others. A week passed, maybe two, then a guard arrived demanding that we confess our crimes. At last, I'd have a chance to explain.

"But even as I tried to reason with the Cheka interrogator, I knew I was in trouble. He accused me of being the fugitive Krumins, who had escaped after being arrested. I said my name was Krastins, but I couldn't prove it because my documents were in my jacket, which had burned in the station fire. 'Liar!' he shouted, 'I know all about you, you Fascist dog, you capitalist lackey!' The more I stuck by my story, the angrier he became. I was questioned, kicked, and beaten every day. They even knocked out my front teeth. Finally, an older man took me aside. 'Listen, son, just admit to whatever it is they are accusing you of, and it will go easier for you.' But I was stubborn and would not confess to a crime I had not committed."

Mrs. Vinerts brought in coffee, and Arvids went on. "I'd certainly listen to the old man today and give the same advice to anyone who tried to resist, because the Cheka will never let you win. I was so naive, I told the truth. But the more I maintained my innocence, the more angry and suspicious they became. I wasn't smart enough to defend myself by praising Stalin and the Red Army. I merely said politics didn't interest me. The interrogation continued, and the more I said, the more they seemed to see me as a revolutionary. I got a twenty-five-year sentence, whereas another man, a property owner and legionnaire, got only five. And still another quick-thinking young fellow went free by pretending to be pro-Communist. It was beginning to dawn on me what a fool I had been."

Arvids turned back to his food. "You must find it hard to believe that a starving person can be so much like an animal," he said by way of apology.

"After several months of living in various basements, we were loaded into cattle cars and put on a slow-moving train that stopped for long periods of time in open fields. There were so many of us that we had no room to sit down; it was hard to breathe, and the stench of sweat was overpowering. Our daily meal was a half-kilo of bread mixed with sawdust. We had very little water. I happened to be near a window, and at every stop I could see the dead bodies of men, women, and children being tossed into the bushes a few yards from the tracks. In time the wagons thinned out enough, so the occupants of two cars could be combined into one, and that was how I met your father. I don't know how long we traveled like that. We didn't know where they were taking us, and, after a while, we didn't care. I was determined to survive so I could carve out a better life for myself. Your father said he just wanted to see his family again."

I couldn't hold back the tears any longer. Until that moment, listening to Arvids's story had been like reading a novel or watching a movie plot unfold. But this was real life—our life—in all its merciless cruelty. And here was a man who could testify to that horror. Yet hundreds, thousands, and perhaps even millions if you counted all nationalities, had been silenced forever. Where were the Americans? Where was their promise of liberty for all?

Mrs. Vinerts made up a bed in the spare room.

"It's all right, I can sleep out here," Arvids said groggily, but allowed Mrs. Vinerts to lead him to the freshly made up bed and remove his outer garments.

"There'll be no sleeping in chairs around here. You are among friends. Now get into bed! I'll leave some crisp bread on the night table in case you get hungry during the night."

As we went back over everything Arvids said, I felt very close to this woman with whom I did not seem to have much in common—at least not until that moment.

The doorbell made us jump. It was Hugo. I had forgotten he said he would come by.

"Good evening, ladies," he said, bowing low.

"Nice to meet you," Mrs. Vinerts said, clipping her words.

"Likewise, ma'am. I wouldn't bother you, but I have a package from Lita's mother, wrapped with her own loving hands, and a note sending lots of love to you both," Hugo said. "Do you mind if I have a cigarette? Would you like one? Modern women like to smoke, I'm told."

"Please, go ahead," I said, pushing an ashtray toward him. "We don't smoke. I guess we're not modern enough."

"Surely you'll take a bottle of homemade wine? I also have sweets," Hugo babbled on, looking smug as he lowered himself into a club chair.

When Mrs. Vinerts got up to get glasses, he leapt to his feet.

"May I help you? We bachelors are good at helping. We are used to fending for ourselves."

"What would you know about that? The chair you were sitting in was just occupied by someone who could tell you a thing or two about hardship."

It was obvious Mrs. Vinerts shared my contempt for Hugo's glib chatter.

"I've been at the front," he protested. "I've seen people die."

"There are worse places to die than on a battlefield. There is starvation and being ripped apart by wild animals on the Siberian tundra."

"How depressing," said Hugo. "But life is also beautiful. Let me tell you something funny that happened this morning on my way to class."

"But why not talk about the serious side of life?"

"Madam, please!" Hugo interrupted again. "When life is depressing, we must make it less so. Drink some wine, sing a song. We are in a transition, so we might as well make the best of it!"

Hugo knew he was losing ground. How differently he came across when he wasn't surrounded by a group of admiring girls. Stammering a bit, he poured the wine. "Let us drink, then, to our hope that Latvia will be free again."

"I'll raise my glass to that," Mrs. Vinerts said and then left us.

Hugo showed no sign of leaving, so I asked about his visit with my mother.

"She is very much alone, and I promised I'd help every chance I get. I feel bad for her. A heavy tax has been imposed on meat, milk, and butter there. Lita, do you know why I'm helping your mother? It's for you. I…we can't allow your parents to lose everything they've worked for."

I appreciated Hugo's sentiments, but I didn't like feeling indebted to him.

He had come up behind me and wrapped his arms around me. I could smell the alcohol on his breath. I turned around and slapped him across the face.

A mean glint came into his eyes. "You'll be sorry for that," he said.

As he strode out, I looked at the half empty bottle of wine on the table and wanted to throw it after him. How dare he threaten me?

◆   ◆   ◆

The next morning, after a hearty breakfast, Arvids resumed his tale. "We traveled for several months before reaching Molotovsk by the White Sea. There, we had to build our own camp with a thick circle of barbed wire around it. The women were taken a few kilometers farther and put to work building their own barracks. Among them was a newspaper publisher's wife. It was probably the only time this woman had ever held a hammer. She was eventually sent to another camp where, I later heard, she died. The former agricultural minister did not survive either.

"My job was to shovel coal, and your father was assigned to building duties. Every night, a brass band met us at the gate, and each of the barracks had a loudspeaker broadcasting the Soviet Union's successes in every conceivable field. Their achievements were indeed something, particularly when it came to our mortality. More people died every day, and their bodies were tossed one after another to the baying wild animals at the edge of the forest.

"Our diet consisted of a half kilo of fried sawdust and a liter of lukewarm soup that tasted more like dishwater. Work was hard. We were divided into small groups, each overseen by an armed Russian guard to make sure we never rested. Most of the poor wretches in our camp worked until they collapsed from hunger or despair. I doubt even a fraction of them are still alive.

"Then, one day, a committee arrived from Moscow. I could hardly believe my eyes, but among them was a Russian officer whose life I had saved when the Germans marched into Jelgava. Separated from his regiment, he had been hiding in my brother's barn. I was visiting and accidentally happened upon the poor devil, who hadn't eaten for days. He started to tremble, thinking I would turn him in. But I didn't, and he soon relaxed a bit. His name was Volodya, and he had been a dedicated Communist who held a responsible position. But politics didn't interest me. When he asked for directions back to Russia, we gave him a map and a ticket, which wasn't that difficult, as I worked for the railroad. In time, I forgot about the incident.

"Now this same officer was in our camp. I could hardly believe it. The poor, frightened fugitive my brother and I had rescued was a Chekist. 'Volodya!' I shouted several times, before a guard hit me with the butt of his rifle. But the Russian heard me, and slowly recognition took hold. 'Arvids!' he said, then lowered his voice: 'You saved my life once; now I want to help you—in a week you will be free.' I was happy beyond belief but told Volodya I also had a deserving friend and gave him your father's name. 'I don't know if I can manage two,' he replied, but I believed he would at least try. I also understood he risked a lot by appearing to be sympathetic to the enemy in the eyes of his fellow Communists.

"The news of my impending freedom spread throughout our camp, and people lined up, wanting to give me messages for loved ones, even if only to let them know they were still alive. Writing letters was not allowed, so I did my best to memorize addresses and messages. Your father made me promise to find you and your mother. He was also hoping against hope that my 'friend' would find a way to free him as well.

"Weeks and months went by, but nothing happened. A year, a year and a half, passed since the Moscow committee visited our camp. I was losing hope. Then a miracle happened. I was called before the commandant and told to be ready to leave in a half hour. I went to say good-bye to your father, and he pressed into my hand a small wooden box he had carved for his daughter. I was given a Russian passport and told to leave. I asked how I was to get back with no money for a rail ticket and was told that, if I didn't want to go home, I was welcome to stay. I said thank you and left. And now you know my story."

21

We Are Thankful

The idea for a philosophy group was born at Olga's son's christening. Our little group, led by Reverend Peteris, met weekly at a different location, each gathering designated as a party.

Parties were not illegal. We were allowed to celebrate birthdays and name days, May 1, the October Revolution, New Year, and weddings. Every two weeks, the Russians even celebrated payday—an unofficial, noisy occasion that was also notable for its brevity. In a couple of hours, the vodka, drunk from tea glasses, was gone, and the revelers under the table along with the empty bottles.

Our fifteen-member group had no problem finding reasons to celebrate. Peteris and the boys managed to come up with a bottle of cheap wine, and the girls brought whatever food was available.

We followed a general format. Having agreed on a theme, we'd start by analyzing a problem, spiritual or otherwise. There was a speaker, then questions that often led to a lively discussion. Peteris said he had rarely heard such intense debate, even in his theology seminars.

We talked about philosophy and examined the works of authors—Ortega, Unamuno, Zenta Maurina, Kant, and Nietzsche. We even analyzed Marxism and Leninism, so that we knew how to identify and avoid the hidden pitfalls of their teachings.

"This is how you learn to become independent thinkers, the very thing the Communists won't allow you to be. Their dogma leaves no room for discussion or dissent," Peteris said.

With his deep faith and youthful spirit, he even taught us to laugh at some of the indignity and inequity in our daily lives. We ended each gathering with a prayer of thanks for that evening and asked for God's guidance in the days ahead.

On this particular night, we had a dual agenda. The first: how Communists intended to prove that Christ did not exist through: (a) the recent university lecture on that topic; and (b) the teachings of the Bible. And second: we would discuss excerpts from (independent) Latvia University's philosophy lectures.

We were ready, but Reverend Peteris had not arrived. It was unusual for him to be late. A half hour passed, then an hour. Maybe his tram had broken down. An hour and a half later, he appeared, his face pale and drawn.

"I am truly glad to be here tonight," Peteris began. "But there will be no more meetings. "I have just spent eight hours with the Cheka. The conversation started innocuously enough about my profession. They assured me that Communism and Christianity were really the same, and the theories of Engels and Marx were based on Christian teachings—not a word against Christ or his teachings. I knew immediately that they were setting a trap and kept quiet.

"They repeated their 'assurances' in slightly different terms. Then came the proposition: I was to sign a paper that my sermons about Christ would include the teachings of Marx, Engels, Lenin, and Stalin. The only difference, they said, was that they were more progressive and, therefore, better suited to our times. I could read verses from the Bible, but gradually I would compare and incorporate them with Communist dogma, finally preaching it as the true path to paradise.

"I knew what they were getting at even before they finished. They wanted me to stay in my profession—but in their employ. They wanted me to sell my soul to the devil, while making the sign of the cross; to use the pulpit to teach the lies of the antichrist. All I had to do, they said, was to report to them anything my parishioners might tell me in confidence. They presented all this in a quiet and persuasive manner, saying they only wanted my voluntary cooperation.

"But I was ready with my own surprise. Comrades, I said, the building of socialism takes a lot of hard work, not only in theory but in practice. As you know, in honor of the October Revolution, construction crews have been formed to rebuild cities destroyed by the Fascists. The victorious army has started to demobilize, and its brave men have earned the right to live in decent housing. Every responsible citizen must help. For some time now I have wanted to leave the ministry to join the rebuilding efforts. I hope, comrades, that you will understand and give me your blessing.

"That caught them off guard. Obviously they were prepared either for my protestations or acquiescence, but not for this. Using their own phrases, I spoke to them for a long time, in the end saying nothing much…just like in Marxist lectures.

"'But you'll earn much less as a builder than working for us,' they said.

"'Comrades,' I replied, 'even the lowest of the low is greatly rewarded in our system.'

"'If you join us, we'll allow you to travel and pay for your trips to meet clergy in other countries.'

"'Ah, what do I care about travel when the best place to be is right here?' I said, and in the end, they backed down.

"Of course, starting tomorrow I must give up my ministry. I know construction work is hard, but at least the physical labor will not burden my soul, as the other surely would. May God forgive me! Tonight, just seeing you all here and thinking back on our past discussions makes me happy that He opened your young hearts to me so I could prepare them and protect them."

There were no more discussions that evening. We said a prayer and then good night.

◆   ◆   ◆

I still couldn't say no to Eugenie. Here I was, helping her prepare for exams.

"My dear, if you only knew what I've been through these last few weeks!" she gasped dramatically, sinking into a plush chair. "You know, my friend the health minister...what wonderful times we had together. But then things got a bit out of hand."

"What do you mean?" I asked.

"I thought I was pregnant, you see, and I told him," Eugenie said, furrowing her brow.

"And he wanted to marry you?" I tried to help her story along.

"Marry me! He punched me in the stomach!" she said with a loud sob.

"How horrible!"

"Not at all!" she protested, dabbing at the mascara staining her cheeks. "That's the Russian method of getting rid of unwanted babies. But it didn't do any good. So he borrowed a motorbike, put me on the back, and drove it as fast as he could on bumpy country roads. That didn't work either, so he tried something himself, though he said he'd never done it before. Finally, he called in some friends...My nerves are shot!"

"But why didn't he want to get married?"

"I don't know," Eugenie said impatiently, then offered an excuse. "My minister believes our lives need to stabilize before we can even think about having a child. I'm still a student, after all, and as his wife would naturally have privileged status, whether I wanted it or not. Anyway, he feels our love wouldn't be so special if it was an everyday sort of thing."

I wasn't convinced, but it was none of my business. Undeniably, she had suffered physically as well as spiritually. She had also entrusted me with her secret.

The first exam was in Marxism-Leninism, and, as usual we drew lots on topics. Mine were just and unjust wars, Communist Party tactics, the Party's eighth congress, and the works of Lenin. The testing committee consisted of Professor Mishke, Dambergs, and Professor Schmidt. Dimanis was notably absent, but whether he had been promoted or transferred nobody knew.

Standing at the long table, I began. "There are just and unjust wars. All wars that are won by socialism are just, because they advance the greater cause—a world under Communist rule, which is the best and highest form of government that can ensure happiness and a carefree life for all people. On the other hand, the wars fought by those who oppose Communism are unjust because they are against progress and would return our civilization to a feudal society. To achieve global victory for Communism, it is permitted and even necessary to find weak spots and zero in on them. To learn what they are, you must first befriend your subjects and gain their trust, appearing to be in agreement on every political point.

Drawing on the analogy presented by Dimanis in one of his lectures, I continued, "Our capitalist enemy, like a pet dog, must at times be allowed to eat from your hand. And then, when he is at his most trusting and least expects it, you can bash his head in. There are still a lot of countries and people who have yet to understand that Communism is the best and only true system in the world. And because they do not understand it, they use force and guile to drive the Soviet Union off its avant-garde path to victory. When we obliterate capitalism, our differences will also be eliminated, and the socialism that now dominates the Soviet countries can be replaced by true Communism, which will provide all people with all the things they need and desire."

"Good, comrade. Very good," Mishke said. "You have understood and explained both parts of your first topic well and your attendance record is good. So, let's skip ahead to the last topic."

Many did not pass the exams but were allowed to try again later.

I wanted to tell Olga I had made it through the most awful part, but I couldn't honestly say I was happy. I felt somehow soiled every time I had to repeat the hateful dogma, but, if I wanted to graduate, I had no other choice.

Olga opened the door and simultaneously Zoya's head poked out of her own doorway. I said hello, but was drowned out by the speakers blaring in Russian about the five-year anniversary and joining the socialist cause to wipe out the backward enemy. Amid the din, Zoya pointed to my feet and then to her room. I understood that she had more shoes she wanted to show me.

A different kind of loud noise emanated from Roberts's room. He was singing "My Heart Belongs to You."

Olga and I slipped into her room, and she quickly closed the door and turned the key. Almost immediately, there was a jiggling of the knob, followed by a pounding on the door. Zoya, as usual, was trying to get in. "Open up, I have something important to say!" she shouted.

"We are trying on some clothes. Please excuse us," Olga replied calmly.

"I am not a man! This is important…"

Olga continued to ignore her.

"So, why is Roberts so happy?" I asked.

"He got his girlfriend registered in one of his rooms, while he kept the other one. Perhaps it was the square-meter rules, but more likely it was greed. Ance's mother died, leaving an apartment, jewelry, paintings, and furniture. Now he can afford to keep singing love songs for quite a while."

"But that's so dishonest! Isn't there some way to warn her?"

"It's too late for that. She's pregnant," Olga said.

"I really don't understand Roberts. They'll probably get married now, and it would make sense to move into her two-room apartment and have more privacy."

"You forget who we're dealing with. I doubt Roberts will marry Ance. Also, if he moved in with her, he'd technically be living on her property. So he'll keep her happy until the inheritance runs out, and then get rid of her. At least that's what he told Andrejs the other night in a drunken stupor."

"But isn't Ance putting pressure on him to get married?"

"Of course, and he always has an excuse. For a start, Roberts is still not divorced from his third wife. But enough about him. Here's some good news: I saw your Gran in Jelgava. Some of the legionnaires hiding there managed to pass filtration. There are two still left.

"That's wonderful news!" I exclaimed. "What about Jaksis?"

"He was the first to get through and is planning to enter university."

"He's certainly brave, but why would he want to study in Riga?" I was puzzled.

"No one can dissuade him. Besides, as he stated emphatically, 'Lita is in Riga!'" Olga smiled as I felt my face turning crimson.

✦   ✦   ✦

Another anatomy exam was coming up.

"So are you prepared?" Laimonis asked, laughing. "Do you know all the best Soviet abortion methods—long motorbike rides on bumpy roads, fists to the stomach? If not, you just might fail."

"What do you mean?" I asked. How did he know?

"I mean that yesterday was Eugenie's turn to take the exam, and she told her sad tale while standing in the doorway of Professor Kalbergs's office.

"She said that in front of all the other students?"

"How else would we know?" replied Laimonis. "Today the whole faculty knows. She seems to enjoy bragging about her tawdry affair with the health minister."

I felt hurt. I had taken such great pains to safeguard Eugenie's big secret.

Ilga, an attractive girl who had spent a lot of time in Kalbergs's office, was standing by the window, surrounded by her classmates.

"Today is my twelfth time," she was saying.

"But how?"

Generally, if you fail twice, you rarely get a third try at the same exam. And you must have had a valid reason, like a serious illness. Usually those students are advised to leave university or, at the very least, to repeat the course. The professor always asks me questions that have little to do with anatomy. And my answers are never acceptable, but he keeps asking me to come back," Ilga said as she shrugged.

Kalbergs arrived and, with a friendly wave, indicated for her to follow him into his office. "Well, Ilga, did you learn your anatomy lesson?"

"Yes, Vasily Alexandrovich."

"So, we will see…"

Usually there were three students at a time in the exam room, but Ilga and I were the only two.

"Ilga Petrovna," the professor addressed her in the Russian manner. "How many teeth does a monkey have?"

Ilga shifted uncomfortably. "I think a chimpanzee probably has as many as…" she said haltingly.

"I was asking about monkeys in general. But we do know that chimpanzees don't have wisdom teeth. It would seem, Ilga Petrovna, that you do not yet have yours either. That was your last chance. I am putting you back two years. If you wish, you can start from the beginning, but there will be no scholarship!" Ilga fled in tears. That was how Kalbergs took his revenge on girls who refused his advances.

Turning to the rest of our group, a jovial Kalbergs asked some straightforward questions we had no trouble answering, and we left with good grades.

◆   ◆   ◆

My mother's letters were full of praise for Hugo and his friends. She said it would have been impossible for her to take care of the house without their help.

I still resented feeling indebted to Hugo but did not object when he invited himself over. It wasn't a good idea for me to visit my mother too often, lest I run into a Communist functionary curious about how the daughter of a deportee came to be studying in Riga. I was finally learning the complexities of the life Latvians were forced to lead.

Hugo arrived early with some alarming news: The previous night, a Red Army unit had broken into my mother's house, and only Hugo's quick action and his friend's knowledge of Russian had saved my mother's life. Frozen with dread, I listened as Hugo told the story in his typically dramatic fashion.

Like it or not, I was now even more indebted to him. "Thank you…very, very much," I said with genuine gratitude.

But it was not enough for Hugo, who went on reminding me of all the things he had done. As he spoke, his good deeds grew in number, as did, in his estimation, my lack of appreciation. I felt terrible. Upset and confused, I finally burst into tears.

"What, exactly, do you want? Do you just want to make me feel bad? What kind of reward are you looking for?" I stammered.

Suddenly, Hugo dropped to his knees. "I want you, Lita," he said, taking a handkerchief from his pocket and wiping his eyes. "I want you to be my wife."

Hugo was crying. I was confused. Was I really as bad as he made me out to be?

As if reading my mind, Hugo started telling me about his own life, his boyhood, school, and army days. His story moved me. He said he had always been alone and looking for someone to love him. His mother had married a second time and transferred all her love to her new family.

"Now that I've found a girl who means the world to me, she rejects me. Life isn't worth living without you, Lita," he raised his voice. "You'll have to live with the responsibility for my death."

Covering his face with his hands, Hugo ran to the door, paused, and then headed for the elevator shaft. My mind was swirling—my mother's brush with death, Hugo's miserable childhood, and now his threat of suicide.

Oh, God, he was near the shaft, though he seemed to hesitate a bit.

"No! Hugo, stop!" I cried.

He turned back toward me. With his flushed face and eyes downcast, he looked so vulnerable I started to feel pity for him. "Don't jump," I said, and then added with some effort, "I will marry you."

"You will? Really?" Hugo brightened. "Let's go to the license bureau right away." He helped me with my coat and pushed me out into the entryway, where he grabbed me and started kissing me. I wanted to push him away, but how could I? I had just consented to be his wife.

We rang Dace's doorbell to ask her to be a witness. She had a visitor, another student, and Hugo invited him as well. The stranger seemed amused but came along willingly, especially pleased by Hugo's promise of drinks afterward. Dace looked surprised, but offered her congratulations. I accepted her wishes somberly, while Hugo was beaming and full of bravado.

One thing was undeniable. Hugo had undergone a total mood change. There was no trace of despair as he regaled us with his latest repertoire of jokes.

Getting married was easy. All Hugo and I had to do was go to the license bureau, and we would leave as man and wife. I realized then that I was still wearing my apron.

"How nice!" the official exclaimed. "I can see you are real working folk. We need people like you in the Soviet Union."

The date was April 30, and it was all over in fifteen minutes. My initial fears had subsided, to be replaced by worrisome thoughts I may have acted too hastily. But I tried to push away my doubts and managed a smile as I took Hugo's arm. I would try to be a good wife.

That night, my name day guests would be surprised to learn that congratulations for the bride were also in order. Dace had some surprises of her own: glowing with happiness, she announced that she and Noldis were engaged. She also brought along her cousin Jaksis and some of his legionnaire friends who had arrived, as promised, with bouquets of flowers.

"I guess we got here too late," Jaksis said. He seemed subdued, while trying to appear jovial. Or was it just my imagination?

I was pleased the boys had succeeded in getting their documents and that the risky venture had ended well. It was probably the only thing that brought me real joy on my own wedding day.

◆   ◆   ◆

After the wedding, I no longer lived with Mrs. Vinerts. When she called to say she had more news from Jelgava, I went to visit her.

"The Communists are always looking for something to keep themselves busy. Their latest venture has to do with divorce. Your mother was called in by the Cheka and interrogated about your father. They told her he was a convicted criminal and that, if she didn't want to stand trial with him, she should submit papers seeking a divorce."

"What did Mother say?"

"She talked it over with some friends, who were familiar with legal matters, and together they came to the conclusion that divorce was the answer. I would have advised her to do the same."

I didn't say anything, but I certainly had mixed feelings.

"We must go on," Mrs. Vinerts continued. "Similar stories are told all the time. The Cheka are routinely calling in the wives of men who are now in the West, and they have nothing to gain by refusing. They'd only be sent to Siberia."

"Do you think I have forgotten my husband?" she asked, her voice suddenly shrill. "Do you think I ever will? And yet I wonder if he would understand me now. The people in the West can philosophize all they like while sitting in their coffeehouses. Let them try living here." For the first time, this strong woman revealed a crack in her facade. But she soon regained her composure. "Your seamstress friend, Ziemele, still hasn't found a job."

"Couldn't she leave Jelgava and go to another town?"

"She'd have to show good cause. The most common reason—pursuit of studies—wouldn't work for a woman her age. Besides, as someone who has been in the West, she can't be trusted. She blames herself for believing the repatriation agent's false promises, but she was glad your mother gave her a home, at least temporarily."

"I'm glad Mother won't be alone," I said. "Did she tell you about the night Hugo and his friend saved her life?"

A strange expression came over Mrs. Vinerts's face. "There was no such attack. Your mother was shocked at how a story like that got started."

I felt a chill even as the blood rushed to my head. I excused myself and quickly said good night. Mrs. Vinerts did not try to stop me, but I sensed she knew that something was wrong, something I didn't even want to admit to myself.

22

A Lump on the Leg

The living-quarters question was still a hot topic, although we all knew it was just a thinly disguised way to alter the demographic of Latvia.

The next goal was to eliminate the "petit bourgeoisie," or small shop owners. Larger businesses were taken over at the start of the occupation, but now even the smallest ones were being nationalized. Lawyers, already in the line of fire, had to fill out long and detailed forms and submit to extensive questioning. Many were jailed or deported. There was no such thing as private practice. Dace told me a story about one lawyer, a friend of her mother's, who had lost his job.

"Zubitis was invited to speak on a radio program to be aired in the West. He was to praise the joys of Communism and urge Latvians to come back home."

"Wasn't he the one who was lured back by a woman pretending to be his wife during a radio broadcast?"

"Yes. I wonder if they—over there—have any idea of the pressures being applied to make us do things we don't want to do. This time, when Zubitis declined the Cheka invitation to participate in the broadcast, he was relieved of his job. I guess they think he might still be swayed; otherwise he'd be in Siberia."

I started to tell Dace about another lawyer, Skritulis, in Jelgava.

"Skritulis? I think my godfather was a friend of his. If he is the same guy, he was pretty liberal in his thinking."

"Yes, it was his thinking that got him into trouble. It seems his idea of socialism was a bit different from the prevailing one. The more he argued, the angrier the Cheka became. Late one night, a woman tapped on his window. She didn't identify herself but told him to get out quickly, because he and his family were in danger of being deported."

"Probably someone like Mrs. Vinerts," Dace said thoughtfully.

"Yes, perhaps. I wonder how many true Communists there really are. Many of them are probably just like us, happy to have food on the table. But few are brave

enough to stick their necks out to help someone else. Where could we go, I wonder, if we knew that—say, tomorrow—we'd be deported?" Dace asked wistfully.

I didn't have an answer. So, I continued my story. "Skritulis and his family
packed some suitcases and fled…to Siberia."

"What? Really?" Dace was stunned. "And he wasn't caught?"

"Well, there is no need for checkpoints for people going into Russia. The next
night, the Cheka found his house empty. The neighbors didn't know anything,
and the whole thing has died down. Skritulis even wrote in a letter that, because
he had relocated willingly, he already had several job offers."

"Yes, life is strange now, but no matter how bad it may be, we have to learn to
adapt," Dace said. "Skritulis didn't wait for help from the Americans, Swedes, or
Brits. He helped himself."

"I wonder what they would think about this in the West? Maybe his friends
and relatives will call him a Communist, especially if he gets a decent job."

◆   ◆   ◆

The clinical studies had begun. Professor Stradins was an excellent teacher.
Occasionally he'd call one of us to the front of the auditorium to diagnose the illness of a patient who had been brought in for that purpose.

One day, it was Eugenie's turn.

"Tell us what you see."

"A lump, Pauls Janovich," Eugenie replied flashing her most dazzling smile
and looking straight into the professor's eyes.

Turning to Laimonis, who was in the front row, the professor asked, "And
how would you characterize the patient's condition?"

"I would say it looks like an infection."

"I would say the same," Stradins said as he nodded approvingly. "But is that a
clear enough diagnosis for those in the back who cannot see the problem for
themselves?"

Without a word, Eugenie took a step forward and touched the patient's leg.

"Remember, first with the eyes, and only then with the hands," the professor
reproached her.

Visibly annoyed, Eugenie stepped back, the color rising in her cheeks.

"What else?" said Stradins, again pointing to Laimonis.

"I would say the inflamed area is located on the upper third of the leg, on the
lateral side."

"Very good!"

Eugenie, nervously scrunching her chiffon scarf, shot an angry glance at the professor.

"Go on," Stradins motioned to Laimonis.

"The redness is about the size of a five-lat piece," Laimonis said and quickly stopped short. He realized too late he had compared the lump to a piece of Latvian currency.

Stradins continued encouragingly, "The redness is about three to four centimeters in diameter."

"Surely we are not using outmoded bourgeois money as a unit of measure!" Eugenie said, narrowing her eyes as she pressed down hard on the swelling, causing the patient to wince.

"A patient must be examined with care," the professor said. "If he feels pain, it is the physician's fault."

Eugenie backed away, spitefully silent.

"Maybe now you could tell us all the symptoms together—the ones you can see as well as the ones you can feel," the professor said, looking at Laimonis.

"A raised area, redness, heat, pain, and interruption of proper function."

"Yes, that's right, but you sound like you're reciting from a textbook. Now try saying it in Latin."

We all knew how much the professor loved Latin.

"*Tumor, rubor, calor, dolor, et...*" Laimonis began.

Before he could finish, Eugenie gasped, "I don't feel well!" and slumped gracefully to the floor.

"So a mere swelling has managed to fell a doctor," Stradins said as he and Laimonis bent down to pick up Eugenie and take her outside.

"You should have saved that trick for the finals!" someone shouted.

"You'll regret that!" Eugenie hissed as laughter echoed throughout the auditorium.

◆   ◆   ◆

When I got home, Hugo was waiting. His scholarship had been taken away because he missed the Marxism exam.

"Maybe if you try harder, you can get the scholarship back." I suggested.

"Try harder?" Hugo raised his voice. "What exactly does that mean?"

"Well, how then do you hope to continue your studies?"

"Things are going to change."

It was Hugo's stock answer.

We could afford to eat only twice a day. In the morning we heated up potatoes in fish oil and put them on a slice of dark bread. In the evening we boiled potatoes and ate them with gravy.

Tonight, I was also boiling fresh cabbage. I was so hungry I could hardly wait for the meal to be cooked. I was always hungry, but even more so since we had gotten married.

Hugo was in an upbeat mood, which meant he had been drinking. When I looked at him reproachfully, he announced with great pomp, "My darling wife, tonight we are having guests—great lads, true patriots. So I started celebrating a bit early."

"How can we have guests? We have nothing in the house."

"Your mother sent us three hundred rubles. I've already done the shopping."

Hugo stood up and opened the pantry door, revealing two half-gallon bottles of whiskey, and slabs of bacon and butter.

"We have fifty rubles left," he explained. "I put them in the desk drawer."

I knew it was futile to object when Hugo was in one of his grandiose moods, but this time I couldn't help myself. "It would be nice if you helped Mother sometime. You used to run up there every week before we were married. I'm ashamed that all we do is take and never give anything back. You know she's not well."

"Ooh, now you're making me feel bad," Hugo said as he pulled down the corners of his mouth. "I'd go if it wasn't for Ziemele. You know I can't stand her. What an idiot to come back here from the West."

"She's just someone who was fooled by false promises. But we can't go on asking my mother—a sick, aging person—to help two young and physically fit people."

"I know, I know. I'm just a leach!" Hugo retorted. "But it's the parents' responsibility to take care of their children. And, if I am your husband, then your mother has to take care of me too." Before I could say anything, there was a knock at the door. Hugo hurried to open it, and two young men came in. He introduced them as Janis and Rudi, true patriots. "They fought the Reds on the Eastern Front," Hugo said, uncorking one of the bottles. "Now, my darling little wife, go make us something nice to eat."

He clearly loved playing host and being the center of attention.

As I was making sandwiches for the guests, I knew Hugo and I would again be eating boiled potatoes for breakfast.

"Well done," he cried as I brought in the platter. "Now come have a drink with us."

I had one drink to be polite.

"Ah, where were we?" asked Hugo. "Oh, yes, the Reds. They begged me to spare them. I almost single-handedly took them prisoner. Don't you think that calls for another drink?"

"Yes, let's drink to that!" the guests echoed.

"We need to keep our memories fresh, so we know what to do when we meet them on the battlefield again!" Hugo said.

"He's right!" his two friends chorused. "*Prozit!*"

When Hugo went to the kitchen to get the second bottle, I took the opportunity to ask them where they had met my husband.

"Just there, in the corner restaurant," said Rudi.

The empty bravado continued into the wee hours. When Hugo found an appreciative audience, he could be generous indeed.

We had only one room, so I moved into a corner and tried to study but found it hard to concentrate. I thought about the night Hugo had threatened suicide. Later he laughed uproariously and said it was all just a show he put on to bring a stuck-up girl down to earth. I had been the only one to ever resist his charms, so he had something to prove. He told me that the day after we were married, adding that now I was just like all the rest of his conquests. My pride was hurt, but I still believed that, if I worked hard at our marriage, things would improve.

Our wedding party took place several months after the civil ceremony. I found out that Hugo had asked each of our relatives—even the ones from the countryside—to contribute to the celebration. I was embarrassed, but it was too late to do anything about it.

Hugo's favorite topics of conversation were himself and his battlefield heroics, though by now I knew that his real heroics came from a bottle. I couldn't discuss our relationship with my mother or even with my girlfriends. I was too ashamed to admit I had made a terrible mistake.

"You're shivering. Are you cold?" asked Rudi.

"Another drink will warm you up." Hugo pressed another glass into my hand. The strong liquor was difficult to swallow. I was also put off by the fact that my husband was making me drink it. "You must also learn to smoke. What kind of doctor would you be if you didn't smoke?" Hugo said lighting a cigarette and putting it between my lips.

Furious, I threw it across the room. Hugo frowned. "A good wife would obey her husband. But never mind, you're still my darling little wife. Boys, if you only knew what a great wedding we had in Gertrude's church. After the photo session, we drove to my wife's home in Jelgava in a car decorated with flowers. My brother had booked a jazz group, and they didn't stop playing for three days!" Hugo rambled on, embellishing the story as he went along.

I retreated into my own thoughts, only vaguely aware that Hugo had left the room, until Rudi's gleeful shouts brought me back to reality. "Another bottle! What a guy!"

I walked over to the desk and opened the drawer. It was empty. My mother's last fifty rubles were gone. We had no money to buy food.

23

The Com-Youth Have It All

I was taking a shortcut across Vermane Gardens, on my way to the old university building, when I saw Olita, a former classmate from Jelgava. She looked as if she had been crying.

"What's wrong?" I wanted to know.

"I am no longer a member of the Com-Youth," she said, looking around uneasily.

"I didn't know you had joined!"

"Well, it seemed like the thing to do. But now they've thrown me out."

"Why?"

"Because of my shoes. I sold my shoes."

"I don't understand."

"Well, I tried to pass my university entrance exams twice and failed both times, so I joined Com-Youth, whose members are registered separately. The next time I took the exam, I passed, though I was still required to pay the fee of two hundred rubles. I didn't have the money, so I went to the market to try to sell my leather shoes. But I forgot to take off my Com-Youth badge, and an officer came over and wrote down my ID number. Today, Kruskops called me in and shouted at me that Com-Youth and Party members are the nation's life force, and they don't lack for anything. I tried to explain that I needed to cover my entrance fee.

'That's not possible!' he pounded his fist on the table. 'You're spreading false propaganda. Everyone has enough of everything here. You don't belong with the Com-Youth. Get out!'" Olita sniffed. "Then he took away my badge and membership card."

"Don't worry, you'll be all right," I comforted her. "You might even be better off."

"I'm not so sure. I was also called in by the registrar and told in the coarsest Russian words that if I wasn't fit for Com-Youth, I wasn't fit to study in a Soviet university. I've been expelled."

Olita was crying in earnest now. One thing was clear to me: It was hardly worth the effort to climb the Soviet ladder, because if you missed a step, you could fall to the bottom rung overnight.

◆   ◆   ◆

Even without Reverend Peteris, our philosophy group continued to meet every week, but, because Hugo didn't approve, I only went occasionally, usually when he was at the pub with his friends.

I was growing resentful and one night decided to defy him. Besides, I had already prepared my assignment for the debate, and my absence would have disrupted the program.

"I said you're not going!" Hugo shouted.

"Just let me go this once. It would be too difficult to explain."

"Tell them your husband wouldn't let you."

"Married people attend our meetings, so that kind of reasoning doesn't make sense. How often have I asked you not to spend our money drinking with your so-called friends?"

"I'm a man, and I can do what I want!" Hugo shouted. The argument escalated from there. I said I was tired of his domineering attitude; he said I didn't understand him, and so it went until we said we couldn't bear the sight of each other and he put on his coat and slammed the door.

When I got home, he wasn't there. The hours passed...midnight, two o'clock...three...still no Hugo. I wondered if our life together would ever change. What if he was lying on the street somewhere, injured? Should I have stayed home? Maybe if I tried to be more understanding, we wouldn't fight so much...

Dawn was breaking. I heard someone fumbling at the door and jumped up to open it. Hugo stood leaning against the wall, smiling. "My darling little wife, what a great night it was." He stumbled across the threshold. "We went joyriding on the police chief's motorbike and parked it outside the Cheka headquarters. What fun! And you say we are not men of action! Afterwards, we had a great meal and toasted our heroics at the pub."

"And how did you manage to pay for this fabulous evening?"

"It was my treat. I sold…" That was as far as Hugo got before he passed out on the sofa. It was not the first time. I undressed him and covered him with a blanket. But what had he sold? Once he traded his leather jacket for a bottle of whisky, but this time I didn't see anything missing.

The next morning, I couldn't find my gold watch, the one I didn't dare wear every day. It had been a confirmation present from Gran. Angry and upset, I confronted Hugo.

He just smiled and said he wanted to teach me a lesson in obedience.

24

We Sell Our Belongings

Farm life was becoming very difficult—not only for older folks like my mother but for younger ones as well. The Communists' goal was collectivization, but they were clever enough not to move too quickly. Besides, they still had some unfinished business in the cities. They were almost done cleaning out the ranks of lawyers, doctors, engineers, and clergy. Now they would offer farmers a choice: if they could not meet production and tax demands, which were impossibly high, they could "voluntarily" join a collective.

One day, on my way to Jelgava, I passed a Russian woman on the road wearing one of my mother's dresses and my school hat. In different circumstances I might have called her a thief, but I just smiled.

Ziemele was still living with Mother and helping out any way she could, though it was clear they couldn't go on much longer. "What will you do?" I asked.

"Well, I'd like to get rid of everything I am allowed to sell," Mother replied. "I spoke to a lawyer who specializes in collectivization matters and that is what he advised me to do."

Ever since she learned that Father was up north in Archangel, I knew that staying in our house was no longer that important to her. But her response still came as a surprise. It took a lot of strength to make a decision to leave familiar surroundings and part with things that had once been held dear. "But what can we sell—legally?" I asked.

"Buildings, if they have not yet been confiscated. Also machinery and tools. The land is already government property, although not everyone is aware of it. The lawyer confirmed that as well."

"So you don't really have much left. Who'll want to buy farm machinery?"

"Buyers have already come forward," Mother said. "A dairy wants to buy the buildings as an annex. They can't pay much, but at least I will get something. Payments will be made over time—with butter."

"I guess that's all right. Butter is more valuable than cash these days. But how can a dairy, which is government owned, use butter as payment?"

"It may not be allowed, but everybody knows they do it anyway."

By the time we parted, Mother and I agreed she should move to Riga.

◆   ◆   ◆

I returned to our apartment to find a letter from Eugenie saying it was urgent that she see me. Hugo wasn't home, so I left him a note telling him where I had gone.

I still liked Eugenie but had mixed feelings about going to see her.

As I approached her house, I saw children playing outside. They were speaking Russian, arguing over a toy horse that had a five-lat piece tied to its tail. I recognized it immediately as the brooch I'd given Eugenie as a present on my first visit.

"Where did you get this?" I asked the children.

"Auntie Eugenie gave it to us," one of the girls replied.

Disappointed and sad, I climbed the stairs to the fourth floor. The door to Eugenie's apartment was slightly ajar, and I could hear a woman's voice pleading from within. "Miss, please, it belonged to my child. If you don't want to give back the furniture, piano, or clothing, then at least let me take something as a keepsake...who knows if I'll ever see my children again. At least I will have something to remember them by."

"Out!" Eugenie shrieked. "If your children are in the West, they are capitalists and Fascists. Our government has ways of dealing with people like you. Now leave my house before I call the police!"

"I was only asking. I hoped you'd understand."

"Get out!" Eugenie ordered.

I had obviously arrived at a bad time. As I turned to leave, the door flew open, and an older woman with red-rimmed eyes stumbled out, an enraged Eugenie on her heels. Seeing me, she quickly changed her demeanor.

"Oh, hello, dear," she said sweetly. "Please, please come in. I've been waiting for you. I am very unhappy and need to talk to someone. You have always been such a true friend. My heart is breaking."

"You mean because of the woman who just left?"

"Oh, no!" Eugenie wrinkled her nose. "She's a pest. My beloved minister gave me this apartment and all the furnishings. It has nothing to do with her anymore."

"What about the things that belonged to her children?"

"Well, they're all mine now," Eugenie snapped, then started to sniffle. "Oh, my darling minister, what is he doing to me?"

"What's wrong? What did he do?" I asked, feeling a bit alarmed.

"That bastard deceived me. He never told me he was married. Now his wife has arrived with their children. Oh, my darling, my love! Why did he do this to me?" Eugenie wailed, writhing on the sofa.

"His wife and I had a fight yesterday at his office. She pulled my hair, so I really let her have it. I slapped her and kicked her," she went on, slowly regaining her composure. "Look at these bruises. And here...this is where she pulled the hair out of my head."

"Are you talking about the wife of Health Minister Grigorash?"

"Of course! Who else? That no-good rat! That's why he didn't want to marry me, no matter how hard I tried to persuade him. And now he brings that old hag, who had the audacity to call me names and attack me in front of everybody!"

"Wasn't the minister there?"

"Of course he was. He took the witch by the hand and left the office. He even threatened to have me hauled away for hooliganism. After all I've suffered because of him!"

"But you used to praise him so."

"What else could I do? He's a man. I had to flatter him."

"I've got to go," I said, rising, "I don't have time to stay today."

"Don't leave, dear. I need to unburden myself. You're such a good friend."

"I thought you already told me everything."

"No, I'm not finished yet. After the fracas, they called me to the ministry and told me I would not be working there anymore."

"That should leave you more time for your studies."

"That's something else altogether, dear. The minister also wanted me to sign a paper saying there had never been anything between us!"

"Why?"

"It's simple. A Party member is always decent and honorable."

"But what if he isn't?" I asked from the doorway.

"Of course, dear, that isn't easy to prove, but, if one does succeed, the punishment can be harsh—expulsion from the Party, and even loss of job."

So Eugenie stood her ground, and Grigorash soon left his job at the health ministry. Though his reason for leaving was never fully explained, it was a very big step down his career ladder.

Eugenie's latest adventure made the rounds of the entire medical school. It was also the last straw for our friendship. My eyes had been truly opened by the woman pleading for a memento of her children.

Eugenie never actually practiced medicine; she simply wasn't qualified. She worked in the health records office for a while, but didn't like it and eventually got a job with the Cheka, who allowed her to work as a doctor for political prisoners. That job she could do, because medical knowledge was not really required. What that job called for was something entirely different.

◆   ◆   ◆

When I got back from Eugenie's, Hugo still wasn't home. Our room, lit by a single electric bulb, was cold and unwelcoming. Hugo had not wanted to move in with me and Mrs. Vinerts, as there was a great antipathy between them.

Now our lives were bleak, like those of most other Latvians. Our central heating didn't work. The bathtub was unusable. We cooked our meals on a gas stove. Electricity was rationed, with a fine levied for every extra kilowatt used. If you exceeded the allotted amount too many times, your electricity was simply shut off.

Dace married Noldis, and we slowly drifted apart. Hugo didn't get along with my friends, and I was too ashamed of how we lived to invite people over. But somehow I was still prepared to overlook the rest of our problems.

The doorbell rang. It was Mrs. Vinerts. I was surprised and happy, as I hadn't seen her since my wedding.

"Good evening, Lita!" she greeted me, warmly shaking my hand. "As I was climbing the stairs in the dark, I almost mistook someone else for you. There was a couple in front of me with the woman carrying the heavy bags, while the young man had his hands stuffed in his pockets. I was sure it was Hugo."

I tried to defend him by saying he was a patriot and believed that Latvian officers did not have to do menial work, but Mrs. Vinerts stopped me short.

"Hugo is a drunk with no morals. All he does is talk, and these days we need more than empty words. The Latvian officers he seeks to emulate would never disrespect a woman."

Before I could say anything else, the doorbell rang again.

"Who is it?"

"Alfons."

"Alfons who?"

"I'm a student. I've come to see Hugo."

He sounded pleasant enough, so I opened the door.

"Hugo's not home. I'm his wife. Can I help?"

"Yes, maybe you can," the slender young man replied.

"Come in. Hugo's probably at a lecture. Please sit down."

"Actually, I'm in a bit of a hurry," Alfons said, "but maybe you can tell me what books he wants to sell?"

"Sell books?" I asked, puzzled. "There must be some mistake."

"He said he had textbooks to sell because he won't need them anymore."

"Textbooks he won't need anymore?" I echoed. "I don't understand."

"It's simple. If he's leaving the university, he won't be needing them."

"Hugo's quitting his studies?" I was aghast.

"He was expelled. Didn't you know?" now it was Alfons's turn to be surprised. He started to squirm in his chair. "I guess I've said too much."

"No, you haven't," I answered mechanically. "When did this happen?"

"Two or three weeks ago. I assumed you knew. He never finished his exams. I'm sorry you had to find out from me," he said, looking at the floor.

"Don't worry, I would have found out sooner or later," I said as Alfons apologized again before leaving.

I was embarrassed that Mrs. Vinerts had witnessed this. I sat at the desk and fidgeted, nervously opening and closing the top drawer. As I opened it a bit further, I saw there was a letter inside. It was from Hugo.

My dear little wife!

You don't seem to understand that I was born to do big things for our country and its struggle to regain independence. It's hard for me to find supportive, like-minded friends here. So Rudi and I have decided to go to Sweden, to make plans for Latvia's future.

With love,

Your Hugo

I was in shock. First, he had not found it necessary to tell me he had been kicked out of university. And then this letter, with words as empty as our relationship had been. Now it was over.

I had no illusions about us, but I still had not expected things to end like this.

Mrs. Vinerts, sensing my distress, held out her hand. "I'll be leaving. I only came to tell you I changed my apartment and now have only two small rooms. Here's the address. Please come and visit."

"You changed apartments? But how?" I was momentarily distracted.

"It's not easy, but it is possible," she replied. "I'll tell you another time. Take care for now."

25

Red Fridis

More Russian professors were joining the faculty. The Party saw to it. And Russian students followed in droves, encouraged by incentives to study in one of the occupied countries.

Much later, when I had the opportunity to become familiar with Western universities, I was able to make comparisons. There were similarities, to be sure. Good students as well as those who simply tried to get by could be found in both places. And, of course, some teachers were better than others.

In other respects, however, learning institutions were very different. In Western universities, for example, someone like Eugenie wouldn't last a week.

Despite the nearly total lack of ethics and morality, the extent of which I'm sure does not exist in any other part of the world, I can't say that I didn't come to respect some of the Russian professors—even if most of them believed that the biggest compliment they could pay a co-ed was to invite her to spend the night. Those invitations were commonplace for the attractive girls, who also knew that any thought of reporting unwanted attentions could have dire consequences, such as counter complaints of sabotage, bourgeois nationalistic activities, or the heinous crime of telling lies about their "liberators."

I much preferred the academic freedom in the West, which made for a much richer learning experience and taught students to take responsibility for their own actions and lives.

But I digress.

At University, our lectures about anatomy, orthopedics, and pediatric illnesses continued, although the dismissal of one of our favorite teachers was disquieting. It was unclear whether Miss Vigante would be brought up on charges after a book published in the West alleged that, during the Communist occupation in 1941, she had helped to hide people who were being sought by the regime. The teacher was puzzled as to why anyone would make such claims and also about the existence of such a book, which, along with so many other things from the West, would not have been accessible to us.

Vigante was replaced by a Latvian from Russia, who was not nearly her caliber and said to be on the Cheka payroll. Needless to say, we didn't like him.

I was chosen, along with a classmate, Livija, to get flowers for our teacher to show our appreciation. I didn't know Livija well, though she seemed pleasant. She lived in a nicely furnished room on Terbata Street. When I arrived, I saw a slender dark-haired girl sitting near the radio.

"Oh, you have company!"

"This is Valda. We've been friends since childhood," Livija introduced us. "Have you never met?"

"Well, I've seen you somewhere before...at university?"

"Yes," she said. "I was studying medicine as well but had to drop out because my husband was also a student, and our little boy was sick a lot."

"You should have married rich like Aina did, then you wouldn't have those problems," Livija teased her friend.

"Oh, sure. I'd be just as free, with a Cheka agent following me everywhere."

"Who are you talking about?" I asked.

"You probably know her. Aina is from Jelgava. She married a Communist convert named Krumins, who is now a very important man," Valda said.

"Oh, I remember her! She was a year or two ahead of me," I said.

"We knew her too," said Livija. "We used to do things together, even take trips to the seashore. But now it seems Aina doesn't recognize her old friends anymore.

"I had a similar experience when I saw her at the Universal store," I chimed in. "I said hello, and Aina looked like she wanted to have a chat, but then a man next to her said something in Russian, and she walked by as if she didn't know me. I must admit I was offended. Soon after, I ran into one of her friends, Laima. She told me Aina has a bodyguard and was forbidden to associate with anyone with unclear political leanings, which might include many of her former friends. Laima said she had also joined Com-Youth and Krumins had helped her get a government job."

"It looks like Laima has paid her own dues just to stay friends with Aina," Valda said after listening to my story. "At least she has a good job."

"Oh, well, we'll get by with our ordinary little jobs," Livija laughed.

We set off for the flower shop accompanied by Valda, because she knew someone who worked there. We bought a large bouquet for Miss Vigante.

The gray-haired teacher was moved to tears by our gesture, which, in the end, must have been small consolation for an educator who had just given her last lecture.

◆   ◆   ◆

With Hugo no longer in my life, I went back to attending the philosophy group meetings.

One night I arrived late and the speaker, a young man named Indulis, had already begun. "Communism teaches you to live for the moment," he was saying. "Spirituality and independent thinking are discouraged in every way for the masses, who are expected to blindly follow any directive, because the people who issue them are 'morally unassailable'. The Communists' goal is to rule the world, and any means to that end are acceptable. Lying, if it advances Party interests, is not only permitted but encouraged. No one is allowed to stay in the same place for long. The Communists want people to be like inanimate pawns that can be moved at will into different settings.

"After work, people are required to attend political classes so they have no chance to pause and reflect on what is going on in their lives. The aim is to make them spiritually empty and apathetic. Great pains are taken to instill fear to keep the masses under control and get them to believe that no other kind of life is possible. And, using any available means, information about life in the West is kept concealed, especially from young people. A situation is created so that a person's most overwhelming concerns became getting enough to eat and avoiding problems with the Cheka. Officially, people are entitled to their loaf of stale bread and a circus performance on holidays.

"People are generally suspicious of one another, lest one of them turn out to be in league with the regime. And for that reason—because Communism is anathema to anything natural or normal—it will remain a Utopian teaching, a castle made of sand," Indulis paused as if suddenly worried he may have said too much.

Reverend Peteris stepped forward and slapped the blond youth on the back.

"I was just expressing my feelings," Indulis said. "And it so happens, I had access to some interesting material."

Nobody asked him to explain, and his speech had run so long we had no time for the usual discussion afterward. In student circles, the tall and muscular Indulis had been nicknamed Bear Slayer, because he looked quite the part of the legendary Latvian folk hero.

"All right, Bear Slayer, enough of the serious stuff," said Peteris. "Now tell us about Red Fridis."

It was well known that the agricultural college had the largest and most nationalistic Latvian makeup, with only a small percentage of Com-Youth.

"Except for a few obvious observers assigned to all faculties, there were no Com-Youth among us," Indulis began. "Then Fridis arrived. We knew he wasn't a Communist and understood that at times we all said things we didn't mean. But Fridis often took it too far and got on our nerves.

"Our summer session was spent at the lake in Talsi, where Fridis cozied up to the organizing committee, even serving as an agitator during elections so he could score a bottle of vodka to satisfy his craving for alcohol. Once he started, he wouldn't stop drinking until he passed out. He got into a lot of fights, and his bad behavior turned the locals against the rest of us. That made us angry.

"So we decided to teach him a lesson using a coffin we found in the attic of an abandoned farmhouse. The next time Fridis went on one of his binges, waving the Communist flag and drinking toasts to Stalin and the Red Army, we were ready. When he passed out, we laid him in the coffin with an empty bottle in his hand, covered him with a red flag, and pinned a note to his chest that said, 'Sleep well, you are now in Paradise!' We put the open coffin on a raft and gave it a good shove out onto the lake. We even took a photo," said Indulis with a mischievous smile.

"And then what happened?" someone asked.

"After a while, Fridis came to and started shouting for help. A crowd had gathered on the shore, and they doubled over with laughter when they realized the 'corpse' was the troublesome Fridis. We let him float for several hours, until the fire brigade came to his rescue. You should have seen his face as he climbed out of the coffin in his hung-over state. It was another photo opportunity, of course."

"But didn't you get into trouble?" Livija asked.

"Fridis never reported us, and the locals weren't about to complain, either."

"And Fridis? Is he still a problem?" I asked.

"No, he's a changed man."

On the way home, Livija turned to me and said, "Remember that reference to having access to interesting material? You'd never guess in a million years what it was! Reverend Peteris gave Indulis a paper that belonged to a Latvian university professor who now lives in the West."

"But how did he get it?"

"I have no idea. Although he treats us all like family, he would not divulge that information, saying only that it's safer this way. Indulis and Peteris have known each other for a long time," Livija said. "On November eighteenth, to mark our Independence Day, Indulis will read patriotic poems, also sent from the West."

"So it will be truly special. He has a nice, resonant voice."

"Yes, Indulis has a truly wonderful voice!" Livija agreed.

◆　　　◆　　　◆

Professor Bune, a Latvian from Russia, taught basic surgery class. He had a heavy accent, but we didn't mind because his approach was generally more sympathetic and had no political overtones. On the other hand, the more advanced hospital surgery lectures were read by another Russian Latvian, Professor Liepukalns. He never missed an opportunity to weave Communist phraseology into the lessons, but his accent was so thick that Latvian students found him difficult to understand.

It was no surprise that Liepukalns was named chief surgeon of the Latvian Republic.

Lectures on eye diseases were read by Professor Balodis, who was popular with Latvian as well as Russian students.

A new arrival, Professor Zdravomislov, who introduced hypnosis as a way to control pain during childbirth, presented the obstetrics and gynecology class for Russian students.

Eugenie wondered out loud if he would demonstrate the effectiveness of hypnosis on the students.

Laughing, the professor explained the procedure and also invited her to his apartment that evening.

"Ooh, he's far more interesting than the health minister," Eugenie gushed the next day. "You should have seen the table he set for me—caviar, exotic fruit, and different kinds of wine!"

It wasn't clear who seduced whom, but it didn't matter because both were willing participants.

The ob-gyn class for Latvian students was taught by Dr. Briedis, who took over for Professor Putnins. We were never able to find out why he left, but his work could be purchased from the cloakroom attendant, along with Latvian and German textbooks, though the prices were high. Still, we liked Briedis well enough and learned a lot from his lectures.

At exam time, Alma was asked to describe the symptoms of pregnancy. Clearing her throat, she began, "The symptoms of pregnancy. Hmm, uh…Well, a large stomach, no monthly periods, feeling ill."

"Stop right there!" Dr. Briedis interrupted. "By your diagnosis, it would seem that I am also pregnant. I have a large stomach and no monthly periods. And I'm feeling ill listening to your nonacademic response."

Alma failed the exam. She also failed the next one and the one after that, and eventually had to quit her studies.

Dermatology and venereal disease were taught in Russian by an elegant German professor called Stein. Those same lectures were read in Latvian by Dr. Apse, who had a sadistic streak. If a female student was obviously uncomfortable, she was the one he would call on. He called on me often to, as he put it, "help me get over my blushing problem." When I missed two classes because of illness, he made me repeat the entire course. Angry, I vowed never to choose skin diseases as my specialty. But even as I made that promise to myself, Gran's words rang in my ears: 'Never say never, child, because it's not possible to know what the future will bring.' As usual, she was right.

◆   ◆   ◆

One day a letter arrived, via a circuitous route, from my friend Karina. Childhood memories came flooding back along with that last telephone call when we planned our escape from the invading Russians. I had thought of her often, but did not know until now what had become of her. Kari was in Germany. I wondered if she had any idea how much we envied her.

I longed to join her in that other world, where people were free to do as they pleased—a place where they didn't have to learn Marxism-Leninism and say that black was white. I didn't know what life was like in the West, but I was certain it was better than ours. Anyway, it was nice to dream. But dreams rarely come true, and I had to keep living in the present.

The doorbell shattered my reverie. To my great surprise, it was Hugo.

"Hello, my dear wife!" he said as if he had been gone only a few hours instead of several weeks. "I've come back."

I stared at him, dumbstruck.

"Yes, I'm back," Hugo repeated. "Sweden didn't work out. Rudi and I got no farther than Ainazi."

"Did you think getting to Sweden was going to be easy?" I finally found my voice. "I really don't understand you."

"Well, Rudi had heard that some people managed to get directly to Sweden, so we wanted to do it, too. We made a sturdy raft, but we just didn't succeed," Hugo retorted. "As far as you not understanding me, I've known that for a long time. Unlike you, the girls in Ainazi adored me."

As I watched him and listened to him, I was never more certain that our marriage had been a dreadful mistake from the beginning and that our interests were so far apart that making our relationship work was never even within the realm of possibility. "You're right, Hugo," I said calmly. "I don't understand you, and you don't understand me. So the best thing for us to do is to get a divorce."

"A divorce?" Hugo recoiled. "My dear little wife, what on earth do you mean? Did you get up on the wrong side of the bed? I have no intention of divorcing you."

"Well, I can't go on trying to earn a university degree while putting up with your nonsense," I stated categorically.

"Ah, so you are jealous."

"How would you like it if I had boyfriends?"

"But I'm a man! I can do anything I want."

"Well, I'm not prepared to accept those terms. I want you to leave."

"No. I am your husband. These rooms belong to both of us."

"All right, then I'll go!" I said, starting to pull on my clothes.

Hugo, puzzled by my behavior, eyed me suspiciously. He was used to my ultimate acquiescence, no matter what the problem.

"You've overestimated my capacity for patience," I said over my shoulder. "It is not infinite. Good-bye!"

◆   ◆   ◆

Some time later, I went to visit Olga. Seeing a young woman in the hallway, I greeted her in Latvian and she returned the greeting.

"A new face?" I remarked when Olga and I were behind closed, and locked, doors.

"Roberts's latest," Olga said as she laughed.

"Another new girlfriend?" I said, surprised. "What happened to Ance?"

"Oh, she's still here but in a different room."

"Now I really am confused," I said, taking off my coat.

"You'll understand soon enough," Olga answered. "As you know, Roberts hasn't worked for a while. He had thirty thousand rubles in his pocket after selling the spare room. He also made money off Ance. Now he has found a job as a press photographer."

"But didn't Ance have a baby?" I asked.

"Yes, she and Roberts have a daughter," Olga said. "That was another reason he decided he had to get out of the house."

"They never got married?"

"Of course not! He wasn't divorced, so he couldn't have, even if he wanted to. I doubt he would have married her, anyway. He already had everything he wanted. She eventually realized what was going on—but what could she do?"

Olga's difficulties over the kitchen she shared with her neighbors had gotten worse. Zoya spent the entire day there. "That's why I have this stove. It's illegal, but my children have to eat. And Roberts won't do anything to upset Zoya because they are in business together."

"Roberts and Zoya? What would a press photographer have to do with her?"

"It's simple. As a member of the press, he has clearance to travel and doesn't have to worry about customs control, so he started bringing in cheap pork from Jelgava and giving it to Zoya to sell at a profit. For a while, these rooms looked like an abattoir. But since Roberts and Zoya are both out for themselves, problems soon developed between them. So he brought in Cousin Milda to sell the meat, and she seems to have managed quite well," Olga explained.

"That's not surprising. Who in his right mind would turn down a slab of pork these days?" I asked, adding, "Is Milda really Roberts's cousin?"

"Of course not! But we have to keep quiet if we don't want Roberts to get upset. He even told Ance that Milda was his cousin. But then..."

"...the truth came out?"

"Yes, in a rather unusual way. Selling the meat was illegal as every animal is registered and can't be slaughtered without part of the proceeds going to the state. In the end, I was glad Roberts never sold me any of it."

"But why?"

"Have you heard about the open pig farm near John's Cemetery?"

"Yes."

"The Russian cemetery guard, who kept pigs, was feeding them corpses. He took the remains out of the coffins, then nailed them shut for burial."

"I find that hard to believe," I said haltingly. "But, if you say it's true, then it must be. And Roberts was selling this meat?"

"We don't know for sure if Roberts was aware of the cemetery guard's activities, but if he was, it didn't stop him from going along with the scheme. After all, there's only one thing that's important to him—making money."

"So tell me how it all came out into the open."

"It started with a distinctive scarf a Russian woman had wrapped around her deceased daughter's shoulders. The mother later saw the cemetery guard's wife wearing it. It seems the couple had become too careless. When the mother demanded that her daughter's grave be dug up, the guard cursed her out, hoping to intimidate her. But the woman turned to the authorities. How it all evolved from there I'm not sure, but they did open her daughter's coffin, and it was empty. They also found large kettles in which the bodies had been boiled to make the flesh more palatable to the pigs."

"What about her other clothes?"

"They had been taken to the market and sold."

"So what did Roberts do?"

"Oh, he just smiled. No doubt his only regret was that his once-thriving business was gone. When they went looking for him, he disappeared. Neither of his girlfriends has a clue of his whereabouts."

"Do they know that they are rivals?"

"Oh, yes! Ever since Roberts made himself scarce, they have talked quite a bit, especially now that Milda has learned she is pregnant.

26

What Do They Think in the West?

All the things I had learned in medical school were coming together, and I was starting to understand the human body for the complicated machine that it was. If I had ever thought that my Latin lessons made no sense at all, I now realized how important they had been in building a foundation.

Back then, Professor Stradins's words had seemed an exaggeration. "For three years, you will have surgery lectures. And from them you will learn just enough to be able to find the right spot in your medical books." I knew now how right he had been. I also grew to appreciate the grueling hours of study by flickering candlelight and the anger I harbored toward professors who were expecting me to learn so many things which at the time seemed trivial or unnecessary.

During the summer months we visited clinics, worked as volunteers, and gained practical experience in hospitals. No one escaped the obligatory bedside diagnosis. The professor stopped by twice a week, sometimes accompanied by an entourage of interns, residents, registered nurses, nurse practitioners, and groups of students. He would move along row after row of patients, listening to each doctor's evaluation, sometimes offering a suggestion or voicing an opinion. When a case was particularly noteworthy, he'd pause and ask brief, direct questions, to which he expected simple but precise answers.

Having spent every day in the clinic, I knew each patient's ailment and felt confident I could take it a step further to a diagnosis. But the professor felt that was premature. He wanted to hear of every possibility the symptoms might cover, and then one by one, eliminate the ones that didn't apply, before finally narrowing it down to one diagnosis.

"Many illnesses have similar symptoms, but they can be totally different," he reminded us, encouraging us to think independently while applying our textbook knowledge.

We became familiar with the medications and medical instruments, treated infected wounds that made us nauseous, and learned to dress them properly. Then came the long-awaited scrub down for the first surgical procedure. We were allowed to participate by holding the appropriate instruments and handing them to the surgeon. I was supremely confident and very proud to be in my profession.

Then came the first patient deaths. Their bodies, however, were nothing like the formaldehyde-soaked ones we had cut apart in anatomy class. These were people with whom we'd had conversations, whose symptoms we had studied, to whom we had given injections or for whom we had dressed a wound. These were people we had come to know—and they were suddenly gone. Although a doctor with no emotions would be well advised to look for another vocation, we had to learn to mask our feelings, as getting too involved with a patient could bring on a different set of problems.

Professor Stradins was a cancer specialist and head of the surgical clinic. And, although it was not officially allowed, he also had a private practice where many—Latvians as well as Russians—came to him for help. Here, the occupying forces seemed to make an exception.

Stradins was known to function on very little sleep, catching naps while sitting or even standing. One afternoon, while I was working, Vaira, Lija, Laimonis, and Velta burst in, chattering excitedly. It seemed Laimonis was the hero of the day. Lija explained. "We were in the professor's office," she began. "We each had to draw a question and then were given time to think about an answer. The professor looked weary. 'Who's going first?' he asked.

"Laimonis stepped forward. As he began his task, which was to describe an operation, the warm rays of the sun were shining directly on Stradins's head, and he soon dozed off. Gradually, Laimonis stopped talking. We stared wide-eyed at him, worried he might have forgotten his lesson. But, after a few minutes of silence, he loudly cleared his throat and said with a flourish: 'And then come the sutures.'"

"And the professor?" I asked.

"Well, not wanting to admit that he had fallen asleep in the middle of an exam, he gave Laimonis a passing grade," Lija said, collapsing with laughter. "The rest of us had to answer our questions from start to finish. Laimonis was the only one who got lucky!"

"Luck had nothing to do with it. He just used the situation to his advantage," said Velta.

Indeed, there would always be students who would take advantage of a professor's weakness, I thought as I laughed along with my friends.

Stradins devoted so much time to his profession and his patients that he had very little left for himself. So, some years later, I was sad to learn that he had been found dead on a bench in the railway station. Apparently, while returning from the seashore on a crowded train, he had felt ill and gotten off to find a place to lie down and rest. He had suffered a heart attack. There were hundreds of mourners at his funeral in Riga.

◆   ◆   ◆

One day in the old university building I ran into another former classmate, Gaida. I'd heard she was studying philology, but she was now there to withdraw her papers.

"You're dropping out? Why?"

"I'll tell you...outside," she replied guardedly.

We found a bench in front of the Opera House and sat down.

"What happened? Were you expelled?" I wanted to know.

She didn't answer my question but launched into a tirade about people who felt it was necessary to take exams in subjects such as Marxism and Leninism. "It will be a blemish on Latvian history if we take these exams from the illiterates who ask us to parrot their doctrine. My relatives in the West won't want to know me if I give in."

"Only the most naive immigrants in the West believe the only true Latvians are in Siberia and all the rest are Communists," I said.

"Yes, but everything has its limits! It's treason to repeat Marxist lies," Gaida persisted.

"I agree that everything has its limits. But I also think wrongdoing begins only when your actions hurt other people. If refusing to take Marxism exams meant I had to leave university, I'd rather suffer through them like a toothache, so I could get an education in my chosen profession." I was getting angry. "I'm one of the people who sat for those exams."

"But what would our friends in the West say?" Gaida was also getting angry.

"I think they'd be happy for any of us lucky enough to avoid the Cheka and get a job to support ourselves. They'd be happy that we are still alive. But they wouldn't like it if we started turning on one another. Now, that would really be something to be ashamed of!"

Calmer now, Gaida waved to a girl striding toward us whistling a German drinking song. "Olita! Where are you going?"

"To the library. I've got to study for my finals."

"It's good to see you're back," I said to Olita, a former schoolmate. "But where have you been?"

"I've been teaching physical education at our old school in Jelgava."

"Did you by any chance see Akermane?" I asked her.

"Of course! She had become even more vocal against capitalism and Fascism. When I reminded Aphrodite of her actions during the German occupation, she reported me to the Party and I had to leave Jelgava."

"See?" I turned to Gaida, "There are boundaries you should not cross, although it is sometimes justified. Akermane was afraid she'd get into trouble because her brother went to America during the independence years."

"She should be shot!" Gaida fumed.

"Too late now," said Olita. "She was found dead. There were some gold coins under her mattress."

"So what did you do after leaving Jelgava?" I asked Olita, changing the subject.

"I went to Dobele and got another job teaching physical education. The director, a Latvian, was a decent guy. He gave me a good recommendation, and it helped get me back into university."

"...and sit for the Marxism exam," Gaida added sarcastically. Then, seeing a young man coming toward us, Gaida quickly said good-bye. He took her arm, and they walked away together.

"That's her boyfriend Ojars," Olita explained. "He loves her, but she still wants to marry Imants. Remember him? They were once very close. But Gaida thinks he has gone to the West."

It was all beginning to make sense to me. "So that explains why she's so worried about what Latvians think over there. She should be more concerned about what they'd think about her living with this boy while she's in love with someone else. It used to be called prostitution, but now, in the Soviet Union, it's an accepted form of life. And, while many Latvians complain, they still go along with it!"

◆   ◆   ◆

Mother and I had found a place to live in Zolitude, between Riga and the seashore, and I took a train the short distance to the city to attend lectures. On my way to the station I would see laborers—German prisoners of war—repairing buildings and landscaping the riverbank from Valdemara Street all the way to the Central Market.

"Those poor men," said Mother, who was more sympathetic to the German people and their culture, as her own ancestors came from there. "I'm sure the average soldier didn't want to fight, but now they are the ones who have to pay," she said as she prepared small packets of food for me to give them. It was Christmas Eve, and, even though we didn't have much ourselves, my mother wanted to share something with those men.

There was a church service that night, and Vaira and Dace were coming along with us. We agreed to wear our shabbiest clothes and cover our heads with large granny-style scarves so we wouldn't be recognized. Going to worship was considered one of the biggest sins, a sin students could not afford to commit.

St. Gertrude's church was full of people, with a Christmas tree at one side of the altar. The candles were homemade, as it was impossible to buy any. The minister read the Christmas liturgy, but his sermon was strangely disjointed. As part of the liturgy, he included a prayer for Father Stalin in the Kremlin and for the homeland. It was obvious he was not speaking his mind.

Whose homeland did he mean, we wondered—Stalin's or ours? We knew the minister was not a Communist, but why was he saying such things? Upon hearing the words "Christ is born," we knelt in unison. But the prayer for Stalin bothered me. It seemed we couldn't escape him…even in church. His "disciples" were standing at the door with cameras. In an effort to blend in, they did not wear the usual red star, but, with expressionless faces like satanic masks, they nevertheless stood out from the others. Suddenly the flash bulbs started popping and we quickly pulled our scarves around our faces. If we were caught, our photos would be posted at the university, along with a notice berating us for falling prey to the lies of the church. Then we would be called in for questioning, and, finally, expelled. Similarly, offices posted photos of employees, along with details of their alleged transgressions.

Arriving home after church, we suddenly felt empty and fearful. Were we in trouble?

As it turned out, the cameras had failed to capture our faces, but the experience taught us to be thankful yet again and to take each day as it came.

◆   ◆   ◆

Vaira received a letter from her sister in Germany, along with photographs of nicely furnished rooms and the latest fashions from Western magazines traced onto transparent paper. Although we couldn't even dream about having a new dress, we were entranced by the fashions and passed them around so we could each make our own tracings.

Dace's marriage to Noldis was not going well, but she didn't seem to want to talk about it. Noldis had also left school. Livija and Indulis announced their engagement and, as I offered my congratulations, I had a feeling that everything would go well for them. They were a perfect match

At long last, final exams were over, and I passed all eighteen subjects. I wrote Gran a long letter telling her the good news. I knew she was always praying for me and was proud of my accomplishments. She would be happy.

But Gran was ailing. I worried that I was not able to do more for her but promised myself that everything would change as soon as I became a doctor.

Sometimes it's better not to know what the future holds for us.

27

Deportations

The highlight of a long stretch of uneventful weeks was the arrival of an invitation to Livija and Indulis's wedding. By now, getting married in church was forbidden, and those rules were strictly enforced. Newspapers wrote commentary on the practice of wearing wedding rings. People who wore them were criticized for wanting to call attention to themselves by flaunting their material possessions. The Com-Youth, the papers said, understood right from wrong and had no desire to decorate themselves with metal rings like farm animals just to show others they belonged to someone. Despite the rules, Livija and Indulis were planning to be married in a church in Vecaki, where her mother was a teacher. And they would wear wedding bands.

When I arrived at the house I was surprised by the extravagant furnishings.

Livija's mother explained, "Livija's father was a foreign ambassador, and we used to live in a ten-room apartment. But he died in 1932, when she was very young."

"Livija is lucky to have such a dowry," I said. "There must be hundreds of books!"

"Yes, these are all hers. My present husband and I have our own things..."

"...which are not nearly so grand," Livija's stepfather finished her sentence as he came into the room. "There are no capitalists in our family, only fishermen," he said as he laughed.

"Oh, there he goes bragging about his proletariat roots again," his wife chided.

"Here come the newlyweds!" someone shouted, and we all gathered to welcome Livija and Indulis, who arrived while a record played the wedding recessional.

Livija's mother cut the cake, and Reverend Peteris made sure the guests' glasses were filled.

At dinner, there were toasts and speeches. We had been told that the thirty or so guests were like-minded, and we could speak freely. Peteris wished the young couple God's help in their new life together and said a short prayer.

After coffee, we danced. What a luxury that was! Not wanting to take part in Communist organized events, Latvians didn't have many opportunities to dance. It was a brilliant evening that I wished could have lasted forever.

In the morning, we walked on the beach, dreaming about a better future—wishing for the kind of freedom that existed just over the horizon.

"We have to ask the gods of the sea to make our wish come true," Livija's stepfather said.

"I'd be happy to toss a coin into the water, if someone would give me one," I offered.

The search through pockets began, and soon I had several coins in my hand. I climbed up on a rock and threw them with all my might out over the waves.

"You have a strong will," said one fisherman. "Your wish will come true."

"And when you get to the West, you'll tell them how much we all want to be free," said another.

It was truly a rare and wonderful day. *Carpe diem.*

◆   ◆   ◆

In March 1949, the streets of Riga were filled with police. There was a buildup of railroad cars in the station and official automobiles standing by. People were saying that there would be more deportations, like those in June 1941.

Should we hide? Where? Was anyplace safe? No one knew.

I had to keep attending classes, as my absence would have been noted. But it was hard to concentrate.

After lectures, some of my classmates came back to Zolitude with me. Our house was near the edge of the forest, and we made plans to spend the night there. At dusk, we put on warm clothing and packed some food before heading into the woods. Mother had a cold and went to stay with a friend. At nightfall, all hell broke loose. Cars came out of nowhere, some with Cheka agents sitting next to drivers, others full of purported criminals. The raids lasted throughout the night.

The next morning, our nerves strained to the limit, we went back to class. Peteris, the nice boy from Latgale, Laimonis's friend Elmars, and many others had been among those taken away. Though the student ranks were visibly thinner, we knew that some hadn't turned up simply because they were afraid.

The next day, deportees, kept down on their knees by soldiers with bayonets, were driven through the streets in open trucks. Dace said she had seen the opera singer Milda Brechmane-Stengele wearing a gown and white shawl around her shoulders and kneeling in the back of one of the trucks. Despite the rifles pointed at her, she had kept her head raised defiantly. It was said that she had refused to sign a paper agreeing to perform propaganda songs. Her anti-Communist stance was so well known that she only had to step onto the stage to get a standing ovation. She had gotten the same ovation after every aria she sang, and, at the end of each of her performances, she had been given a bouquet of red and white flowers, the colors of the Latvian flag.

Her biggest operatic rival was Elfrida Pakule, who was married to the Russian baritone Dashkov. Pakule's coloratura was commendable, but she had become sympathetic to the Party and was known as Stalin's nightingale. There was a strong suspicion that she had something to do with Stengele's arrest, and audiences kept silent whenever she performed.

The arrests went on for several more days and nights, and we continued to sleep in the forest. On the third night, exhausted and apathetic, we went home to try to get a decent sleep. Though our house had remained unscathed, some of our neighbors had been taken away.

The frightening roundups ended as quickly as they had begun.

When I next saw Livija, she was in tears. I knew something bad had happened.

"My mother is gone," she sobbed.

"Where? I thought she was with you in Riga."

"She was here on Ministry of Education business, but she wasn't trying to hide," Livija said. "They were looking for her in Vecaki. There was a warrant for her arrest because my father, who died seventeen years ago, had been in the diplomatic corps."

"That's insane! How could they blame her for anything her late husband may have done?"

"Well, since she wasn't there, they arrested my stepfather and his parents. When my mother heard the news, she asked the Vecaki police to free them and deport her instead, if they really thought she was to blame for having the bad judgment to marry her first husband. The police chief, who had always been polite to my mother, just shrugged helplessly. 'The orders came from a higher level, ma'am. You were not there, so we had to take your husband and his parents. The numbers have to match up.'

"'I can understand taking my husband,' my mother argued, 'but an elderly couple?'

"'Your neighbors were on the list, but they ran away, and we had to fill the quota.'

"So my mother came back here to see the head of the Cheka but was told it was too late to change anything. The quotas were filled, and the numbers had been submitted to Moscow.

"Mother then went to the rail yard and bribed a soldier with a hundred rubles and a bottle of vodka to toss one of the people out of the car my stepfather was in." Livija was crying again.

"What about your mother's house?"

"Someone has already moved in."

"And your things?"

"All I have is what I'm wearing now...I've not only lost what my father left me, but everything else as well...clothing, dishes...I took it all to Vecaki for the wedding."

"At least you still have Indulis," I tried to reassure her.

"Yes, I could not have survived this without him," Livija agreed.

The tragic stories were everywhere. In just three nights, a thousand people had been taken away—this time mainly from the countryside, although a fair share of city dwellers were also arrested.

I called on Mrs. Vinerts in her new apartment. The place we had shared had been subdivided and housed five families. She now held the job of building superintendent, which had previously existed only on paper.

"Were many people from your district arrested?" I asked her.

"Fortunately, I was able to control the situation," she replied. "I was asked to provide information about each resident, so I took the opportunity to alert them. There was only one who didn't heed my warning, and he was the only one arrested."

"But they could still come back."

"I have always said we have to be thankful for each day. But I have also noticed they pretty much operate according to plan. Once the plan is executed, they are done, at least for the time being.

28

Butter for the POWs

"Homo homini lupus est, medicus medico lupissimus." (Man is man's enemy; a doctor is a doctor's biggest enemy.)

With these words, the new Health Minister Krauss began his lecture. He was talking about medicine as it was practiced in the West, where doctors were in competition with each other. It was quite the opposite here: there was no private practice, and doctors received a monthly salary.

"Here, patients can go to a free clinic and get free treatment. Each section of the city has its own polyclinic, and each doctor there is responsible for certain neighborhoods," Krauss said.

But what did free treatment really mean, I wondered, when ambulatory patients still had to buy their own medicine, which was prohibitively expensive and often not in stock? The doctor's fee was the only thing they didn't have to pay. And patients had no choice but to use the doctor geographically assigned to them, whether or not they found him competent or sympathetic. It was an even bigger problem for elderly Latvians, who found it difficult to communicate with Russian doctors because of the language barrier. If a patient preferred to use a certain doctor, he had to engage him privately and pay for his services—even though, officially, that was forbidden.

"We have no class system in our clinics, like capitalist countries do," Krauss droned on.

Ah, but you're leaving something out, I thought. It's true there is no class system at ordinary hospitals, but what about the special clinics that exist only for Communist functionaries?

When Krauss finished, a group of us walked together to the next lecture. On the way, we were joined by a student who had recently arrived from Russia.

"So what do you think of our new health minister?" she asked.

"Maybe you should ask Eugenie. She's the expert," Laimonis remarked.

151

"I meant his lecture," said Tamara, ignoring the inside joke. "Did you like it? He did such a wonderful job of comparing the two systems—but I wonder if it's really like that."

She paused as if waiting for a response but got none as we arrived at our next lecture.

"She's a spy," said Laimonis when we met up again afterward. "I know that for a fact. She's always listening to conversations and pretending to be anti-Communist to get people to open up."

"But I've never even seen her before." I was puzzled.

"Her name is Tamara Vlasova. She's Russian but knows how to speak Latvian. She was probably specially trained."

By now life had taught us to keep quiet about a lot of things and to talk freely only among our closest friends. Now it looked like we'd have to be even more careful.

◆   ◆   ◆

A dairy worker to whom my mother had given some farm machinery had brought us several kilos of butter. Since it was so valuable, Mother took it to the central market halls.

She told me what happened. On the way, she saw a group of German POWs at hard labor. Whenever the guard looked away, they'd reach out their hands. Mother swiftly sliced off a chunk of butter, wrapped it in paper and pressed it into the open hand of one of the prisoners, who thanked her and hurried away.

A moment later, a Russian plainclothes officer approached my mother and told her to follow him to headquarters. "Things must be going too well for you, since you are willing to throw butter into the mouths of Fascist dogs."

"I gave the butter to someone in need."

"Ah, but real Soviet patriots hate their enemies—Hitler's servants."

"It was only a small morsel. Besides, not all Germans support Hitler."

"Shut up. You're just like the capitalists, defending Fascists. There are still too many of you here. We'll have to deal with you later."

Then she said he told her she could go, but to "leave the butter here."

◆   ◆   ◆

Much to our surprise, Ziemele was back. We thought she had been deported, but her departure from Jelgava had only coincided with the arrests, causing some to come to the wrong conclusions. She had had no luck finding work and begged us not to turn her away.

"I suppose we'll get by somehow," Mother said. "You can help milk the cow to earn your keep."

Ziemele thanked us profusely. We couldn't know then that her attitude would soon change.

◆　　◆　　◆

The nearest polyclinic to Zolitude was on Kalnciema Street. The entire area from there to Babite, a half-hour from the outskirts of Riga, was served by one Russian doctor. So if anyone got sick they preferred to call me or one of my colleagues, and, almost every day, on my way home from lectures, I would look in on a patient.

One of my tuberculosis patients was the daughter of an organizing committee member. With the sanatorium overcrowded and up to three months' waiting time, it was not possible for her to travel several kilometers back and forth to the clinic.

In the house next door was a heart patient.

These "illegal" appointments helped me gain experience and earn some extra money. Not the least of it was the pride I felt because Latvians had more confidence in me—a medical student—than they did in a full-fledged Russian doctor.

One night on my way home I was called to a house where an elderly woman was running a fever. One of her hands was swollen to three times its normal size. I recommended that she go to a hospital immediately.

"I've never been in a hospital, and I won't go now," she said. "If I have to die, I'll die at home."

I tried to convince her that an operation was necessary.

"You can do that right here! I gave birth to five children at home—I'm not afraid of pain.

"Please help her." The patient's sister looked at me beseechingly. "If you don't…"

She was right. If nothing was done, blood poisoning would soon set in. She might lose her hand, or worse.

"All right." I finally gave in. "I'll see what I can do."

A friend who worked in a pharmacy lived across the street. I returned from her house with a scalpel, alcohol, iodine, penicillin, a syringe, and rubber gloves.

The penicillin, from America, had cost one thousand rubles.

I made a small incision, and, when I had finished doing all that was necessary to drain the infection, I was satisfied. The patient seemed to be improving.

◆   ◆   ◆

I returned home, eager to share my experience with Mother, but she wasn't there.

Instead, there was Ziemele, wide-eyed with fear. "Your mother was taken away," she said. "Two military police arrived soon after you left. Where have you been?"

I froze for a moment, then started pacing from room to room, looking out the window every few minutes. I realized how futile that was but I didn't know what else to do. I went outside. As if following an inner voice, I went to the corner bus stop. The Riga bus would be arriving soon.

In the dark, I heard someone call my name and saw the shadowy outline of a woman. She came closer and I recognized her—it was Kasejeva, the committee member whose daughter had tuberculosis.

"I'm glad you came outside. I've been trying to think of a way to speak to you. I wanted to wait until dark," she said.

"They've arrested my mother."

"I know," Kasejeva replied. "But she will come back."

"She will?" I clutched her hand. "Really?"

"Don't get too excited. They'll let her go, but then she must leave again—tonight. They are planning to make an example of her for trying to befriend a Fascist soldier. She suits their purpose at the moment. I must go, but I had to warn you. You've helped my daughter so much. But if they find out I said anything, it would cost me my life. So, please, think of me as well."

"Thank you, kind lady," I whispered as she slipped away.

Mother did indeed return—pale and frantic. Like many others who had undergone interrogation, she seemed to be in shock and didn't say much. We threw some things into a canvas bag, and she was ready to go. Where? We didn't know.

I watched helplessly as, bag in hand, my mother disappeared into the darkness.

29

My First Job

A notice was posted at university: Students had to report to the assembly hall. No reason was given, but we found out soon enough. Before we would be allowed to take the national exams, we first had to sign a paper saying we would willingly accept a job in any location the ministry chose for us.

While waiting my turn in the hallway, I watched the first of the students emerge. Some had signed on for good jobs in Latvia, while many others had "voluntarily agreed" to go to Russia. Two senior-year students, a married couple, turned down jobs in the Kolima region of northeastern Siberia and were told they were no longer eligible to take the national exams.

My lab partner Sergei was posted to Kazakhstan. He protested—his wife had tuberculosis, and they had two small children aged two and six months—and was told that a change of climate was just what he needed. Several years later, when he was allowed to return, he came back alone. His wife and their children had died.

Eugenie, confident she would stay in Riga, had to take a job in Tukums, a provincial city in western Latvia. She was not happy.

From our small circle of friends, only Laimonis was assigned to one of the "brother republics." He mounted a strong protest, but the authorities just laughed. "We really should put you in jail for that," they said. "But, instead, we offer you—like any other free citizen—a job in the Urals."

Laimonis argued that he had paid his own way by working nights with ambulance crews.

"So, you also have capitalist tendencies—just as we suspected," they said.

Seeing that he was not going to win, Laimonis signed the paper.

It was my turn. With great trepidation, I approached a row of officials seated at a long table covered with a red cloth.

"Saldi or Ventspils?"

"I have no preference," I replied, relieved that at least both places were in Latvia.

"Good! Soviet students are agreeable. But we will still allow you to choose."

"All right then—Ventspils," I said, remembering it was a Baltic Sea port, and someone had escaped to Sweden from there. As absurd as the thought may have been at that moment, no one had yet succeeded in imprisoning our minds. We were still free to think what we wanted. Of course, it was also smart to keep our thoughts to ourselves.

◆   ◆   ◆

A short time later, I was summoned to Kruskops's office. He stared at me for a long time, then asked, "Did you know your husband is going to be tried as a capitalist spy?"

"No. We haven't lived together for several years, but I find it hard to believe he would do anything like that," I said with total conviction.

"Where was Hugo last Christmas?"

I honestly didn't know.

"How long have you been living apart?"

"More than three years."

"Why did you separate?"

"Our marriage was a mistake. But why are you asking such personal questions?"

"A Soviet citizen has no secrets from the Party. If you really don't get along, as you say, why aren't you divorced?"

"I submitted the papers two years ago. My request was denied. You can check the records."

I remembered that Hugo and I had agreed to save the cost of hiring an attorney and seek an amicable divorce. Also as agreed, I was to base my request on irreconcilable differences and our mutual wish to stop living together.

Then it had been Hugo's turn.

"Honorable members of the court," he had said with great pomp. "There seems to be a misunderstanding. I never wanted a divorce. I love my dear little wife very much. I'll confess, I'm no angel and have caused her distress. But I have begged her forgiveness. Show me a man who has never made a mistake. I know she still loves me but is just too shy to admit it."

I was too shocked and flustered to say what I needed to say—that we had never really had a marriage in the true sense and that our physical relationship had lasted only a few months.

So the court had decreed that my complaint was unfounded.

Adding insult to injury, a Russian factory worker then came over to offer me advice. "If your husband takes a drink, you should too. A good Soviet wife wouldn't say no. And remember, if a man hits his wife, it just means he loves her. Even if he takes up with some other bitch, why get upset over it? You do the same! He'll get jealous and come back to you."

I had an answer for him but thought better of it. In the Soviet Union it was better to keep your opinions to yourself. But it was equally important not to stop having them.

Hugo had been waiting for me at the door.

"Well, my high-minded little wife, I just wanted to teach you another lesson. You should have seen your face. It was so funny. Come on, this will make a great story at the pub."

"Are you crazy? I can see you're already drunk. What were you trying to prove, anyway?"

"All right, so I've had a drink. I needed some courage. And before you cast any aspersions on my intellect, you know I outsmarted you today, even if you are the one with the university education."

"So what are you doing these days?"

"I teach in a machine shop. Everything is good…and there is no shortage of fabulous women."

"So why don't you just leave me alone!"

"I need to get even with you because you are the only woman who has left me," he said simply.

◆　　　◆　　　◆

"Do you still want to divorce your husband?" Kruskops asked.

"Of course I do!"

"Submit your request to the high court," he advised. "Without the decree, you won't be able to take the exams because your husband has committed a serious crime against the Soviet Union."

That was it. I was free to go. As I walked home, I felt relief, as if I had just dodged a bullet. If Kruskops had asked about my parents I would have certainly been barred from taking the exams. Maybe I was just lucky, or, as Gran would say, it was God's hand at work.

◆   ◆   ◆

The next day was the Marxism-Leninism exam. If I didn't pass, I would have to wait a year to try again. It was late, and my study table was heaped high with the "classics" of Stalin and Engels when, suddenly, there was a tap on the window. I listened. There it was again, more insistent this time.

My room faced the garden, so I went to the veranda door. It was Jaksis. "Shh," he whispered. "May I come in?"

"Of course," I whispered back. "What's happening? I have an exam tomorrow."

"I was called in for interrogation. One of the architecture students said I was using a false name, but I insisted he was mistaken."

"You're very brave."

"Maybe I was just desperate. You know I'd do anything to keep up my studies…"

"I know that. Tell me, did the Cheka ask you to become an informer?"

"Yes. It's the most demeaning thing I can think of," Jaksis said, clenching his fists.

"I agree. I'd rather die first. Yet the Communists think you should feel honored. Now they'll be even more certain you have a false identity."

"I was just hoping I could finish school first."

"Let's forget that for now," I said. "I have that awful exam in the morning, and you need to get some rest. Go to the little room in the attic. It's just above mine, and from there it'll be easy for you to jump to the roof of the veranda, if necessary. I can warn you by tapping on the ceiling with a broom."

◆   ◆   ◆

My head ached and my ears were still ringing with Communist ideology, but my nightmare was over. I had passed the Marxism-Leninism exam, albeit with a mark of Satisfactory.

When I told Jaksis, he was happy for me, but we still needed a solution to his problem.

In the meantime, Ziemele was glowing like a teenager. Her frequent visitor, Klumpis, spent a lot of time in our kitchen every night. Always naive, she was sure that this time it was the real thing.

"He is so smart and so inquisitive. He even wants to know about you and your medical studies. There was only one question I couldn't answer. Who is that young man in the attic room?"

I quickly made an excuse and left. It was clear Jaksis had to leave.

That was the last time I would see him. Later, I learned he had hidden with relatives for a while, but the Cheka had tracked him down. After that he was sent to a labor camp in Narilska, the northernmost town in Siberia, and forbidden to write letters or receive packages. There were hundreds of thousands, maybe millions, like him.

30

A Doctor in Ventspils

I was always hungry. Thinking back over the last few years, I realized the only time I had not been hungry was while I was staying with Mrs. Vinerts. I comforted myself with a vision of the large pork chop I would buy with my very first doctor's paycheck. Then at last I would be able to eat so I wouldn't feel hungry a half hour later.

I was still in Riga, waiting for official clearance to go to Ventspils. Security measures were extremely tight for port cities, where Russian military secrets were kept. I might have even enjoyed the break, if it hadn't been for the ever-present gnawing hunger.

One evening, I eagerly accepted a dinner invitation from Mrs. Vinerts. She could still manage to put together an impressive meal. When she asked me to come back soon, I was too proud to let on how much I wanted to—how hungry I was. I simply replied that I was a doctor now and would soon be leaving to start a practice.

Another day, I had lunch at Olga's. I think she also noticed how quickly I wolfed down my food. Yet my pride kept me from confiding even to my closest friends what a sorry state I was in. I politely refused her very tempting invitation to stay for dinner.

After Mother left, I sold everything of any value. All that remained was our rickety furniture and the cow. It had been a long time since Ziemele had let me have a glass of milk, claiming that the income from the cow's milk was just enough to buy more feed. But then I unexpectedly walked in on her and Klumpis in the kitchen eating hot milk soup. I also saw her making butter, and him slipping into her room with a loaf of bread. I had such a craving for a buttered slice of bread that I broke down and cried like a baby just thinking about them devouring an entire loaf.

The Soviet rules were strange indeed. Student allowances ended with the last exam, but there would be no income until we started work. Meanwhile, it was endlessly repeated that there was no need for jobless benefits because everyone in the Soviet Union had a job.

Another day passed without food. I couldn't stand it any longer and looked in the kitchen cupboards. There were some boiled potatoes in a bowl and home-made sour cream. The potatoes were the same kind as the ones that Ziemele told me had earlier disappeared from the basement.

My mother had bought those potatoes, and the sour cream had come from our cow! I pried the potatoes open with my fingers, spooned on the sour cream, and shoved them in my mouth, skin and all. I was so busy eating, I didn't notice that Ziemele and Klumpis had come in.

"Thief!" shouted Klumpis, accusingly pointing his finger at me. "Thief!"

"You are a thief only if you steal property that belongs to someone else," I replied, stuffing the last of the potatoes into my mouth. "These potatoes and sour cream are mine."

"We'll see about that," he retorted, slamming the cupboard door shut.

◆   ◆   ◆

I was destitute, but my student transportation card was still valid, so I decided to use it to go to Riga and ask Mrs. Vinerts for advice. I was trying to summon up the courage to tell her that I had no money and no food. I could offer to sell her my doctor's diploma, even though I didn't actually have it yet. There was another rule that said we had to work for three months before we could collect our diplomas.

At the bus stop, I felt a light touch on my elbow. It was Kasejeva, the mother of the girl with tuberculosis, and the one who had warned me of the danger my mother was in. "I'm afraid I have bad news. Ziemele has lodged a formal complaint against you—though the handwriting on the complaint is different from her signature."

"It's obvious Klumpis wrote it," I said flatly. "What do they want?"

"They are asking for the cow and the rest of your mother's things. Ziemele claims she was pressed into servitude and is entitled to have whatever is left."

I started to laugh. Kasejeva stared at me as though I'd lost my mind.

"I have to laugh," I hastened to explain, "about how many ways that woman can twist the truth to suit her purpose. I remember not so long ago when she said she was starving and pleaded with us to take her in. But never mind. A woman in love, whether she's seventeen or seventy, is and always will be a fool."

Little did I know that my own words would one day come back to haunt me.

"What will you do?" Kasejeva asked as I started to leave.

"Nothing," I said calmly, getting on the bus. "We've lost everything anyway, so these last few things won't make much of a difference. I'm just eager to start my job."

"I wish you well." Kasejeva squeezed my hand. "Thank you again for helping my daughter."

◆   ◆   ◆

There was a graduation party for our class at the Astorija restaurant. It cost fifty rubles to attend, so I didn't go. Anyway, my shoes were shoddy and my only dress—the one I was wearing—was made from an overcoat. The restaurant probably would not have let me in.

But I didn't mind. My clearance papers had come through, and I was on the train to Ventspils and the next stage of my life—working as a doctor.

I thought again about what I would buy with my first—long-awaited and much-needed—paycheck. First I would have a good meal and then perhaps buy something new. But 600 rubles was not really a lot of money, considering that a pair of shoes cost 400 to 500. A winter coat was 1,500 to 2,000. Of course, I would have to try to put some rubles aside.

As I was busy making plans, the four-hour journey passed quickly.

My first task after arrival was to register for my job. While waiting to see Dr. Kuchumova, the head of the health department, I struck up a conversation with the young secretary, who told me there were thirty doctors in Ventspils, but only two of them were Latvian—Miezis the internist and Zukovskis the surgeon. The rest, including Dr. Kuchumova, were Russian. I was the first of five new doctors expected to arrive.

"What is your specialty?" Kuchumova looked me up and down with a critical eye.

"Children. I want to be a pediatrician," I said.

"That job has just been given to an officer's wife."

"What else is available?"

"You'll have to speak to the director at the hospital," she said and walked away.

I had been dismissed.

The director, Dechterevs, was a surgeon. He asked about my studies.

When I told him I had worked as a volunteer with Professor Stradins for six months, he said he wanted me to work with him in the surgery.

"I'm not so sure it's the right field for a woman," I protested.

"Are you anti-Russian?" Dechterevs voice took on an odd undertone.

"I only meant surgery might be too difficult for a woman," I said.

"It would not have been easy working with Stradins, but then he's Latvian, isn't he?"

"Volunteer work and a permanent job are two different things."

"Yes, like a Russian and a Latvian are two different things," he retorted and left the room.

I didn't know what to do. I still had no directive as to where I'd be working. I didn't know the city or anyone there to whom I could go for advice.

I crossed Vasarnica Street, with medical buildings on both sides, and headed toward the sea. I walked past some trees and crossed a grassy area before I could finally see the huge, frothy waves rolling into shore. I wished they would pick me up and carry me away—away to freedom. Lost in thought, I didn't realize that someone had come alongside me.

"Good evening. I believe we met this morning. You're one of the new doctors?"

"Yes," I replied, recognizing the young secretary.

"I am Marga Ziedina," she introduced herself. "How was your meeting with the director?"

I told her what happened.

"Oh, that doesn't sound good!" she said. "Dechterevs is a competent surgeon, but he suffers from complexes, among them that Latvians dislike Russians, himself included."

"Do you think I should go back and say I'd be willing to work in surgery after all?"

"No. I'm afraid it's too late."

"But I'm not allowed to leave Ventspils. And now it looks as if I might not be able to work here. What if they deport me?" My lower lip was trembling, and the tears were starting to roll down my cheeks.

"Perhaps it's not as bad as all that. But your job prospects don't look good. Usually, the only way to get out of breaking a work assignment is to volunteer to work in Russia."

It seemed all my efforts had come to naught. I was so physically and mentally exhausted I felt I was nearing a nervous breakdown. If my life had been a pebble, I thought how easy it would have been to toss it into the roiling sea. But Gran had always said it was a sin to take your own life.

"I've got an idea," Marga said brightly. "A Russian officer's wife who worked in the dermatology and venereal disease section left her job yesterday. It's the only division that works independently of the hospital, so you wouldn't have to report to Dechterevs."

It seemed that in the darkest moments, when things appeared truly hopeless, someone would always reach out. Gran used to say that, too. "There is no such thing as chance," she would say. "A person doesn't lose a hair from his head without God knowing about it." When I asked if the horror that had been visited upon our little country could really have happened with his knowledge, Gran also had an answer. "It is the struggle between good and evil. Sooner or later, good will emerge victorious."

◆   ◆   ◆

My request for a job in the skin and venereal disease section was met with a frown from Kuchumova. Nevertheless, after many questions, phone calls, and an excruciatingly long wait, I was given permission to start working there.

There were no familiar faces among the other new arrivals at the clinic. Asking for any specific duties was futile. I remembered the Liepins couple who had been my classmates in medical school. The jobs committee gave her a job in Daugavpils, southeast of Riga, and placed him more than a thousand miles away on the other side of the Ural Mountains. When he objected, the committee member smirked and, not taking her eyes off the floor, said, "Do you think there's a shortage of women in Russia?"

"But I'm married!" he objected angrily. "My wife…"

"She'll find someone else, too. For Soviet citizens, the state comes before personal interests."

And Laimonis, who had "willingly" signed a job agreement hoping later to change it, was arrested on trumped-up charges of treason. Within three days, he was convicted and sentenced to twenty-five years. It was probably meant to deter others from trying the same course of action—a warning that instead of accepting a doctor's job in Siberia, you might end up in a labor camp there.

Dace was working in rural Talsi in northwestern Latvia. As students we had been best friends, but more recently we had grown apart. I had heard she and Noldis were divorced, and wondered how she was doing. I thought a lot about my friends while taking frequent walks along the sandy beach. The sea drew me like a magnet, fueling my desire for freedom somewhere on the other shore.

"*Kuda?* (Where are you going?)" a harsh voice barked. I was so startled I nearly bolted, as I had done when I first arrived in Riga. But years had passed and, although I had become accustomed to Russians, my fear of them had not subsided. And now in the twilight with no one else around, I was frightened.

It seemed I had come too close to forbidden territory—the confluence of the Venta River and the Baltic Sea. I hurried away to avoid the same fate that had befallen some of my colleagues the night before. The two young doctors had gone for a swim when armed Russian guards had suddenly emerged from among the trees with attack dogs and ordered them out of the water.

With one of the guards carrying their clothing, the others herded the women, still in their bathing suits, trembling with fear and the cold, about five kilometers to headquarters. There the women were told it was a crime to swim after 10:00 PM and were labeled "capitalist spies." Finally at 4:00 AM the guards phoned Dechterevs and allowed the two doctors to return to the hospital.

Ignorance of the law is no excuse, but it was safe to assume that more things were forbidden than allowed. Even staring in genuine awe at a ship in the harbor could be viewed as a crime.

My offices were in a two-story building at 66 Pils Street. On the ground floor was a treatment area, and upstairs a sizable recovery room with fifteen beds. There was also a small barn with guinea pigs and two rams.

Two Russian women worked as doctors; both were planning to leave—one of them very soon, and the other in a few months. I didn't have much time to learn my new duties, so I closely observed the other doctors and studied the relevant medical books.

My room was only about seven square meters, but that was more than adequate since all my belongings fit into one suitcase.

One day a letter arrived from my mother. It was short, with no signature, and had obviously been rerouted many times. Things had not been easy, she wrote, but she would soon have permission to travel and wanted to know where we could meet. I was overjoyed.

I asked Marga, a Ventspils native, for help. We had become friends and, with her connections, we found a suitable room on the edge of town. I asked Mother to come as soon as possible.

31

The Voice of America

Mother and I sat together at the dinner table and cried. I wasn't sure if it was because we were so glad to see each other or because we were able to have a decent meal at last. The fish, cooked in pork fat, was dark and succulent. And the potatoes were swimming in real fat instead of that disgusting, smelly fish oil.

I had my first paycheck—six hundred rubles. It didn't go far after deductions. Under the Communist regime, nobody was paid enough to cover daily expenses, so people of all occupations were always looking for ways to supplement their income.

When we finished our meal, Mother filled me in on what had happened since we had last seen each other. "When I left you that night, I didn't know where to go. I was cold and feverish and found a barn to sleep in. At daybreak I found the nearest road and flagged down a truck. The driver asked me where I wanted to go, and I told him it didn't matter. He gave me a strange look but didn't ask any more questions. He said he was making a delivery somewhere near Mt. Munamegi in Estonia, just across the northern border of Latvia.

"We drove for two days, stopping to pick up other riders. I lost track of time and distance. The other passengers got out before me, and I must have dozed off when I felt the driver shaking me. He told me it was too risky to take me any farther, lifted me out of the truck, and put me down at the roadside on the edge of the forest. He said there was a village a few kilometers away. I sank onto the carpet of soft green moss and must have passed out.

"When I opened my eyes, I was surrounded by a group of young men trying to speak to me in Estonian, German, and Russian. I didn't understand much, but they seemed kind. I doubt I would have survived without their help. They wrapped me in a blanket, took me to a nearby house, and left me by the front door.

"The Estonian woman who lived there said she had also found some sulfide and expensive American penicillin wrapped in my blanket and was using it to

166

help me get better. Her house was some distance from the road and had not yet been collectivized.

"Slowly I regained my strength, and it was time to think about what to do next. Then something happened that provided me with the answer. The chimney had become soot-choked, and smoke was backing up into the house. A chimney sweep was called out from the village. I was home alone when the sweep—a man of about eighty—arrived, and we communicated in fractured Russian as I explained to him what needed to be done. As he climbed up on the stove, he slipped. '*Vai, Dievs! Gandriz vai...*' (Oh, God! I almost...) he cried out in Latvian. I stared at him in shock. 'You're Latvian?'

"'No, but I spent my youth there,' he said, equally shocked. 'My foster parents were Latvian.'

"We talked and talked, until we felt we could trust each other. I told him my story and that the Cheka were looking for me. He said he had an idea. 'If it will help make your life easier, I could give you my last name. Then you won't have to be afraid anymore.' I gratefully accepted his offer, and the next day we registered as man and wife. I thanked him, and we never saw each other again."

Marriage for convenience was not unusual. Many of my classmates had done that with men who held influential jobs—engineers, doctors, or teachers—just so they wouldn't have to leave Riga, or at least so they could stay in Latvia. It worked more often than not. And when this marriage on paper had served its purpose, the parties filed for an uncontested divorce.

Mind you, a Western clergyman might say that my mother acted immorally. Oh, those self-righteous Westerners! If they could just spend one week in our Communist-oppressed skins!

I thought about the young men in the forest who had saved my mother's life and wondered who they were. I was grateful to them for helping her.

◆   ◆   ◆

Marga attended music class in the evenings. I went with her several times and decided to take lessons myself. It would make a nice change from the everyday drudgery of life.

My voice teacher, Vanda Ivanova, soon also became my friend. I learned from her that the opera singer Milda Brechmane-Stengele had not been deported after all, just briefly detained. Vanda had been her pupil at the esteemed Music Conservatory in Riga. To make ends meet, she would sing in restaurants.

One evening, Vanda said she had been performing in Staburags when a man had complimented her performance and asked where she was studying. "I told him I was a student at the conservatory, but also needed a job. He said he thought the state took very good care of students. I laughed and told him he was being naive if he really believed that. We exchanged a few more pleasantries, and he left.

"The next day, I was called into the conservatory office, where I was told I had besmirched the name of the Soviet state and would have to quit my music studies. That was several years ago, and they haven't allowed me to return. At least I was able to get this teaching job," she said.

"You have such a beautiful voice. It's a shame you couldn't have obtained your music degree."

"I know," said Vanda, her eyes welling up. "If only I hadn't said I needed the money."

◆   ◆   ◆

Then I got some terribly sad news—Gran had died quite suddenly. I ran over to the hospital to ask Kuchumova for some days off to attend the funeral.

She looked at me as if I had demanded the moon and all the stars in the sky.

"You just started working here. How can you even think of asking for time off?"

"But I'm not asking for a vacation, only a couple of days, so I can say goodbye to my grandmother. She was the dearest person in the whole world to me."

"What kind of bourgeois sentimentality is that?" Kuchumova slammed her fist on the table. "What does it matter who buries your dead babushka? Your duty is to socialism; you must work hard to repay the state for all it has given you." The conversation was over.

I went to the seashore and cried. My dear, wonderful Gran! How I had wanted to repay her kindness so she could live her last years in comfort. But she was gone, and I couldn't even be there to put a songbook into her hands and a handful of Latvian soil under her pillow.

The Baltic hissed and foamed near my feet as I sat on a rock trying to deal with the pain of my loss and my constant longing for freedom and a decent life. I knew that those same waves, on the other side, were breaking onto a shore where people were free.

◆   ◆   ◆

It was not uncommon for a port city to have many VD cases, and I spent six hours a day in the treatment center, with fifteen critically ill patients.

My helper was Tamara Ivanovna, a Russian head nurse. She was very helpful and diligent, the opposite of Maria Petrovna, another nurse who was always getting medications mixed up. On one occasion, I was summoned to help a young syphilis patient in severe shock. I asked Maria what had happened, and she just shrugged. Then I saw an empty ampule of cardiazol meant for veterinary purposes. Maria had injected its entire contents into the patient's vein.

"Maria Petrovna!" I shouted at her. "Why did you do this?"

"The patient was complaining of nausea."

"You're playing with a human life! Don't you know that only doctors are allowed to give intravenous injections?"

"I was allowed to do it at the front."

"We are not at the front now. If you keep making these mistakes, I will have to report you."

"I've already spoken with Kuchumova," Maria replied haughtily. "I told her you hate me because I am Russian. She was very sympathetic."

And, sure enough, a few days later Kuchumova called me in and gave me a warning. When I tried to explain, she dismissed me with a wave of her hand.

As I was leaving her office, Marga caught up with me.

"You know, Maria never even finished nursing school. She was a sharpshooter and during the war got to be a nurse after becoming a doctor's lover. She is also in the Party."

"I don't care if she's in the Party," I said. "All I want is a competent nurse. If she hasn't got a nursing degree, she has no business working here!"

"I guess she'll leave sometime, but not as long as Dechterevs and Kuchumova are here. They follow the letter of the law that in any disagreement, Party members are always right, because they are the 'most competent, moral, honest, and polite.' We've had many complaints about Maria from Dr. Kundzins and your predecessor, but they weren't Party members either."

After that incident, I tried to do much of the work myself—even the nurse's duties. Sometimes I asked Tamara to help, and Maria didn't seem to mind; she preferred to read romance novels.

32

An Invitation to the Party

I had lost nearly everything I ever owned, but I still had my beloved books. If I could have put them onto shelves, they might have covered an entire wall. But I didn't dare, because they were all published in pre-Communist times. So they languished in boxes in an attic or a basement. Occasionally I'd take out a couple to read or trade.

One evening, I was reading when there was a knock at the door. Thinking it was a routine visit from one of the Russian nurses to get a signature on a medical supplies form, I made no effort to hide my books before opening the door.

I was surprised to see the chief accountant Eglis, and made a vain attempt to block his view. But I wasn't quick enough. I could see his eyes taking in the titles and authors such as Reiner, Maria Rilke, Jose Ortega, Andrejs Eglitis, Charles Morgan, and Anslavs Eglitis."

"They say that people are judged by the company they keep. The same might be said for their choice of books," Eglis said, walking to the window and looking out. As I had never exchanged more than a few words with him, I had no idea where his sentiments lay.

"May I sit down?"

"Yes…please," I pushed a chair toward him. "I'm sorry. I didn't mean to be rude."

"I've suspected for some time that you were not a Communist," Eglis spoke in a low voice. "Now I see we have similar tastes…in books, for one. Take Morgan's *The Source*…"

"He's one of my favorite foreign authors," I said cautiously. "I've read him over and over again, yet each time I discover something new!"

"Indeed, that is the difference between good literature and the stuff that now fills the bookstores," Eglis mused as he leafed through the Morgan book. "Peace. Contentment…what joy to be free, without bonds, untouched by the evil in the world…"

"But is that possible—I mean really possible? I think one can only strive for such a state."

"You are young and looking for happiness. That's not easy these days. I'm at least twenty years older than you. I was a student in independent Latvia. It seemed I never made time to enjoy the things life had to offer—concerts, theater, literary evenings, parties. Now? If the Almighty would grant me just one wish, I would wish for my life to end."

"But why?"

"You could say I am a pessimist. I often feel like I am suffocating. Once I considered suicide after a lengthy period of interrogation and torture in a Cheka prison. Yet it was there, in the throes of hopelessness, that I learned to pray, really pray, on my knees and from my heart. I felt I truly spoke with Him and suddenly He was not a distant and stern taskmaster, but a true father, helper, and savior. Ten months later, when the prison doors were opened, I said a prayer of thanks, but—and this may sound strange to you—not because I was leaving prison at last, but for the deep faith that the experience had given me."

I didn't know what to say, because I knew my own faith was not as strong. Beset by doubts and uncertainty, I had asked myself countless times whether the terrible things that were happening to hundreds of thousands of innocent people in our country could truly be God's will.

Eglis continued, "At that time I also learned to rise above everything that was happening to me and around me. I suppose that is inner peace. But I must go now," he said, rising to his feet. "I came here to give you the new work schedule, but I have stayed too long."

"Oh, no!" I cried. "I enjoyed your visit."

"If it is all right with you, maybe we could continue our conversation sometime," he said hesitantly.

"I would be so glad if we could."

"Then may I invite you to visit at a time that is convenient for you? Please don't misunderstand my intentions. I live on the outskirts of town with my mother and an aunt. They will also be happy to see you."

"Thank you! I would like that very much."

◆　　　◆　　　◆

I had a music lesson that evening. My teacher, Vanda, had called several times to remind me, which I thought was odd, as I was hardly likely to forget.

Had something happened? I had asked Vanda if it was urgent and she replied that it was. Should I bring my doctor's kit? No, no, it was nothing like that. I must come for my lesson, though.

I couldn't imagine what could be so important.

Finally, my work was finished for the day.

"Lita Heinrikovna!" Tamara called out from the adjacent room.

"Yes. What is it?"

"I have something important to tell you."

"Can it wait until tomorrow?"

"No, it really is very important. It's such wonderful news that I'm fairly bursting to tell you."

The dark-haired woman came in, smiling broadly. Tamara was a good assistant. I was genuinely satisfied with her work, and she was well aware of that. Thanks to her I was able to carry a heavy patient load, often seeing three at a time. We communicated well, and it helped that she was able to write prescriptions in Latin. Educated and capable, she was a rarity in the Soviet system. I also respected her as a person. But, even though she courted my friendship, it was hard for me to accept it—not because she was Russian, but because she was a Communist.

At the start of the occupation, we equated Russians with Communists, but now we were able to tell the difference. Not every Russian was a Communist or our enemy. Often the worst Judases were from our own midst, because only they could know our true weaknesses or innermost secrets to pass along to the enemy. It was toward them we felt the most hatred.

"Let's sit down, Lita Heinrikovna," Tamara said cheerfully. "This may take awhile."

"But I really must hurry," I protested. "I have a music lesson tonight."

"Oh, that," Tamara shrugged. "If you knew what excellent news I have, you wouldn't give your lesson a second thought. Anyway, you must be hungry."

"Yes, actually I am hungry," I said, still hoping that Tamara's news could wait until tomorrow.

"I just happen to have some piragi," Tamara chirped. "It was my husband's birthday yesterday, and I baked them myself. Our patient from the corner store gave us some flour. It's not the whitest, but I added some oil to soften the dough and supplemented the meat filling with sauerkraut. They turned out well."

She put the piragi on a white sheet of paper on the table.

"And," she added mysteriously, "I have something else. Look!" She pulled out a bottle of Caucasus wine. "I got it from the wife of a sea captain, whose syphilis I cured."

Doctors and nurses often had private patients on the side. Some, wanting to avoid long lines at the clinic, invited us to their homes. I also believed the red light at our door and the signs "Prophylactics and venereal clinic" were a cause of embarrassment to many of our patients—particularly those who only had skin problems.

The atmosphere was not the best, especially late at night, when the aide had her hands full with drunken, cursing sailors breaking windows and getting into fistfights. Worst of all, there was no guarantee of confidentiality. Just about everything that happened in the clinic was soon known to everyone else.

In our studies, the Hippocratic Oath had been mentioned only in passing, depending on who taught the course. Professor Stradins taught us that Hippocrates was responsible for laying the foundation of medical practice, while Krauss merely said there was once a man named Hippocrates, who had adhered to one or two outdated dogmas.

To fend off boredom, nurses frequently chatted about patients among themselves or with other patients. Their conversations were overheard by cleaning staff, who knew nothing about medicine but wanted to impress their friends. They would often repeat what they heard, sometimes confusing dermatology patients with VD patients.

So it was not surprising that many patients did not want to come to the clinic. And, by treating them outside the clinic, we were able to benefit, if not monetarily, then in barter. And that was how Tamara came to have the bottle of wine and the flour and oil to make the piragi that were now on the table in front of us.

Politics aside, I was aware that Russians could be enormously generous, as well as hypersensitive to any rebuff.

"All right, Tamara Ivanovna, I'll stay for a little while."

She had already filled two ceramic cups with the highly touted red Caucasus wine. "To the new head of the clinic, Lita Heinrikovna!" Tamara raised her cup.

Putting my cup down, I stared at her, puzzled. "Dr. Kundzins is leaving?"

Tamara's eyes were sparkling like a child's. "Yesterday, at the Party meeting, it was decided that you'll be the new boss! And we will also accept you as a candidate to join the Party, because that post is available only to members. As for Kundzins, he has already been asked to resign. He had an important job during Ulmanis's presidency, so he is not eligible. The main thing is that Mikelsone will be your first sponsor. With twenty-five years in the Party, she has a lot of clout. I will be the second sponsor.

She raised her cup again, and I quickly grabbed mine to try to hide my discomfort at the unexpected turn of events. How odd they should make that decision without my showing the slightest interest. So I was to replace nice old Dr. Kundzins. That sort of thing was happening a lot; younger people educated under the Soviet system were being given job priority.

Tamara was looking at me, waiting for a response, but I was practically speechless.

"Thank you, Tamara Ivanovna, but I have no administrative skills and still need to study more about dermatology and VD. I also don't feel right about accepting a job that has been taken away from a more experienced colleague. For now at least, I'd like to stay outside the Party."

Tamara was taken aback, but not ready to give up. She had been taught well in the active as well as passive methods of recruiting new members. There were certain privileges to be gained, of course, but you also had to denounce your mother, father, sister, or brother. And you had to swear to turn in any "former" relatives if their views differed from those of the Party, with no mercy shown to anyone who strayed from the line. Punishment by the Party was far more severe than any handed down by the courts.

"Don't worry, Lita Heinrikovna," Tamara assured me. "You'll get assistance in your administrative duties from Comrade Kuchumova or Comrade Dechterevs, or the town polyclinic director, Comrade Lazinskaya, who is very fond of our new crop of doctors. And don't worry about Dr. Kundzins. Anyway, if it's not you, it will be someone else. But we are all very proud of you. To help you gain additional experience, we have already arranged a six-month course this fall at the university clinic in Riga, and in two years' time we'll send you to Leningrad or Moscow to sharpen your skills even more.

"But I didn't think Comrades Dechterevs or Kuchumova approved of me," I stammered, trying to find the right words, as I was well aware that an outright refusal could have grave consequences. But at that moment I honestly couldn't come up with any other reason for not accepting. The wine was also doing its work. It was not only delicious, but very strong.

"My dear Lita Heinrikovna, you will be ours!" Tamara went on giddily. "I know it!" She suddenly threw her arms around me and kissed me on both cheeks.

I noted with considerable concern that it was already dusk. I stood up and said I really had to go. Vanda would be very worried.

"If you become the new boss, Dechterevs will be your colleague," Tamara burbled on as if she hadn't heard me, "and everyone knows there are no feuds among Party members."

She said the words with absolute conviction. The Party voice had spoken.

"But all this must remain our secret for now," she added. "I just couldn't wait to tell you the fantastic news. The official part comes later."

We said good-bye at the dispensary door. As I hurried along to the music school, I saw Dr. Dechterevs walking toward me, accompanied by a middle-aged Russian woman.

"My wife...Our new, dear, and much-lauded colleague, Lita Heinrikovna," he said jovially.

I stared at him dumbfounded.

"Why are you looking at me that way?" he said as he laughed. "Have I aged that much since we last saw each other? My new job is indeed taking its toll, so my wife and I decided to get some fresh air. You were wise not to become a surgeon; you'd be as gray as I am. And you've done such a fine job at the dispensary. It will only get better...but it's still a secret, so I won't say any more." Dechterevs patted me on the shoulder and walked away.

At last I reached the music school. I felt my way along the dimly lit hall to the classroom and knocked on the door, but there was no response. I walked across to Vanda's room on the other side. I saw a sliver of light under her door and knocked again. The door flew open. "Where have you been? I've been waiting for you," she exclaimed.

"Oh, Vanda, I simply couldn't make it earlier," I replied. "I will explain, but you go first."

I leaned back on the mattress propped up on wooden blocks that served as a sofa as well as a bed. Against the other wall of the tiny room were a small table and two wooden chairs. Nails driven into the walls served as clothes pegs for a coat and dresses.

Looking exhausted, Vanda sat down at the other end of the mattress. "My apartment in Riga is even smaller than this, since they took away two of our rooms and gave them to Russians. Now there are four of us—my mother, half-brother, half-sister and myself—in one room. When I go there, we sleep on the floor, side by side, like sardines. This space may be small, but at least I have it to myself.

"Vanda, you know there are times when I go to sleep wishing I would never wake up," I said. "Our lives seem so meaningless and hopeless."

"I admit I felt that way myself this morning," Vanda said, "but now there is hope."

"How is that? Tell me!"

"We all have our problems. I am being pressured to resign 'voluntarily'—all because of a student who got too familiar. I slapped his face. He told me that he was with the Cheka and that I would regret what I did. So he reported that I am politically untrustworthy, and that was enough. But none of that matters now, because we're going to Sweden!"

"What? How?" I jumped up, suddenly full of energy.

"I told you about the captain of the fishing boat and his brother-in-law Krastins, who is also one of my students. It seems Krastins has been able to organize something. He works as a statistician at the Seamen's Club. There's a concert there now featuring Freibergs from the Riga Opera. I told Krastins you and I would go there."

As we hurried along, we made plans for our new lives in Sweden.

"I could finish my education and become whatever I choose. I wouldn't have to starve. We wouldn't have to be afraid to see private clients anymore. Everything is forbidden here—even protecting yourself from unwanted advances becomes a political issue! Did you hear on the radio that Cukurs and some other people managed to get to Sweden?"

The Seamen's Club was opposite the music school, and we usually made it a point to avoid it because of the drunks. Even tonight our arrival was greeted by unwelcome comments and propositions. It was clear why Vanda had not wanted us to meet there.

It was intermission, and people filled the stairs. We squeezed through the crowd and were finally in the wings of the stage. Off to the side was a room with a small group of men, and Freibergs was sitting on a table finishing up a half-empty bottle of vodka. He motioned us over.

"Would you girls care for a drink?" he asked in Russian.

"We know how to speak Latvian as well as that other language," Vanda said firmly. "But I'm afraid we haven't learned to drink straight from a bottle yet."

The singer looked startled, then, speaking in Latvian, quickly excused himself as he was being summoned to go back on stage. Moments later we heard a spirited rendition of "Ridi, Pagliaccio" in Russian. His voice was beautiful and, had it not been for the bottle, he could certainly have been very famous. Maybe the drink made his problems more bearable.

Most of the audience had gone back inside when Vanda made eye contact with Krastins. We left the club immediately, and the blond young man caught up with us at Vanda's apartment.

"Can you really get us to Sweden?" I looked at him hopefully.

"Yes," Krastins said somberly. "I've been thinking about how to do it for a long while."

"I'm very grateful to both of you," I said, and then brought them up to date on the Party's plans for my future.

"That's how they work," Krastins said. "Now they won't leave you alone, usually alternating flattery with threats. And don't believe for a second what Tamara Ivanovna said about it being a secret. It has all been carefully planned. You are being prepared and will be tracked like an animal. But let me give you some advice: Don't make it harder for yourself by protesting. In two or three weeks this will be just a bad memory."

33

A Friend Grows Distant

I was on the train on my way to Riga and a five-month course at the First City Hospital. In my first year of work, I had been back to Riga four times. Those times Dr. Kundzins was there to back me up, but now he had been pushed aside.

I wondered by what miracle I was being allowed to keep my job—and for how much longer? I felt the Party noose tightening. I worried about what would happen to my career and my family when I officially turned down their invitation.

During the time Vanda and I were planning our escape to Sweden, my life took on new and positive meaning. But then came the bad news: After the Cukurs family escaped, the rules were changed and Krastins's brother-in-law, along with many other fishermen, lost their permits to go out to sea.

Vanda and I spent many evenings pondering the turn of events. We heard from reliable sources that things were not going well for the Cukurs family and other refugees in Sweden. It seems they were regarded with suspicion and shunned by Latvian society there.

"Vanda, what do you think about those stories?" I asked her pointedly.

"I don't believe them."

"Neither do I," I agreed. "It's probably just more disinformation to stop others from trying to escape."

I also thought about my friendship with Eglis, the accountant. After he walked in on me and my collection of books, I visited his family several times, until one day I was called in by the Party committee. Clearly people were under their jurisdiction, whether or not they were members.

I was scolded like a schoolgirl for keeping company with bad elements. I wasn't even sure who they were talking about. Eventually, from oblique references to has-been corporals mired in outmoded bourgeois traditions and religious mysticism, I gathered they were probably talking about Eglis, though his name was never mentioned. I was sent off with the by-now familiar praise that I was a bright new light with a promising future, but I had to allow myself to be shown the right path.

◆   ◆   ◆

The train pulled into Talsi, where I had planned to stop and visit Dace.

I was waiting in her tiny attic office when the sound of footsteps made me jump to my feet in anticipation of seeing my good friend. I stopped short when I saw Eugenie.

"Hello, dear. I came to see Dace as well. I work for the health department, inspecting stores."

She lowered her voice to a conspiratorial half-whisper. "I treat them like they treat me…If they're good to me, I am good to them. It's the only way, really."

Opening a large tote bag, Eugenie took out a coffee can, a sausage, and a half loaf of white bread and placed them on the table.

"Poor Dace works like a slave, and she only makes pocket change compared to me."

I was happy when Dace finally arrived, but a private conversation was out of the question, so we chatted about inconsequential things. And, every time there was a pause, Eugenie jumped in.

"Remember my health minister? Well, he's nothing but a small cog in the Institute of Medicine these days. My new friend is a young MVD officer. You can't imagine how Kolya adores me! With him, I will have new opportunities. I'm going to be a nurse for the security forces."

Through the chatter, I found one thing puzzling. Dace didn't say a word. She used to make fun of Eugenie, parroting her Communist phrases. But now she kept her eyes fixed on her coffee cup.

I had hoped to discuss some things with my old friend but saw that it was not going to happen. Eugenie showed no signs of leaving.

It suddenly struck me that Eugenie and Dace were themselves friends.

As if reading my thoughts, Eugenie chimed in, "Dace and I see each other a lot. She is a candidate to join the Party."

"You're joining the Party?" I asked her directly.

Dace nodded slowly, not taking her eyes from her coffee.

Stunned, I mumbled an excuse and hurried away.

Huddled in my seat in the half-empty night train, I thought back on that afternoon's events. Was Dace being pressured to join the Party? Noldis, for whatever reason, had become a Party candidate while we were still students and, soon afterward, had been rewarded with a directorship. I was certain Dace still loved him. Maybe this was her way to get him back.

I learned the answers to those questions much later—the day before I left Latvia. Until then, Dace and I remained on cool but polite terms. The Soviet system could chalk up yet one more success in its ongoing efforts to destroy friendships and tear families apart.

34

My Biggest Humiliation

The dermatology clinic in Riga had one hundred and fifty beds, and fifteen doctors worked in the venereal disease section. Assigned to the women's division, I was honing my specialty along with four other female doctors. Those months were very productive and professionally satisfying. Unfortunately, they also coincided with another extremely difficult time in my life.

It seems that when a woman is betrayed by a man, her view is always thought to be more subjective. Perhaps mine is as well, but, nevertheless, I must tell my side of the story.

By then I was living in Asari, near the seaside. My neighbors, Gaida and Ojars, were still together, while she continued to hope that her childhood sweetheart would return. I couldn't imagine how she could walk away from someone who had been so good to her, but I had long since stopped passing judgment on people and things I didn't understand.

In the evenings, Gaida and I would go for walks along the shore, discussing our shared passions for literature and politics. We differed somewhat on when our country's situation might change—she thought sooner, while I believed it would be later—but in the end we wished for the same result.

Gaida's birthday was approaching. It was November 18, the same as Latvia's Independence Day, and it gave us a reason to have a party on a day it would otherwise be illegal. Among the guests was Olita, who had once been in Com-Youth. Surprisingly, she was the first to lead us in singing forbidden patriotic songs. Another guest, one of Gaida's distant relatives, had served with the freedom fighters and entertained us with his stories.

There was also a stranger, a dark-haired young man who wouldn't take his eyes—his brooding dark eyes—from mine. He sat across the table from me, and his gaze was so unsettling that, if it hadn't appeared impolite, I would have gotten up and changed my seat. But I didn't.

Though darkness descended early in November, we all decided to go for walk. As we set off, the young man, whom I will call Adolfs, came up beside me and took my arm. Without a word, we walked on the path, along the towering, rustling pines and the crashing waves. The cold wind whipped my hair and tore at my shabby coat, but I was oblivious to any discomfort.

◆   ◆   ◆

There was a buzz around the clinic.

"We have been chosen for a great honor—to willingly and enthusiastically order copies of the combined works of Lenin and Stalin," one of the head doctors said.

"Willingly? What do you mean?" I practically shouted, initially missing the irony in her tone.

"As willingly as we give everything else—the so-called loan to the government and all the other deductions they take from our wages. A Party lackey arrives with a paper that says you respectfully seek permission to donate two months' salary to the government, and all you have to do is sign at the bottom. It's the same with these books. A Cheka agent arrived with a letter saying that we humbly request the opportunity to become more familiar with the teachings of Lenin and Stalin and would like to receive their complete works at a price of 15 rubles each—to be deducted from our wages," she explained.

"Can't we refuse?"

"I think you know the answer to that one. I must be careful. My children are in the West."

Facing a double problem were Livija and Indulis, who nevertheless managed to accept the situation with humor. They were married, but since both of them worked at the hospital, each was expected to "willingly" order a set of fifty volumes of Marxist "wisdom."

I didn't have to order the books as I was on temporary assignment, yet my friends never missed an opportunity—a birthday or holiday—to try to present to me with great pomp, a set of their books. Each time, feigning somber piety, I declined their "great sacrifice," saying that I couldn't possibly accept a gift of "such magnitude."

The months flew by. I spent my days at the clinic and most evenings with Adolfs. Oddly our meetings were never arranged; it was always as if we met by chance.

Sometimes we found ourselves on the same train going to the seashore. I particularly enjoyed the evenings and Sundays we spent there. Adolfs was very knowledgeable about literature and music. And, though I still found it unsettling to be with him, we were never bored in each other's company. He often disappeared as suddenly as he arrived, with a quick check of his watch, a hurried excuse, and a squeeze of my hand. He never waved good-bye, and never looked back.

Perhaps it is what we least understand that draws us like a magnet. I knew very little about him, but I found myself thinking of him often and wondering what he was really like. Conversant on every subject, he was also a very good listener and even better at drawing out people's thoughts.

Gaida said he came from a family of Latvian patriots, and so it would seem that Adolfs, the youngest of the lot, was like the others, only more reserved. She talked about him in such glowing terms that Ojars often seemed annoyed, but I didn't pay too much attention because I also enjoyed talking about Adolfs, as well as hearing good things about him.

My special training was coming to an end, and I was worried about the pressures that awaited me back in Ventspils, especially the Party's efforts to get me to "willingly" join. I shared my concerns with Adolfs, who was supportive and reassuring.

Adolfs had taken a genuine interest in every aspect of my life—even in my broken marriage. No detail was too small. He wanted to know what it was about Hugo that upset me the most. Indeed, the more time we spent together, the more I was convinced he was the total opposite of Hugo. I didn't hold anything back as Adolfs had entrusted me with his greatest secret—he had a brother in the West who had graduated from university there and was working for an American company.

He made me feel I was very important to him and even suggested that the best way around the Party problem was for us to get married, the sooner the better. As a director of the Kirov school district, he had a stable job in Riga, and, if I were to become his wife, they couldn't make me stay in Ventspils, at least not longer than one year. And I could certainly keep putting off the Party's efforts for that long. While Adolfs reassured me he wanted us to be together, there was just one obstacle—his mother, a devout, old-fashioned woman, who would not approve of us rushing into marriage.

One day, I brought up the subject of our marriage with Gaida, who responded with an uncharacteristically stony silence. Ojars, however, was overjoyed at the prospect. Adolfs, apparently having learned of the conversation from Gaida, was upset that I would discuss such private matters with others. It wasn't the right time, he said, as we had not yet told his mother.

I was hurt by his reaction but tried not to let it show.

Little by little, Adolfs had found out everything about me—personal details that, with the rarest of exceptions, were guarded with the utmost ferocity in the Soviet Union. He knew that my father had been deported and that my mother was on a wanted list. He knew my views—political, philosophical, emotional, or otherwise—on every conceivable subject. He even knew that Gran had left me her house and what remained of her belongings.

Apparently there was nothing more he needed to know. He now owned me.

Armed with all the information I had so willingly confided, Adolfs became my master. In short, from that point on, I lived under constant threat that he would divulge my secrets—unless I gave him money.

And so, I eventually lost everything Gran had managed to salvage for me. But even that wasn't enough for him. Nothing was ever enough! Even later, when I was an instructor at the Institute of Medicine, Adolfs would turn up unexpectedly and demand money. And, as I learned soon enough, I was not the first of his conquests, nor would I be the last.

What it meant to fall into such a dire trap in occupied Latvia is almost impossible to explain to those who haven't experienced it. My nerves were shattered. And not the least of what bothered me was the fact that I had been so terribly, terribly wrong about him.

In my predicament, I felt that the only people I could turn to were Gaida and Ojars, who were both there when Adolfs and I met. But, cleverly, Adolfs had driven a wedge between us. Gaida received a letter (allegedly from me) ridiculing her relationship with Ojars, that caused her great pain. And, as I had long ago begun to suspect, she also had a weak spot for Adolfs and had already become his next victim.

It was a perfect example of how hatefully and skillfully some Latvians were capable of using their compatriots' weaknesses to achieve their personal aims. Even now, many years later, I find it difficult to dwell on that emotionally devastating time of my life.

◆   ◆   ◆

I eventually became the head of the serology lab at the dispensary, but I did not find laboratory work very interesting so I left after six months. My next job was on the faculty at the Riga Institute of Medicine, which by 1950 had become the highest bastion of learning.

But let me back up a little.

One day, a strangely dressed man arrived at my door, asking repeatedly if I was the Lita he was looking for. His face was swollen, and his feet wrapped in rags.

"Are you a deportee?"

"Yes," the stranger replied, pulling a piece of paper from his pocket. "I've spent the last two years with Hugo."

The note said that Hugo wanted to know if I could do him a favor. The stranger would tell me what it was.

"Nothing you could say would shock or upset me. Hugo and I were married only a short time, but there is no enmity between us, and, if I can, I will help him."

I offered the visitor lunch and, as we ate, he related his story. "After you and Hugo separated, he found a series of jobs but couldn't hold any of them for long. His problems with alcohol didn't help, as it made him a little too, shall we say, talkative?"

"That certainly sounds like Hugo."

"He was eventually arrested, tried, and sentenced to twenty-five years. I had been in Magadan (a sub arctic port and major transit center for prisoners being sent to labor camps) for several years when Hugo arrived with the latest replacements for the many who had died."

As it turned out, luck had not entirely deserted Hugo. Though he had only briefly studied veterinary medicine, he was made head of an ambulance corps and worked as a doctor.

Then came the request. Hugo wanted some books on medicine.

I was glad Hugo was alive and well, and of course I got the books for him. But to this day, it remains a mystery to me that he was able to function as a doctor. That kind of situation could only exist in the Soviet Union.

35

The Death of Stalin

On March 3, 1953, like a thunderbolt from the leaden Soviet skies, came a news flash: Stalin had suffered a massive stroke.

Did it really mean the end was near for the biggest despot and mass murderer in history? That maybe Stalin was already on his way to hell? Most Latvians felt that when he reached the end of his journey, the devil himself would be looking for an escape route.

We heard hourly updates on the "beloved father and teacher, war hero, and leader of the happy Soviet people." There were detailed reports on his vital signs, pulse rate, and frequent lapses into unconsciousness. "Everything possible" was being done to help him.

As the bulletins became more frequent, it was clear he would not last much longer. People were nervous and on edge. The most apprehensive of all were Party members, political functionaries, and the military—all those who had managed to grab the biggest slice of the pie for themselves. The rest of us, though we dared not let it show, were in a state of delirious disbelief.

The presence in the streets of MVD men in red and blue hats brought back horrific memories of the deportations in 1941 and 1949. Plainclothes Cheka were also out in force.

Finally at 6:00 AM on March 6 came the announcement: "The heart of the Party's and people's teacher, leader, and Comrade Lenin's valiant follower has ceased to beat. Our duty now is to avoid panic and unrest, guard our Party's unity, and ensure strong leadership."

It was over.

What would the Party lackeys do now? What would Lacis, Sudrabkalns, and Grigulis—those fabricators of nonsense—write about? Would all the torturers and slave masters have to re-educate themselves? I couldn't help but feel a sense of satisfaction.

Party members, military, and political underlings gathered in groups on the streets, weeping copious tears. I wondered if their emotions were genuine or if it was just an act they had perfected over the years. "Our dear leader has left us…Oh, no…Oh, no," could be heard in Latvian as well as in Russian.

"Stay calm. Don't panic," the radio broadcasts cautioned every hour on the hour, along with reporting details of grandiose funeral plans while Chopin's Funeral March played incessantly. To this day, the somber strains of that music bring back memories of this evil, bitter, and happy time. The killer of free Latvia and tens of thousands of Latvians was dead. He no longer had any control over us.

But the Cheka were not about to relinquish control of Riga. They were everywhere—at railway stations, ministries, the post office, and the bridge. Change was inevitable. Stalin was dead, but it looked as if the Cheka would be in charge as long as Communism was alive.

◆   ◆   ◆

There weren't many job openings for doctors in Riga, and Party members and officers' wives always had priority. I had been without work for several months, though I did have several private patients.

So, when Riga's Institute of Medicine had a vacancy for an assistant, I applied for the job. While waiting for a response, I stayed with friends near the hospital. One afternoon, the doorbell rang and Adolfs strode in.

"I need something from you," he said, making himself comfortable in a club chair.

"I don't have any money," I said. "You know I'm not working right now."

"Ah, but you'd like to work, wouldn't you? At the Institute of Medicine."

So he knew about that, too.

"Whether they hire you or not is in my hands," he said smugly. "As is whether or not you ever work as a doctor again."

I looked at the dark-eyed young man I had once adored with all my heart. What a brilliant actor he would have made, I thought. He had truly missed his calling.

"My girlfriend Meta is pregnant," Adolfs continued. "You have to help her."

I nodded wearily, realizing I had no other choice. Abortions were not prohibited in the Soviet Union. In fact they were as common as going to the dentist to have a cavity filled.

The next day, at the appointed hour, a beige Moskvich pulled up at the front door. The car was a painful reminder—I had paid for it with my grandmother's house. There was also a note, signed by me, saying the car was a present for Adolfs. A young blonde woman got out.

Meta was a seventeen-year-old art student. In her naïveté, she told me how much in love she and Adolfs were, but then stopped suddenly, explaining that it was supposed to be a secret, lest others—especially his mother—find out. She seemed like a nice girl, and she was so young. I felt sorry for her.

I assured her she needn't worry about me telling anyone. And, although I had to help her out more than once, I was afraid to warn her.

In between, there was another girlfriend, Zenta.

Not surprisingly, the time came when Meta, under threat of being expelled from art school, also fell victim to Adolfs's cruelty and greed. He used her skills to provide beautiful hand-woven blankets, tablecloths, napkins, and pillows to furnish his house in the suburbs.

But young women were not Adolfs's only victims. He also befriended Verners, a religious man who would refuse to give up the names of the people in his prayer group. Adolfs, like a chameleon, was capable of adapting himself to any person's needs or interests, as long as the end result meant his own personal gain.

His modus operandi was always the same. After carefully studying his quarry, he would become whatever he needed to be. Like a black spider lurking behind a red star, he pulled victim after victim into his deceitful web. Did Adolfs really have nothing to fear? What were the circumstances that allowed him to conduct his operations so boldly? How people from respectable Latvian families could be so evil is something no normal human being can possibly understand.

Some time passed and, with help from my former boss, Dr. Mazkalnina, I got a job as a professor's assistant. But I continued to live under threat from Adolfs, who had instilled such fear in me that I didn't dare speak with anyone about anything.

One day I ran into Vanda, who was in Riga on vacation, and she brought me up to date on our mutual acquaintances in Ventspils. I muttered something vague in response.

"Lita, what's wrong? You're acting so strange," Vanda said. "I want to know how you really are. And then I have some things to tell you as well."

I agreed to have lunch with her, and we went to Vanda's tiny room, where we had delicious smoked fish she had brought from Ventspils and a bottle of Caucasus wine. We ate and drank and commiserated over our failed escape plan and the terrible state of things in general.

"I'm so tired of this life," Vanda complained. "The lies and the betrayal—it's always the same. This little room is all I was allowed to keep after my apartment was subdivided. When I started working in Ventspils, I allowed my adopted brother, Rudolfs, to live here in my absence. He got married a few months ago, when he thought he had the opportunity to buy his own apartment."

"He bought an apartment?" I asked incredulously, knowing that officially it was impossible.

"No—even though it was practically guaranteed by his best friend, for whom he would have done anything. He was from a good family, with a brother in the West. Rudolfs still doesn't want to believe that Adolfs was at fault..."

"Adolfs! What does he look like?"

"I only saw him once. He was a slender, dark-haired, dark-eyed young man. I don't even know his last name."

"It's him!" I shouted and began to pace about the room.

"What? Who?"

Then fear set in again, and I tried to change the subject. But the wine had done its job and I had said too much already, so I finally told Vanda everything. The more I told her, the more agitated she became. "I must speak to Nikolai," Vanda cried.

"Who is Nikolai?" I asked, frightened again.

"My classmate. He's Russian, but he was born and raised in Latvia. He's all right—he's not a Communist. He works in the criminal courts and has often told me how much they would like to arrest the real criminals, not just the ones who are only designated as such."

"Don't do it, Vanda. Please, don't do anything. Maybe your friend is a good person, but you can't even begin to imagine what Adolfs is like!"

But there was no calming her down. She told me about her adopted brother's friendship with Adolfs. They met at the boat club in Kisezers, and, as their friendship developed, Rudolfs told Adolfs he was thinking of getting married but didn't know where he and his wife would find a place to live. His new friend took a sincere interest, even confiding that he had a brother in the West. He showed him letters his brother had written, though it had been necessary to mail them to an address in the countryside, where some of his relatives lived. Adolfs said he had also asked his brother to send packages to help an aging minister rebuild his church. That finally convinced Rudolfs of Adolfs's unwavering patriotism.

There were no blemishes on Rudolfs's own life. He never knew his parents and was raised by Vanda's family. He had been discharged from the army for health reasons. But Adolfs was very patient and persistent, and Rudolfs finally told him about his fiancée, along with some "useful" details about her family.

Adolfs said he could arrange a meeting with a woman on the housing committee, Herta Adukone, who could help. Rudolfs paid her thirteen thousand rubles. She gave him a receipt and told him to be patient. When there was no progress and Rudolfs became more insistent, she threatened to expose his fiancée's family. In the meantime, Adolfs was nowhere to be found.

Some time later, when Rudolfs ran into Adolfs by chance and told him his problems, Adolfs expressed shock and dismay and swore he didn't know Adukone, that he had only heard about her and was still eager to help if he could. Rudolfs was genuinely confused.

The woman was eventually brought to trial for "selling" apartments to thirteen other people while impersonating a member of the housing committee. Her name wound up in the newspapers in the Soviet Union as well as in the West, and she was sentenced to six months in jail.

But never was there any mention of Adolfs.

◆   ◆   ◆

My job was interesting and challenging, but I was not happy. Indeed I wondered if I could ever be happy again, or whether I could ever again trust anyone.

Stalin was dead, but Communism was still alive. There was no revolution, and our lives continued more or less unchanged.

At the institute every Monday there were so-called educational gatherings that began and ended with politically oriented speeches and announcements. In between, professors and their assistants shared the results of their latest experiments and findings, which were then opened to discussion. These discussions led to what eventually would become the basis for a thesis for candidates to earn a higher degree.

On Tuesday night, we had compulsory courses in Marxism-Leninism that had to be completed in three years. It was considered an honor to be allowed to earn a second university diploma. On Wednesday, we read or sometimes listened to the latest findings in foreign medicine. This was something new that had not existed in Stalin's time. Thursday night there were political studies.

On Friday, each of the faculties assembled individually to discuss that week's most interesting developments. The head of dermatology was Peteris Janovich Jakobsons—a Latvian from Russia who lectured in both languages. As his assistant, one of my duties was to translate the Russian into Latvian, which he spoke with a very thick accent. Students found it so difficult to understand what he was saying that in the end it always fell to me to explain his lectures.

My own patients also took up my time. Yet having such a busy schedule was a blessing. It left me less time to dwell on my problems.

Adolfs's threats and blackmail went on for several years. Knowing that I had a job, he knew where to find me if he ever needed money.

36

Smashing an Idol

It was 1956, March—a dreary time. Spring was coming, but the interim chill was too much for our thin coats. The melting snow formed large puddles of dirty water that soon became swiftly running streams along the gutters.

There was new excitement at the university. A group of people with no apparent common denominator had been invited to a meeting in the old auditorium. Everything was shrouded in secrecy, but rumors were rampant. My boss, Professor Jakobsons, was expected to attend but, as usual, was trying his best to avoid going. His solution this time was to give me his invitation.

When I arrived, I found myself caught up in the stream of people entering the auditorium, which was filling to capacity. At the front was a table covered with a red cloth and behind it the usual assortment of prominent people. Only this time, their faces had a worried expression.

Then Comrade Skapars, a man of about thirty with a thick shock of brown hair stood up with a stack of papers in his hands. Clearing his throat, he adjusted his red tie and spoke in Russian. "Comrades, I will now read for you a historic document—Comrade Khrushchev's speech at the Party's twentieth congress held on February 25."

So it was nothing out of the ordinary, we thought, just more of the same old boasts about a slew of Soviet "accomplishments." As it was likely to take at least an hour, we settled in with our private thoughts.

But all that changed after the first couple of sentences.

Khrushchev, in his speech, had praised Lenin and Leninism, the Party, and peoples' collective leadership methods. Then we heard that back in December of 1922, Lenin had asked the Party's thirteenth congress to remove Stalin from his post as general secretary because he was too coarse and vulgar.

That caused ripples throughout the auditorium. Lenin's request, I later found out, was no secret in the free world yet had been kept hidden from Soviet citizens. We didn't dare look at one another.

Skapars carried on in a monotone, reading other documents, including a letter from Lenin's wife, Krupskaya, in which she complained bitterly that Stalin had cursed at her. He also read Lenin's letter to Stalin, threatening him with bodily harm if he didn't take back his insults. That would also explain the frosty relationship between the two major proponents of Communism. Yes, he went on, all of Lenin's dire predictions had come true—Stalin had abandoned his teaching methods and replaced them with force and repression, which he used to terrorize and control the masses.

After Lenin's death, Krupskaya occasionally dared to criticize her husband's successor, whereupon Stalin issued the following threat: "If you keep talking like that, I'll have to find Lenin another widow!"

I smiled, inadvertently catching the eye of one of my pupils, who smiled back. But then we both quickly changed expression, fearing we had revealed too much of our true feelings.

Skapars continued reading. "From the seventeenth congress' elected 139 central committee members and candidates, 98—that is 70 percent of them—were arrested and killed in 1937 and 1938. These victims made valuable contributions to the Party and had joined it before the October revolution in 1921. So how was it possible that 70 percent of those central committee members were enemies of the Party and the people? The only explanation could be that they were the victims of lies and false accusations. The same fate befell the 1,966 congressional delegates, when 1,108—more than half—were imprisoned for counterrevolutionary activities."

Here and there, people started picking up pencils to take note of the numbers that had previously been so secret. Who knew? They might be useful someday.

There was a loud knocking at the main auditorium door. The presiding professor, Golbers, stood up and motioned for the speaker to stop. He opened the door to admit a middle-aged woman dressed in work clothes and carrying a broom. She was on the university's janitorial staff. The two carried on an animated but hushed conversation, and afterward Golbers announced, "It has been proposed by the people that under no circumstances are we to take notes. I strongly urge you to heed that request."

Without a word, pencils disappeared back into pockets and briefcases.

Skapars resumed reading Khrushchev's speech about the unsolved killing of Kirov. And then we were told about the Latvian Communist Eiche, a name not familiar to us. Apparently he had worked his way to quite a high level in the Party and was a government minister under Stuchka, a politburo candidate and more. We learned of Eiche's reports to Stalin, his broken ribs and torture, all ending in his execution by firing squad. Then came another tale of the Communist Rud-zutaks, who met the same fate. The detailing of Stalin's horrors lasted for several more hours. Then the meeting ended with a rousing cheer, "Long live the flag bearers of Leninism!"

As we dispersed, we were obviously afraid to discuss what we had just heard. But I had an odd feeling as I walked past Stalin's bronze bust in Vermane Gardens that his facial expression had altered. It seemed that, at last, some kind of change was afoot.

Conversations at the hospital were guarded, to say the least. For so many years, even a single bad word about the "dear father and teacher" had resulted in arrest or deportation. Yet the man who now held the highest office in the country had publicly flouted that directive. While it created confusion among Party members, that development raised real hopes for the rest of us.

Even if we had been forgotten by the freedom-loving Western powers, it now seemed possible that the breakdown of Communism could come from within. There were whispers of a revolution among the occupied countries, including anti-Communist Russians, Ukrainians, Georgians, and others who felt crushed by the regime. It was a confusing time.

Then I was sent to Moscow's First Institute of Medicine to learn about the latest breakthroughs in dermatology. I had been given the address of a Latvian pensioner who had lived there since before World War I. Although she had only one room and a shared kitchen, she offered a reasonably priced place to sleep for visitors from Latvia. It was her main source of income.

Upon my arrival, Sofia Petrovna told me one bed had already been taken by a young man from Riga. It was bad enough to share sleeping quarters with women strangers, but a strange man? I was ready to leave to try my luck at finding a hotel, which would have been difficult on a tight budget.

Then the pensioner told me how quiet and pleasant the man behind the Spanish screen was and repeated her invitation for me to stay. I was tired from my journey and the room looked clean and was affordable, so I gave in.

But no sooner had we retired for the night than the third occupant arrived, visibly intoxicated. I was shocked to see it was Valda's brother, Helmuts—one of the only two Communists I knew who was not in the Party for personal gain. I almost didn't recognize him. His face was pale and expressionless, and, until now at least, he had never been known to drink.

He fell into his bed and passed out almost immediately but soon started shouting and moaning as if in the middle of a nightmare.

"And all this because of that murdering despot," Petrovna whispered. "You know, my husband believed in Lenin, but Stalin had him killed. This entire six-story house was once filled with Latvian families. Now I'm the only one left. How I hated that Red monster! But..." she stopped talking, and a fearful expression came over her face. "Please forget what I just said."

The following morning, Helmuts showed me the way to the institute. At the entrance, he took my arm and pulled me aside. "Tell me, Lita, what are people saying in Latvia? I've been here for a few weeks and am looking for work. I've always believed in Communism and in Stalin, but now...now I don't know what to think."

I felt sorry for Helmuts. It seemed his world was coming apart, as it was for many others. "But, why are you asking me?" I said. "You know the answer, even if you don't want to admit it."

"I know," he said quietly and hurried away.

37

A Memorable Christmas

There are times when you don't want to be alone, when you have an overwhelming need to share with someone, no matter how ordinary the experience.

On this Christmas Eve, I felt lonelier than ever. I had nowhere to go and no one to see. No one was waiting for me, eager to spend time with me.

My windows were tightly shuttered, so no one could see that on the table—like in days gone by—there was a beautifully decorated Christmas tree. What a feat it had been to get it, because, before the holidays, selling fir trees was illegal. After the New Year, of course, that "law" changed.

Olga's husband, Andrejs, had managed to smuggle in two trees in a burlap bag—one for his family and one for me.

The sale of candles was also forbidden just before Christmas, so a few months ago I had managed to buy some, along with just enough ornaments to make the tree look festive.

Everything was ready. I had even spent a day's wages on a half kilo of shiny red apples. They looked so beautiful hanging from the branches of the tree. I would eat them later.

My Christmas dinner consisted of potatoes fried in pork fat. At least I didn't have to use that smelly fish oil. I also had a pickle. In the best of circumstances, I couldn't afford to eat meat more than twice a week. Tonight, I had wanted to have sausages, even the least expensive kind. But the political speeches had run too long, and every store I passed on my way home was already sold out of meat.

I longed for the aroma of freshly baked piragi, but there were no ingredients to make them. Yeast was not available for months before Christmas, and then miraculously reappeared for the New Year. The flour was gray and pasty, and milk was too great a luxury to use in making dough.

Christmas Eve brought back memories of my parents' home, the tree, sweets, Christmas songs, and Gran's special prayer. I willed myself to stop thinking about things the way they used to be. There was nothing I could do to change anything...yet. Usually, thinking about the past made the present too hard to bear, but tonight I allowed myself to remember, if only to try to regain some holiday spirit.

I tried several stations on the radio. The announcers were talking about peace, about a 200 percent improvement in work output. I had heard it all ad nauseam. I couldn't tune in any foreign stations, as the signal jammers were working overtime at this time of year.

Suddenly, my doorbell rang. Who could that be tonight of all nights? Was there someone else as lonely as I was? I answered the door with some trepidation because of my illegal tree.

Outside were several of my students. I took a step backward, and they came inside carrying a package—a cake and a bouquet of golden wheat tied with a ribbon. I was so touched that I took a long time arranging the stalks in a clay pot, while I composed myself.

When the candles were lit, we sang Christmas songs, forgetting, at least for the moment, the things that were forbidden. And although at least a third of the young people wore Com-Youth badges on their lapels, the only thing that showed in their faces that night was sheer joy.

It was a moment so magical that it was hard to put into words.

As I sliced the homemade cake, I thought about how much thought and love must have gone into baking it. We felt so close that it was easy to drop our guard.

"I wonder if they celebrate Christmas over on the other side?" someone asked quietly.

The question started a lively discussion. None of us really knew the answer. How could we? Western books were not sold in bookstores. If a book occasionally turned up in the market, you could be sure it contained something negative about the capitalist system. Those books also came with a written caveat and guidance on how the reader should interpret their contents. It was the same with movies and Western music. Religion was for fools. We were told that even Westerners were turning their backs on such nonsense and that the only ones who celebrated Christmas were lazy people looking for another excuse to get out of work.

Some of my young guests had been in the countryside, where radio signal jamming was not so effective, and heard Voice of America broadcasts that gave them an idea about the lives of Latvians over there.

"They drive their own cars, and have their own homes, and have trouble deciding which clothes to wear, but still they call themselves refugees. I could get used to that kind of deprivation!" said one boy.

"Couldn't we all!" another one piped up.

"So much for the material part," the first boy continued. "But from the broadcast, it was clear they can say whatever they like—even criticize the president if they don't agree with him."

Could that possibly be true? Again, we didn't know the answer.

A boy with dark, mischievous eyes got up to demonstrate America's latest dance—the Calypso.

Then, all too soon, the night was over—the candles had gone out and the guests had gone home. It had been so unexpected…their arrival, the open conversation. Had we gone too far? I thought about acquaintances who were arrested for celebrating Christmas. What if the Communist bosses found out about my little party? My walls were thick enough, and the other families in the house were Latvian. But what if one of the youths just happened to mention something?

The human mind is a strange and complex thing, particularly within a Communist regime. I worried if I would have to pay dearly for my Christmas wish come true.

But a week went by, then several weeks, and there were no repercussions.

◆   ◆   ◆

One evening one of the doctors and I stopped in Vermane Gardens at a restaurant that was popular with students, perhaps because they could listen to Western music. But all the tables were taken. As we turned to leave, Gvido, a Music Conservatory student, stood up.

"Come, join us at the musicians' table," he said. "I'll introduce you."

We joined the other musicians, some of their friends, and a woman named Marika.

Marika wasn't beautiful, but there was something appealing about her. She was about twenty-six, dark-haired, slender, and animated. Only her voice, which was harsh and metallic, was unpleasant.

"You're a doctor?" Marika began. "Ah, then we have a lot to talk about. I wanted to study medicine, but fate decreed I should become a lawyer.

It turned out she was a former classmate of my friend Olita.

After an hour or more of conversation, I was getting up to leave, when Marika, fixing her gaze on Gvido, suddenly said, "Why don't you all come to my house next Saturday?" Gvido accepted right away. Then she turned to me. "And you, Doctor, don't even think of staying home. I promise you won't be bored."

Marika was true to her word. She was a good hostess; the food was delicious, and the conversation was stimulating. Then she excused herself to prepare the sauna.

She returned wearing only a light robe and held out her hand to Gvido. "Come, darling, we've had enough to eat."

Gvido did as he was bid, leaving the rest of us in an awkward position. Should we leave? We stayed and pretended we didn't know what was going on.

When they returned from the sauna, Gvido looked a bit sheepish, but Marika regaled us with a detailed report about their escapades.

After that Saturday, I vowed to stay as far away from Marika as possible. But, again, fate decreed otherwise. Marika sent me a letter.

As someone whose job it is to uphold the law, I am aware I am breaking it by making the following request. But, as a member of the Party, if I were to go to a public clinic to take care of my problem, it would create a lot of gossip. So I am asking you to help me privately.

I make this request in writing so you'll know how serious I am but also as a promise to you that I am ready to return the favor if I can ever help you in any way.

I remained resolute. I wanted nothing to do with her.

◆   ◆   ◆

It had been a busy day at the institute. I was tired and in no mood to be jostled on a crowded bus, so I decided to walk.

I was enjoying the fresh night air when I heard someone calling my name. It was Olita, bubbling over with enthusiasm just like in the old days. But I also knew her mood could change very quickly if anything displeased her. Things were going well. She had a good job in Riga. As we chatted, I brought up Marika's name. Olita doubled over with laughter.

"Come, let's go sit by the canal," she said.

"You know, of course, that Catherine the Great earned her place in history as Russian royalty, but there was another reason for which she is remembered…her name has also come to describe women who can never get enough. She was a nymphomaniac."

"Why are you telling me this?" I asked.

"It's simple. Marika is a miniature version of Catherine the Great," Olita said.

"You can't be serious! Surely the university would have found out. How was she ever allowed to graduate? How did she get a job?"

"Well, there are ways…and then there are ways," Olita said slowly.

"Marika's father owned a pharmacy in Riga during the independence years. The house on the banks of the Daugava and the apartment in Riga were left to her. How, coming from such a typical middle-class family, do you suppose she got that way?"

I thought of Adolfs and knew it was possible. "I'm sure that phenomenon will keep sociologists and psychologists busy for years to come," I replied.

"Did I mention that her brother is head of the Cheka at the port of Liepaja? That should tell you a few things."

"Oh, my!" I gasped. "If I had known all that before, I never would have set foot inside her house. Poor Gvido."

"Up until now, Marika's personal doctor helped her with any difficulties. But several weeks ago, the doctor had an accident and died."

"Oh, God, what will I do now!" I groaned. I still hadn't learned to hide my emotions.

Olita didn't take long to put two and two together and work out that I must have something to hide. Would she be able to offer sound advice on how I could avoid becoming Marika's personal physician? Oddly enough, she said I'd be better off to try to help her.

"Don't forget, her handwritten letter is a valuable document. Hold on to it. Maybe someday you can exchange it for a special favor."

Totally confused, I went home. As I debated on what to do, I was struck by the idea that I might have been presented with an opportunity to break my cycle of misery. I accepted the job.

Marika's tumultuous personal life being what it was kept me quite busy. She had many lovers, and some of them—like Catherine's hapless officers—suffered a similarly unfortunate fate at Marika's hands. At least four times, in seeking personal revenge, she brought about the arrest and deportation of former lovers. One of the unlucky ones was Gvido, who had graduated from the conservatory with honors and otherwise might have had a bright future.

Only once did I feel any satisfaction at one of Marika's acts of retribution. Olga's brother-in-law, Roberts, had continued to change women friends, discarding them when they no longer served his purpose. Though he wasn't in Adolfs's league, he had mastered a few of his tricks. Somehow, his and Marika's paths had crossed. His coarse manner had intrigued her at first, but he hadn't lived up to her expectations. And so, Roberts, who had always found a way to weasel out of life's difficulties, was on his way to Kazakhstan in north-central Eurasia.

38

Theater in a Church

The arrival of a group of Western clergy in Riga was generating a lot of excitement. A church service would be held to welcome them.

That evening Mrs. Vinerts filled me in on the day's events. "When I got to the church, I was told it was closed to non-members that day. I started to walk away but ducked into a nearby building entrance. I saw the Westerners and also observed that anyone who was middle-aged or older was being turned away. Then the younger generation began arriving. They showed a note concealed in the palm of their hands and were admitted right away. Among them was the daughter of one of my former classmates. I decided to ask her about it later."

"Tell me more about the Westerners," I said.

"They were accompanied by our so-called Archbishop Turss and a Cheka agent dressed as a church elder. He speaks Russian, Latvian, German, and English. When he is around foreigners, he pretends he doesn't understand but stays nearby and listens to everything they say."

"So did you ever talk to your friend's daughter?"

"Oh yes! I have known her for quite a few years. We developed a close relationship after her mother died. The first time she applied to university, she was turned down, so she joined Com-Youth and was accepted. But it never affected our relationship, and we were always able to speak openly. So when I asked her about the church service, I was surprised that she lied and denied being there. I told her I knew she had been there because I saw her enter the church."

I smiled, thinking how the girl was no match for Mrs. Vinerts.

"She finally admitted being at the church, but said they had been threatened with severe retribution if they spoke to anyone about it. Nevertheless, I was able to learn that the students had been handpicked and specially trained in religious practices. They had previously 'performed' for the Orthodox and Catholic clergy, telling them how they enjoyed complete freedom of worship under the Communist regime. As the Orthodox and Catholic services required knowledge of specific rituals, the best-prepared ones were seated in the front, while the other Com-Youth remained in the rear pews. Some couples even asked the visitors if they would conduct a marriage ceremony for them or christen their baby.

"Do you think they put on the same shows in Moscow, Leningrad, and other cities?"

"Certainly," Mrs. Vinerts said with conviction. "Wherever there is Commu-nism, the story is the same, though the presentation may vary. Stalin's regime was characterized by violence and terror, which is why Khrushchev is using lies, guile, and feigned ignorance. And the next Ivan Ivanovich will invent yet another twist—all to advance world Communism, the one cause in which they are united. The easiest way to lull the world into a sense of complacency is by pre-tending the Soviet Union is changing. They know they particularly need to appeal to the spiritual senses, so they are putting in a big effort with the Western clergy."

"Actually, one of my colleagues was called in and reprimanded for wearing a shabby dress and run-down shoes while speaking with Danish journalists," I interjected. "Since we are supposedly far better off than our counterparts in the West, her scruffy appearance was viewed as a malicious betrayal of the socialist homeland."

"Your director must have forgotten how little our doctors are paid," Mrs. Vin-erts said as she laughed heartily. "It reminds me of something that might have been humorous, in different circumstances.

"The other day, I was nearly hit by a car hastily pulling into a driveway. It was filled with men and women in fashionable eveningwear. Later I learned why they were in such a hurry. Apparently, some visiting Western diplomats had expressed a desire to dine out. So a group of well-dressed 'ordinary restaurant-goers' was hastily assembled. But the dignitaries had a last-minute change of plan and chose a different restaurant from the one that had been recommended. Consequently, their hosts had to stall the visitors until the actors could be transported to the right restaurant."

I laughed along with her, but couldn't help but wonder if the diplomats had any idea what was really going on. Only later, when I was in the West, did I come to realize that the naiveté of Westerners—especially when it came to Commu-nism—was truly boundless.

As it turned out, that was the last time I would ever see Mrs. Vinerts. Not long afterward, she had a heart attack and died. There were a large number of mourn-ers—as many as her good deeds, because in her roles as a building supervisor and a Russian general's widow, she had been able to help a lot of people. Sadly, one of her own wishes would remain unfulfilled. On the day she died, a letter arrived from her husband and son.

I held it in my hands for a long while. Should I send it back with a note? But then questions would follow, questions I was not prepared to answer.

I decided to let Mrs. Vinerts's secrets be buried along with her. Her loved ones would never know the kind of life she had. I wondered if they would have understood.

And so, together with the flowers she had loved so much, I placed the long-awaited letter in the coffin, under her pillow.

39

The Road to Freedom

It's wonderful to dream—even if dreams rarely do come true. I was lucky, because, out of all the thousands upon thousands of people who shared the same dream of one day being free, mine came true.

I was in a train carriage on my way to East Berlin, from where I was certain the road would lead to freedom. At last, I would be free of the suffocating red fog.

I watched the scenery slip by and thought back on the events of the last years.

Vanda, who had so longed for freedom and had organized the escape boat to Sweden, was dead. She had a heart attack and, regaining consciousness for only a short while, used her last breath to condemn the Communist regime.

Valda's brother, Helmuts, felt betrayed and never found his way back to Communism. While he was in Moscow, he met a girl from one of the democratic countries. A few months later he married her, so he would be allowed to leave the Soviet Union.

Livija and Indulis remained devoted to each other and were as happy as it was possible to be in the circumstances. Indulis was put under great pressure to join the Party, but kept coming up with reasons why it was not possible. When he ran out of excuses and they still didn't relent, he submitted a formal letter asking to be relieved of his job, giving up his life's work.

We paid silent tribute to his great sacrifices, in admiration of his strength of character. We understood why as a student he had been called the Bear Slayer; he never gave up the fight against the Red devil. And in the end, Indulis won his battle. Acknowledging his near-genius skills as a researcher, the Communists allowed him to return to his job without joining the Party. It was rare, but these things did happen occasionally.

Dace, after joining the Party, had become head of a hospital in one of the provinces. Shortly before I left Latvia, I was surprised to find her waiting for me. The news that I had permission to travel outside the Soviet Union had spread like wildfire.

"Lita, don't say anything, but listen to me, please. In the spirit of the friendship we once shared, I beg you to believe me that this is not a provocation. If I were you and got to East Berlin, I would not stop there. I would keep going and never come back! And, above all, tell everyone about the suffering and oppression we have to bear here. I wish you all good things, and God speed."

She gave my hand a squeeze and hurried away.

Lija and Vaira were both married and working as doctors also in the provinces. Reverend Peteris kept working as an engineer but never lost his spirituality.

My father returned from the labor camp blind. He never spoke about what happened during the years of his deportation. And I never asked any questions. He sat expressionless, gazing off into the distance at things no one else could see. Yes, the Soviet regime had succeeded in working another one of its miracles—it had created the walking dead. My poor father, what are you thinking? I sometimes wondered. But the invisible wall always remained between us.

My mother also returned after the "amnesty." She lived with my father, but was very bitter and unable to forget all the things they had lost. Perhaps the compassionate part of her had frozen somewhere in time, like the Siberian tundra.

I could not have continued to bear Adolfs's blackmail, or my mother's coldness, indefinitely. In fact, I had considered applying for a voluntary posting in Siberia, where there was a shortage of doctors in addition to everything else.

Now here I was on the train hurtling west and toward freedom.

Until the last moment I had feared that news of my imminent departure would reach Adolfs. He had turned up a few days before. My knees buckled when I saw him, and I thought all was lost, but he didn't seem to know anything and simply demanded that I give him one hundred rubles. With trembling hands, I took out my purse and counted out one hundred. He grabbed it away from me and, having ascertained that it contained one hundred and fifty rubles, he stuffed the entire purse in his pocket.

Summoning up my courage, I took a deep breath and asked, "Has it never occurred to you that things might change?"

"Of course. But then my brother will help me get as good a job as I have now."

As I watched him turn and walk away, I knew he was probably right. He was one of those people who would always land on his feet. But, most importantly, he didn't know about my trip! Gran would have said it was part of God's plan. Yes, wasn't it odd, in retrospect, how I came to meet Marika, without whose help I would not be sitting on this train.

Before I left, I went to say good-bye to Olga, whose growing family was squeezed into two small rooms. She and Andrejs both worked, and even their boys helped.

As I stroked the littlest one's hair, he said, "You know, Auntie Lita, we were in the country visiting my uncle and we heard a radio news broadcast in Latvian."

My eyes darted fearfully towards Olga, but she reassured me. "Don't worry, they know not to say anything to strangers. And they know about the revolution in Hungary and have some understanding of what's happening there. Maybe…someday. I know we thought it would happen before, but…It seems that other things took priority for Americans, who speak too glibly about freedom. But talk is cheap.

"Did you know your ex-husband is coming back here?" Andrejs said.

"How nice it is that Latvians are again allowed to return home!" I said. "How did that come about?"

"Well, it was with the help of his girlfriend, a Russian doctor. She got him into medicine and then fought for his release."

"Ah, so that would explain why his friend felt so awkward about asking for my help," I said. "By all means, give Hugo my best if you see him."

I noticed that Olga was staring at me rather intently.

"I mean, of course, if you see him before I come back," I added hastily.

My friends pressed my hand in a prolonged good-bye, and when Zoya poked her head through the door, I knew it was time to go. I thought about all these things as the train sped toward Berlin.

But freedom did not come as easily as I'd thought. I still did not know how to cross the invisible border that separated the Communist world from the West. And there was no one to go to ask for advice.

With Marika's help, I had gotten permission to have surgery performed by a specialist in East Berlin. When I arrived at the hospital, I had a hard time trying to persuade him to operate on me, as he didn't seem to see it as a priority. I persisted, although it later turned out that the operation did me more harm than good.

But at that moment, on the threshold of freedom, no price was too high.

While convalescing, I learned how to get to the West.

I was physically ill and spiritually drained, but at long last I had emerged from the oppressive red fog and was able to breathe free.

Afterword

While strolling in a large European city, I pause in front of a florist shop window. The blaze of color brings back a flash of memories. But the lavish floral arrangements, along with many other things, no longer amaze me. I nod my head knowingly and my reflection nods back.

Many years have passed since the moment when, in a similar setting, I got the idea to write about life in occupied Latvia. There was my illness, surgery and a lengthy convalescence. Since then, I had also come to know a number of Western countries and how their people think.

Nothing much surprises me anymore, although I continue to be amazed at Western egoism and lack of empathy, as well as the petty squabbling and in-fighting, as if their worst enemies were the family next door, or the people in the neighboring town or country where opinions may differ.

Underlying this seemingly trivial discord, I see Communism at work. It's easy to provoke ill will by sowing seeds of suspicion or slandering a specific individual or group. It continues to amaze me that people cannot see through this rather crude and obvious subvert-from-within method of operation.

The lack of morals is at the very core of Communist dealings. From an early age they teach that "there are just wars and unjust wars. Those that oppose Communism are unjust; but wars waged against capitalists are just. Guile and lies are acceptable tactics and smart strategy to achieve victory.

While that bit of "wisdom" was meant for the Party faithful, common folk were expected to follow blindly in the belief that the Communist Party knows best and is infallible in every way.

To perpetuate this unstable system, children are turned against parents; colleague pitted against colleague, and clergy against congregation.

Any means justify the result if it keeps Communists in power and advances their global ambitions. Things are not always what they seem. One could ask, for example, why so much effort is expended before political elections to introduce fear and suspicion and create an atmosphere of instability.

But I will not keep silent. I also will not go along with the view of so many Western intellectuals who naively maintain we must use ethical and moral methods so the Communists will recognize and adopt our model of decency. As if their amoral and brutal deeds were done out of ignorance, or there was ever any doubt that Communists understand only one way of dealing with things—their own.

So, if the florist shop window now leaves me a bit indifferent, it re-ignites my sense of righteousness.

I want to tell the passersby to stop their pursuit of material wealth. I know too well what it is to have nothing, but acquiring possessions should not be our primary goal in life. I have learned a lot. I know that Westerners themselves are not all-powerful and all-knowing and that small nations cannot change the political course set by world powers. I also know the storied might of Communism is, in fact, as fragile as a soap bubble and only as strong as the power ascribed to it by the West.

No totalitarian government has lasted for long, because its foundation, built on subjugation, is weak. The human soul yearns for freedom. Having experienced life under the Communist regime, I can state unequivocally that everyone wants to be free.

The struggle is not over, but we must stop quarreling over unimportant things. Communism is destined to crumble. The time will come when the red fog will be dissipated by the bright light of freedom.

—L.Z.

978-0-595-40257-1
0-595-40257-7